Apocalypse TV

Apocalypse TV

Essays on Society and Self at the End of the World

Edited by
MICHAEL G. CORNELIUS *and*
SHERRY GINN

McFarland & Company, Inc., Publishers
Jefferson, North Carolina

ALSO OF INTEREST AND FROM MCFARLAND

Marvel's Black Widow from Spy to Superhero: Essays on an Avenger with a Very Specific Skill Set, edited by Sherry Ginn (2017); *Spartacus in the Television Arena: Essays on the Starz Series*, edited by Michael G. Cornelius (2015); *The Worlds of Farscape: Essays on the Groundbreaking Television Series*, edited by Sherry Ginn (2013); *Power and Control in the Television Worlds of Joss Whedon*, Sherry Ginn (2012); *The Sex Is Out of This World: Essays on the Carnal Side of Science Fiction*, edited by Sherry Ginn and Michael G. Cornelius (2012); *Of Muscles and Men: Essays on the Sword and Sandal Film*, edited by Michael G. Cornelius (2011); *The Boy Detectives: Essays on the Hardy Boys and Others*, edited by Michael G. Cornelius (2010); *Nancy Drew and Her Sister Sleuths: Essays on the Fiction of Girl Detectives*, edited by Michael G. Cornelius and Melanie E. Gregg (2008)

This book has undergone peer review.

LIBRARY OF CONGRESS CATALOGUING-IN-PUBLICATION DATA

Names: Cornelius, Michael G., editor. | Ginn, Sherry, editor.
Title: Apocalypse TV : essays on society and self at the end of the world / edited by Michael G. Cornelius and Sherry Ginn.
Description: Jefferson : McFarland & Company, Inc., Publishers, 2020. | Includes bibliographical references and index.
Identifiers: LCCN 2020004683 |
ISBN 9781476678757 (paperback : acid free paper) ∞
ISBN 9781476639963 (ebook)
Subjects: LCSH: Apocalyptic television programs—
United States—History and criticism.
Classification: LCC PN1992.8.A67 A66 2020 | DDC 791.45/615—dc23
LC record available at https://lccn.loc.gov/2020004683

BRITISH LIBRARY CATALOGUING DATA ARE AVAILABLE

**ISBN (print) 978-1-4766-7875-7
ISBN (ebook) 978-1-4766-3996-3**

© 2020 Michael G. Cornelius and Sherry Ginn. All rights reserved

No part of this book may be reproduced or transmitted in any form or by any means, electronic or mechanical, including photocopying or recording, or by any information storage and retrieval system, without permission in writing from the publisher.

Front cover image © 2020 Shutterstock

Printed in the United States of America

*McFarland & Company, Inc., Publishers
Box 611, Jefferson, North Carolina 28640
www.mcfarlandpub.com*

Sherry says that this one is for Larry, in whatever future,
and
Michael says that this one, as all things, is for Joe

Table of Contents

Acknowledgments — ix

Introduction: Apocalyptic Saturations; or, The End of the World Will Not End
  MICHAEL G. CORNELIUS and SHERRY GINN — 1

Apocalyptic Television, Hobbes's Moral Psychology and the Tenuous Nature of Liberal Democratic Values
  WILLIAM S. ALLEN — 23

Post-Apocalyptic Competition and Cooperation in *The Handmaid's Tale* and *The Walking Dead*
  SHERRY GINN — 40

The Long Winter of Discontent: The Changing Society of *Survivors*
  FERNANDO-GABRIEL PAGNONI BERNS, JUAN IGNACIO JUVÉ and EMILIANO AGUILAR — 58

Risk Without End? The Seriality of Risk, the Outbreak Narrative and Serial Post-Apocalypse in Guillermo del Toro and Chuck Hogan's *The Strain*
  SEBASTIAN MÜLLER — 71

Driven to Extinction, Again: *Cadillacs and Dinosaurs* and the Irresistible Apocalypse
  TONY PERRELLO and C. ANNE ENGERT — 86

The End of Everything: Survival Narratives and Everyday Heroism in *Battlestar Galactica*
  E. LEIGH MCKAGEN — 102

Apocalypse(s) Already: Doomsday Preppers at the End of The(ir) Worlds
  JZ LONG — 113

Reinvesting in the Rapture: Apocalypse and Faith in *The Leftovers*
  CHRISTINA WILKINS — 124

Social Life and Death in *The Leftovers*: Surviving
the Personal Apocalypse
    Derek R. Sweet   137

"How many times have I died?": Time Loops, Post-Human
Reversion and the Editable Self in *The Magicians*
    Michael G. Cornelius   149

Westworld and the Apocalyptic Cycle
    Adam Ellerbrock   163

Postnatural Comedy in *The Last Man on Earth*
    John Elia   174

Appendix 1: Apocalypse Television Series   185
Appendix 2: "Darkness"
    Lord Byron   189
About the Contributors   191
Index   195

Acknowledgments

Michael G. Cornelius: I would like to thank my good friend and colleague Sherry Ginn for pestering me about this project for several years, as the experience has been incredibly edifying and enlightening, even if all of this end-of-the-world talk has turned me into an ardent pessimist. Thanks to all our contributors for their amazing work in this collection. Thanks to McFarland for being great partners in the realm of popular culture studies. Sherry and I both want to thank our anonymous readers, who made everyone's work all the better. And thanks to my 12-year-old pug Knox, who puts all of this into perspective by reminding me that, should the apocalyptic poo really hit the fan, the first thing we must do is secure the dog food, lest it be raided by the marauding corgis next door.

Sherry Ginn: I would like to thank Michael Cornelius for agreeing once again to coedit a collection with me, especially since I have been pestering him about this one for several years now. Wouldn't you know this would be the time I experience a severe case of "writer's block?" Thank you, Michael, for helping me through it and getting this collection finished. I also extend my thanks to our contributors for their awesome essays. I am often surprised at what people see that I don't when we are all watching the same show. Like Knox, the Monster of Monroe—my cat Madison—has her own perspective, which is something along the lines of "provide me with food or you will meet your own personal apocalypse."

Introduction

Apocalyptic Saturations; or, The End of the World Will Not End

MICHAEL G. CORNELIUS *and* SHERRY GINN

> "Turns out I suddenly find myself needing to know the plural of apocalypse."
> —"A New Man," *Buffy the Vampire Slayer*

If current trends hold—and they show no sign of abating for now—then determining the plural of the word "apocalypse" may indeed prove useful for all of us, surrounded as we are by repeated and recurring incarnations of the end of the world.

Truly, the end times have arrived. Visions of the apocalypse inhabit every aspect of our ultra-medial society. As consumers of media we have become inured to representations of the end times on television, in movies, in literature, and in comic books. Yet our apocalyptic surroundings extend far outside the traditional realms of fiction: trappings of apocalyptic narratives highlight our 24-hour news cycle, dominating discourse on everything from national politics to international conflict to the weather. The worse the event, the more coverage it ensures; the more hopeless any resolution might seem, the more we talk about it, and the more it dominates our culture, our news, our media, and our lives. Our discourse has taken on the hyperbole of extreme characterization, and we seem to seek continual confirmation of our encroaching belief that things cannot improve in the political, social, scientific, and cultural news and developments of the day.

In short, we are surrounding *ourselves* with the end of the/our world(s).

This is hardly surprising. A cursory glance at news headlines from the previous few years only reinforces this feeling of impending doom. Violent, seemingly uncontrollable manifestations of the three "realistic" causes of the apocalypse—natural disaster; human-made (generally nuclear) cataclysm; and plague/disease—have happened, and keep happening, with alarming frequency. The last three full years were the hottest on record (2016, 2017, and 2018, with 2019 threatening to displace them), with significant portions of the

2   Introduction

globe experiencing severe, life-threatening drought; yet under U.S. President Donald J. Trump the United States pulled out of the Paris Agreement. Hurricanes, tornadoes, and wildfires have destroyed large stretches of the United States and left people and communities devastated. Puerto Rico still has not recovered from the depredation wrought by Hurricane Maria in September 2017. Whole towns in California were destroyed by wildfires in the fall of 2018. Australia has been devastated by fires that have raged across that continent since July 2019. In six months more than 7 million acres of land have burned—equivalent to an area the size of Belgium and Denmark combined—and a conservative estimate indicates that at least half a billion animals have perished (Young). Experts predict that disasters such as these are only going to increase in number and severity with time, primarily due to global climate change. A 2019 report in the *New England Journal of Medicine* concludes that the death rate due to climate change first reported by the World Health Organization (WHO) in 2014 is an underestimate. The planet is likely to see an increase of 500,000 adults dying from food shortages alone by 2050, with over 100 million people sliding into extreme poverty by 2030, resulting in an increased vulnerability to myriad other health problems (Haines and Ebi).

Climate is not the only pressing concern. In 2019 the United States pulled out of the Intermediate-Range Nuclear Forces (INF) treaty, heating up the arms race, increasing the possibility of nuclear Armageddon. The lessons learned in the past, whereby 120,000 (±30,000) people living in Hiroshima and 60,000 (±20,000) people living in Nagasaki were killed in 1945 during World War II by the atomic bomb, have been largely forgotten. Even if humankind never experiences another nuclear event arising in warfare, the use of nuclear power is not without its risks. Fifty-six deaths (forty-seven accident workers and nine children with thyroid cancer) are directly attributed to the Chernobyl disaster, which occurred in Pripyat, Ukraine, in April 1986. Estimates are that another 4,000 deaths due to cancer were attributable to the exposure people experienced during and after the event.[1] Media analysis of the March 2011 Fukushima Daiichi nuclear disaster five years after the event estimated that anywhere from 1,232 to 1,656 deaths were attributable to outcomes related to the nuclear event.[2] Scientists have even reported that another nuclear accident is believed to have occurred in Argayash, Russia, in September 2017, based on recordings of large quantities of the isotope ruthenium-106 in the atmosphere, though Russia initially denied the event, their subterfuge adding to the apocalyptic undertones of the event.

Diseases once thought to be eradicated are rearing their heads, primarily because of the unwillingness of people to vaccinate their children (Pannaraj). Highly contagious illnesses, such as measles, can be deadly; the state of Washington declared a public health emergency in January 2019 because of the sheer number of cases diagnosed there (Vera). People often consider the flu to be slightly more discomfiting than a bad cold, but influenza is the eighth leading cause of death in the United States.[3] An estimated 50–100 million people died of the "Spanish" Flu in 1918; that was 20–40 percent of the world's population.[4] Scientists believe that the next pandemic could kill over a billion people, especially in overpopulated areas (20 percent of the world's 2018 population is 1.46 billion people) (Hunter). Various strains of the flu have been more deadly than others, especially for the animals believed to be disease vectors, which are often slaughtered by the thousands in an attempt to stop the spread of the disease; such actions result in food shortages. The most notable examples of these strains are the "bird" flu pandemic of 2006 and the "swine" flu scare of 2009. Epidemiologists predict that as habitats shrink and the human population reduces resources available to sustain living, more serious and deadly strains of diseases may emerge and may not be easily suppressed or cured. Indeed, the Centers for Disease Control (CDC) report that more people in the world die of influenza than once believed: approximately 650,000 people worldwide (to put that number into perspective, it is slightly more than the population of the state of Vermont or the country of Montenegro) (Santhanam).

Ecological collapse; nuclear disaster; viral outbreaks; a population equivalent to entire countries (or maple-syrup producing states) wiped out of existence. These facts and figures may seem harrowing, and we are of course only addressing the tip of the proverbial apocalyptic iceberg here. And yet, if a rational individual wished to accuse us of both pessimism and hyperbole, that person would be right. Harrowing as these numbers may seem, we are really only discussing tiny fragments of the population, and none of these events rose to a true apocalyptic, "end of the human race" level. After all, even in the worst apocalyptic scenario, some people will likely survive. As Annalee Newitz points out, there have been multiple extinction level events (ELEs) throughout the 4.5-billion-year history of planet Earth, yet numerous species have survived these cataclysmic events, and life still flourishes on this planet. And humanity has faced serious threats in the past, both globally (Spanish Flu, the Bubonic Plague) and locally (the volcanic eruption of Mount Tambura in Indonesia in 1815, for example), and has survived. Bubonic Plague (which is alive and thriving in the world today) is hypothesized to have killed 60 percent of Europe's population in the 14th century (Benedictow). Following Mount Tambura's eruption, global temperatures dropped, on average, five degrees. The year 1816 was known as the "year without a summer"—certainly an apocalyptic scenario—a time immortalized by Lord Byron in his poem "Darkness" (truly a masterpiece for the apocalypse; see Appendix 2). Crops failed worldwide because of the cool weather and a dust cloud blocking out the sun in the upper atmosphere.

We certainly do not require such global cataclysms to feel the grasp of the apocalypse. As we put the finishing touches on this introduction, the United States suffered two mass shooting events—in El Paso, Texas, and Dayton, Ohio—in less than 24 hours. While the number dead does not begin to reach the totals of any of the cataclysms listed above, the tone and mood surrounding these events indicate helplessness, despair, anguish, and futility. Events like these both signal and confirm that, indeed, things are continually getting worse on planet Earth. If—as a culture, as a species, as individuals, and as creators and consumers of narrative—if we believe we are living in the apocalypse, and the very real, very bleak news of everyday life seems to confirm that we are, does it truly matter whether the world is actually ending? Or is it already doing so, because we believe it is?

We are not the first to make the observation that we are living in the apocalypse, or that our belief in such may very well be the lynchpin cause of these end time feelings. In some very real, very tangible fashion, the allegorical power of the apocalypse as an event, as a thing to happen, that has happened, or that *is* happening, has always acted in this way. Apocalypse has always required the power of belief to make it come to fruition. The religio-mythic traditions of most faith systems feature stories of annihilation that occurred both in the past (such as tales of the Great Flood, which can be found in the Christian bible, in Mesopotamian stories, in Greek mythology, in Hinduism, in Chinese mythology, in the Norse tradition, and in the lore of indigenous peoples in North America, South America, and Australia) and are slated to occur in the future (the Rapture, Ragnarök, Frashokereti, etc.). Though traditional apocalyptic fictional narratives do not emerge until the 19th century, tales of wholesale destruction and annihilation feature in our earliest literary traditions, such as the *Epic of Gilgamesh*, which includes the figure of Utnapishtim and his tale of surviving a Great Flood. Even in our most hopeful, most utopian narratives, the end of the world—the destruction of mankind—looms. Frederick Kreuziger suggests that the realms of speculative fiction, especially science fiction, generate vital "central myths" which "should be understood in religious terms" (84, 15). Kreuziger divides these myths into two broad categories: the apocalyptic and the utopian (100). And yet the apocalyptic and the utopian are, in essence, the same thing, or—at the very least—two sides of a very thin coin. Both essentialize a narrative ending, the culmination of the social experiment, resulting in either destruction or perfection—a conclusion all the same, even if the outcomes vary. Connor Pitetti suggests that apocalyptic narratives "tell a story in which the falling bombs have destroyed the old world of the past and prepared a *tabula rasa* upon which the future will be built from scratch … [thus] 'the end of the world' offers the opportunity to escape from an imperfect past into a new and better world," a reading that is simultaneously apocalyptic *and* utopian (437). These apocalyptic accounts are ultimately little different from utopian narratives, which Pitetti aligns with "a more optimistic vein, millennial fantasies of rebirth, renewal, and the advent of a golden age" and which "proliferate just as widely and diversely" as their more damning fictive cousins (437). Either way, the tale reaches a conclusion and society moves on—presumably, and preferably, to something "better."

This intimate relationship between apocalypse and utopia proliferates science fiction narratives, and can perhaps best be demonstrated by one of the most enduring utopian science fiction visions of all time—Star Trek. Dozens of scholars have connected the vision of the Star Trek franchise to the utopian school of science fiction narrative; Dan Hassler-Forest, for one, suggests that the series

> is structured by a teleological view of history in which human development is synonymous with modernisation and technological advancement, resulting in a post-capitalist technological utopia. In *Star Trek*'s "visionary" future, humanity has essentially progressed beyond its own dialectical nature: class struggle, warfare, poverty, famine, sexism, racism and all other aspects of human history's struggles with itself have been eradicated. The United Federation of Planets' flagship *Enterprise* with its multi-ethnic (and indeed multi-species) crew therefore represented for many a meaningful ideal of human progress ["*Star Trek*, Global Capitalism" 371].[5]

Of the various Star Trek series, *Star Trek: The Next Generation* (1987–1994) is often viewed as the most utopian; and yet, the series' entire narrative frame is apocalyptic in nature. In the series' pilot episode, "Encounter at Farpoint," the crew of the *Enterprise* is pursued by an omnipotent being named Q, who places humanity on trial for being a "dangerous, savage child race." What is initially at stake is not the destruction of humankind, but the end of the vaunted Starfleet and the cessation of a particular way of life that has come to define human existence, as Q intones: "Thou are notified that thy kind hath infiltrated the galaxy too far already. Thou art directed to return to thine own solar system immediately." At one point, under threat of Q, *Enterprise* Captain Jean-Luc Picard frustratedly suggests that Q "finish us" already, with the antecedent pronoun referring to both the crew of the *Enterprise* as well as the entire human race—an ominous portent, indeed. And though the *Enterprise* crew manages to "pass" this initial test, the episode suggests that from the onset of *The Next Generation* the fate of all humanity dangles in the balance—a fate that is revisited in the final episodes of the series, "All Good Things...":

> Q: The trial never ended, Captain. We never reached a verdict. But now we have. You're guilty.
> PICARD: Guilty of what?
> Q: Of being inferior. Seven years ago I said we'd be watching you, and we have been, hoping that your ape-like race would demonstrate some growth, give some indication that your minds have room for expansion. But what have we seen instead? You worrying about Commander Riker's career, listening

> to Counselor Troi's pedantic psychobabble, indulging Data in his witless exploration of humanity.
>
> PICARD: We've journeyed to countless new worlds, we've contacted new species, we have expanded our understanding of the universe.
>
> Q: In your own paltry, limited way. You have no idea how far you still have to go. But instead of using the last seven years to change and to grow, you have squandered them.
>
> PICARD: We are what we are, and we're doing the best we can. It is not for you to set the standards by which we should be judged.
>
> Q: Oh, but it is, and we have. Time may be eternal, Captain, but our patience is not. It's time to put an end to your trek through the stars, make room for other, more worthy species.
>
> PICARD: You're going to deny us travel through space?
>
> Q: You obtuse piece of flotsam. You are to be denied existence. Humanity's fate has been sealed. You will be destroyed.
>
> PICARD: Q, I do not believe that even you are capable of such an act.
>
> Q: I? There you go again, always blaming me for everything. Well, this time I'm not your enemy. I'm not the one that causes the annihilation of mankind. You are.

Clearly, the stakes have been raised. No longer is a way of life threatened—life itself is on the brink. Picard and his crew are called upon to avert an apocalyptic event—the same event foretold in the first episode of the series—or else the very existence of humankind will be eliminated. Of course, Star Trek being Star Trek, and *The Next Generation* being *The Next Generation*, the crisis is averted. Only then, after the danger has passed, does Picard learn that averting disaster has crafted other possibilities:

> Q: You just don't get it, do you, Jean-Luc? The trial never ends. We wanted to see if you had the ability to expand your mind and your horizons. And for one brief moment, you did.
>
> PICARD: When I realized the paradox.
>
> Q: Exactly. For that one fraction of a second, you were open to options you had never considered. That is the exploration that awaits you. Not mapping stars and studying nebulae, but charting the unknowable possibilities of existence ["All Good Things..."].

Here, just the aversion of apocalypse brings new potentialities to the utopian world of *The Next Generation*. Thus, even without wholesale destruction, apocalypse accomplishes what Pitetti notes it is meant to: to shift the nature of civilization itself, to alter society and open it up to new possibilities, new modes of being, new forms of enactment.

Pitetti is hardly the first scholar to point out the correlation between apocalypse and utopia. Pitetti himself cites Frank Kermode's thesis, "developed in *The Sense of an Ending* (1967), that storytelling is a mechanism for making sense of the overwhelming and unstructured experience of lived history" (438). Kermode suggests that narrative endings—simply by virtue of presenting an ending—are all, in some sense, apocalyptic, referencing both the concluded nature of the protagonist's story line as well as the liminal awareness of the reader that the narrative has come to an end and thus ceases to persist (at least until a sequel may be printed). Kermode suggests that "the paradigms of apocalypse continue to lie under our ways of making sense of the world," and thus that endings, the finiteness of conclusions, allows for humanity to comprehend that which may seem otherwise incomprehensible (26). Or, at the very least, endings provide a sense of completeness that allows for the digestion of a narrative, an idea, a thought, a concept. Rather than being consumed by the potential vastness of—whatever it is we may be consuming, whether history, fiction, politics, religion, story, etc.—endings dictate reflection and retrospection, forcing us to conclude the act of consumption and re-examine or rehash that which we have just exhausted. This suggests that life itself, then, is something we cannot truly comprehend unless we can see the back of it, or, at the very least, understand that it exists in a finite system, that it, too, will end, that both ourselves as well as our entire species and planet will end, giving us an opportune moment to examine all that came before.

This is all perhaps more metaphysics than physics, and thus it is no surprise that, for millennia, the apocalypse suggested religious overtones and divinely inspired events; whether the Rapture or Ragnarök or Kali Yuga, most major systems of faith delineate eschatological events that foretell "end times" or "the end of the world." In the Christian bible, these events are depicted in the Book of Revelations, which is particularly fitting, since the Greek word for revelation is *apokalypsis*. In their introduction to the collection *The Apocalypse in Film: Dystopias, Disasters, and Other Visions About the End of the World*, Karen A. Ritzenhoff and Angela Krewani note that the Christian apocalypse "tells the story of the destruction of the earth by God and of the final judgment. The good people are united with God; the sinners are confined to hell"—a model along the lines of utopia (heaven) and apocalypse (hell) (xii). Because of this bifurcated structure, Ritzenhoff and Krewani argue, "the apocalypse has become a strong allegory, a rhetorical figure that enables us to speak of the present in terms of the past" (xii). This metaphor is key to understanding those modes through which apocalyptic events have filtered down through the centuries. Indeed, while eschatological versions of the apocalypse all prophesy violence, death, and destruction, their common moniker of "end times" is not wholly accurate. In most faith traditions the end of the world does not result in the total cessation of life, but in a transformation, or even a rebirth, of life itself. The religious apocalypse, really, is about change—bloody, violent, protracted change—that usually results in a reaffirmation of the faith or the reconstitution of life itself.

Hence for thousands of years the "end of the world" has been perceived as not quite what it seems—the great flood (to select one pan-religious/mythic example) is both an end and a new beginning. In the 19th century, however, authors of science fiction began to speculate about the humanistic response to events that might, indeed, spell the doom of all humankind. Jean-Baptiste Cousin de Grainville's 1805 novel *Le Dernier Homme* (*The Last Man*) is often considered the first "modern" apocalyptic tale, but the work is essentially a re-telling of the story first penned in the Book of Revelation, and does not reflect a significant departure from eschatological tradition. It is Mary Shelley's 1826 novel, also titled *The Last Man*, that reflects the first secular apocalyptic tale, centering on a few survivors of a plague that has wiped out mankind. But this type of literature really came to fruition in the works of such authors as H.G. Wells, whose seminal 1898 novel *The War of the Worlds* depicts a humanity that is helpless before the onslaught of an alien invasion. Wells' novel captures the "moment of," portraying the apocalypse as a singular event that humans struggle to survive. In many ways, the notion of the apocalypse as the true and literal "end of the world" was created and then popularized through the work of Wells and other science fiction authors of the late 19th and early 20th centuries, extending into the filmic representations of alien invasions, attacks by giant monsters, and zombie hordes that dominated drive-in science fiction and horror cinema in the middle part of the 20th century.

This is the sort of apocalypse that the character Riley Finn ponders in the epigraph to this introduction from *Buffy the Vampire Slayer*—the apocalypse as singular event, usually as something to be overcome or defeated, and always just in the nick of time. Filmic depictions of these apocalypses, such as *Independence Day* (1996), *The Day After Tomorrow* (2004), or *2012* (2009) often highlight the great destruction caused by alien invasions or ecological cataclysm, but, in the end, the traditional apocalyptic narrative is maintained: humanity rises from the ashes, perhaps—presumably?—to create society anew. Serial television representations of this same apocalyptic narrative—highlighting series from *Doctor Who* (1963–present) to *Buffy the Vampire Slayer* (1997–2003) and its spin-off *Angel* (1999–2004) to the Star Trek franchise, etc.—use the apocalypse in the same metaphorical manner, generally averting impending disaster and allowing the protagonist heroes of these series to right all necessary wrongs and rescue humanity yet again (there is a palpable and poignant reason—narratively speaking—that Buffy's tombstone reads, "She saved the world. A lot") ("The Gift"). Interestingly, by forestalling the apocalyptic event itself, these television narratives also forestall any societal alteration that may result from the cataclysm; as such, heroes like the Doctor and Buffy and the *Enterprise* crew are maintainers of the status quo, for good and for ill. They do not seek to save humanity from itself, but only (merely?) and continually rescue mankind from those external threats—aliens, demons, spatial anomalies—that threaten it with (forcible) change.

These apocalyptic narratives dominated visions of the end of the world for decades (and still do; even recent superhero films like *Suicide Squad* [2016], *X-Men: Apocalypse* [2016], and *The Fantastic Four* [2015] all feature apocalyptic scenarios at the heart of their narratives). In film, the apocalypse became a singular event, whether resulting from a viral pandemic, nuclear holocaust, an astronomical catastrophe, an environmental disaster, or the work of preternatural beings: zombies, vampires, aliens, monsters, mutants, etc. In these tales, the crisis is either averted or the human race is (more frequently) decimated, and the narrative thrust is on the fragile, continued existence of small groups (often familial groups) or individuals whose endurance may or may not guarantee the ultimate survival (and hopeful alteration) of humanity itself. They represent change. On television, the apocalypse was usually averted through the efforts of a singular protagonist hero or small band of heroes. Avoiding the onslaught of changes that would be necessary to survive in such altered worlds, the televisual version of apocalypse long represented fearful change and fear of change, and that the most important work of our world's heroes is the maintenance of the status quo and the maintenance of the world itself.

Yet the notion of the apocalypse as a singular event to be survived or forestalled has not always been the enactment of the apocalypse. Though its duration varies among different faith traditions, the tribulation of the Christian rapture is indicated to last years; the Kali Yuga of the Hindu faith lasts 432,000 years. These extended periods are marked by violence, discord, conflict, and yet, at the same time, the notion that life must simply endure; during these periods of great strife people must survive, come together, live their lives, bear children, and continue on with the business of living, even if that business is tinged with harsh and unpleasant realities. The belief that human beings must "live through" an extended period of trial, rather than "survive" a singular apocalyptic event, is not born simply of the notion that the apocalypse is longer in duration than many contemporary science fiction films and televisions series would lead us to believe. This period of suffering is an important part of the eschatological belief; though different faith traditions differ as to why this is essential, they mostly agree that the apocalypse, when it comes, is here to stay.

Such duration of events is difficult to capture in films that last at best a few hours; and even difficult to capture in novels, especially before the more recent resurgence of popular series literature (recent dystopian series like James Dashner's *The Maze Runner* [five books; 2009–2016] counter the literary tradition of singular apocalyptic titles dating back to Wells and his ilk, though in their culminating volumes they often revert back to the filmic concept of the one-and-done apocalypse). Briefer works constitute narratives with a sense of commencement and termination, and as such it is no surprise that the particular moment of apocalypse—the moment the end arrives—

dominated these texts for almost 100 years. If narratives require conclusions (of a sort), then an apocalyptic narrative must reach some sort of terminal point as well, at least as far as the unfolding of events and the pleasure of the reader is concerned. This is not to say that all apocalyptic visions of the late 19th and 20th centuries fit this pattern—this is hardly the case. And yet even in works such as Richard Jeffries' *After London* (1885) or the various literary and cinematic re-tellings of Richard Matheson's *I Am Legend* (1954), the focus is still on singular events, even if those events occur after the apocalyptic devastation of the planet.

Serializing the apocalypse on television, however, necessitates a re-envisioning of the apocalypse; it is a return, in many ways, to the eschatological tradition of duration and suffering. Thus, even though most of these series do not have their genesis in faith narratives (though, as the essays included here will attest, some do), this extended period of strife is very much part of and an allusion to the eschatological, sacred tradition. Of course, one genesis of this is simply the function of television: the walkers on *The Walking Dead* (2010–present) have been "walking" for the better part of a decade, and will continue to "walk" until the series' ratings or the series' creators deem otherwise. And yet the real key to these new forms of televisual apocalypses is that no longer would the world or the human species be saved; no longer would a singular actor alter the doom that is to come. While post-apocalyptic narratives have existed on television for decades, the trend now is to eschew any notion of the "happy," world-saving ending and to instead embrace the nihilism of destruction and the doom of humanity. The ascendance of these apocalyptic visions and re-tellings of these "end of the world" scenarios afford a unique opportunity for scholars. Unlike the previous common medial representations of the apocalypse, extending back to Wells and moving forward to popular films like *Independence Day* and *The Day After Tomorrow* and *Suicide Squad*, serialized versions of apocalyptic events dwell in the realms and stories of the apocalypse for (potentially) years and years, reliving, re-enacting, and rehashing the apocalyptic events over and over and over. In short, in many of these series, it seems that the end of the world may never end.

Critics and scholars of apocalyptic texts have been pondering the notion of the post-apocalypse for some time, questioning the meaning of those texts where the end of the world simply will not end. As Teresa Heffernan observes, "If the 'end' has traditionally secured a sense of order, meaning, originality, and autonomy to the narrative as it progresses from start to finish, what is at stake in a world that no longer offers up narratives with conclusive endings?" (3). She adds, "Apocalypse as the story of renewal and redemption is displaced by the post-apocalypse, where the catastrophe has happened but there is no resurrection, no revelation. Bereft of the idea of the end as direction, truth, and foundation, we have reached the end of the end" (11).

The end of the end—but of what? For, indeed, what is perhaps novel about current iterations of the post-apocalypse on television is that, indeed, the "end" is usually not in sight. This is significant because these texts, on a narrative level, reflect not only the eschatological belief(s) at the heart of apocalyptic narratives, but also reflect the highly personal experience of the apocalypse as well. Many studies of the resurgence of apocalyptic cinema and television over the last 20 years have focused on the psychological, historical, and cultural events that have shaped our fascination with "end times," including the turn of the new millennia and Y2K, the terrorist attacks of 9/11 (and other similar incidents), the rise of global pandemics, the exacerbation of meteorological disasters caused by climate change, etc. These studies have all largely been causal and psychological in nature, focusing on *why* we—as medial consumers, and as a culture—are fascinated by discourse on the end times.[6] Most scholars link this apocalyptic saturation to social and cultural anxiety—but anxiety over what? Ritzenhoff and Krewani commence this list by noting that these "social anxieties [can be] linked to economic, ecological, and cultural factors. In the aftermath of 9/11, film directors have dealt with the trauma of terrorism, the explosion of technology, war, and ecological disasters in many different ways" (xiii). Other scholars have suggested the loss of identity and self-identity (Garry L. Hagberg); loss of spatial and psychological territories and borders (Ana Moya and Gemma López); and the perpetual fear of the Other (Jennifer Rickel) or even becoming the Other, to name but a few emerging, interconnected social constructs and factors that heighten collective anxieties and suggest embracing myriad narratives reflecting such dystopian outcomes mirrors not just our current mood, but our anticipated belief in how the future will transpire as well.

Ana Moya and Gemma López suggest that the "common anxiety" (broadly construed) among post-apocalyptic works is that "they speculate with the possibility of human society disintegrating." They add that, in such instances, "the known becomes unknown as society reverts to chaos and wilderness. What has emerged after disaster and mayhem is presented as other to human beings who are constantly threatened not just by the possibility of death, but rather by engulfment into the chaos they strive to avoid" (n.p.). This, in their estimation, is the reason for the proliferation of post-apocalyptic texts: the fear of emerging chaos. Our collection, however, takes a slightly different approach from these previous studies. We view the apocalypse as not (strictly speaking) a metaphor, but as a given. We posit that the reason why these texts abound is that as a society we have seemingly reckoned with the notion that we *are* currently living in the end times.

As we previously noted, in some ways, this reflects a function of medium. Television series are usually designed to persist; if Rick and his cohorts in *The Walking Dead* save the world from the walkers once and for all, the series (like societies after the apocalypse, *post* the apocalypse) would need to change, to adapt, or to stop narrativizing altogether. Yet this functional response also reflects a key component of their consumptive viewership. Perhaps the one essential difference between apocalyptic narratives like *Star Trek: The Next Generation*, *Buffy the Vampire Slayer*, and *Doctor Who* and post-apocalyptic works like *The Walking Dead*, *The Strain*, *The Leftovers* and so many similar series is not that the former are utopian and the latter apocalyptic/dystopian, or that the former allows for heroes to save the day while the latter does not; these differences, though easy to depict and visualize, are shallow reflections of larger matters. For, indeed, what these post-apocalyptic series most say is that we, the viewers, can no longer perceive of the chance of rescue. Pessimistic? Definitely. Nihilistic? Quite possibly. More than this, though, the contemporary emphasis on the post-apocalypse only reflects what seems to be felt so keenly in the psyche of those cultures that generate them: society is broken.

Or, at the least, society is *perceived* to be broken. The actual status of society we will leave to sociologists and anthropologists and political scientists and statisticians and those better suited to address such questions. Narratives, we feel, are more reflective of societal perception, of how the larger whole views society itself, and, it seems safe to say that, right now, society perceives itself as threatened, fractured, and ill; that things are not getting better; that, indeed, we are living through the end of the world. These apocalyptic narratives reflect, affirm, and create this notion that the world may very well be coming to an end.

The word "through" is a signifier here, a notion that the event is transpiring. Indeed, the phrase "post-apocalyptic" may be a misnomer when applied to the current crop of serialized "end-of-the-world" narratives. "Post-" implies after, subsequent to, that the event has concluded. There are post-apocalyptic narratives and post-apocalyptic television series represented in this collection, such as *The Handmaid's Tale* or *Cadillacs and Dinosaurs* or *The Last Man on Earth*, set in worlds where some past cataclysm has radically altered society. There are also works that one might almost deem *intra*-apocalyptic, such as *The Walking Dead* and *Westworld* and *The Strain*, since those events are unfolding, or continue to unfold, as part of the narrative. Can one truly consider *The Walking Dead* to be post-apocalyptic when the apocalyptic event—the invasion of what is essentially zombie hordes—is still ongoing?

This is important in understanding the cultural and narrative state of the current end of the world. Both post- and intra-apocalyptic narratives strive to tell stories infused with suffering and torment, reflective of tremendous and disruptive social and personal change. Yet while the end result of eschatological apocalyptic narratives is societal change that results in a type of rebirth, the contemporary post- (or intra-)apocalyptic television narrative never reaches a state of change. In these works, there is no hopeful resolution or revolution; there is no transformation. In most of them, there is only suffering and continued tribulation, further threats that are designed to disrupt whatever temporary, fragile peace the main characters may find for themselves, resetting the narrative of ordeal for the characters, so that they might relive the(ir) apocalypse all over again.

This form of narrative forestallment—of revisiting the same structure and style of events over and over—hearkens back to the significance French philosopher Gilles Deleuze places on the construct of the middle: "What matters on a path, what matters on a line, is always the middle, not the beginning or the end. We are always in the middle of a path, in the middle of something" (Deleuze and Parnet 28). As Betti Marenko and Jamie Brassett, writing on this important Deleuzian vision, explain, "For Deleuze it is not the beginning or the end that counts but the middle, the multiple middles, and the milieus they describe: intersections, crossings, inflections, where a multilinear complex folds back on itself and where philosophy can interconnect with what is outside itself" (8). Contemporary television narratives of the apocalypse tend to focus not on the moment of the event itself, but on the duration of the apocalypse, on the *middle* of the apocalypse, on living *in* the apocalypse.

Living in the Deleuzian middle(s) is key here. In his essay in this collection, one of the authors of this introduction examines Syfy television's adaptation of *The Magicians* (2015–present). *The Magicians* is an archetypal rendering of Delueze's "middle" in these types of narratives. Each season of the series presents a world-ending problem that the central characters of the series must overcome or correct; and yet, as if by cue, as the characters triumph in the final episode of the season, their actions spark yet *another* apocalyptic scenario, one even more daunting than the first, which they will then spend the next season working to overcome. Continually trading one apocalypse for the other, the characters veer from one disaster to the next, barely pausing to either enjoy any hard-fought victory they have striven to achieve or the manner in which their experiences may have changed them and/or the world around them. They simply must keep going, averting disaster whenever possible, and learn to live with the outcome when it is not.

Similar constructs abound in apocalyptic television series. Rick and his cohorts on *The Walking Dead* establish a peaceful settlement, only to be overrun by the walkers, the Governor, the Saviors, the Whisperers. The threats, the terrors, and the dangers keep coming. It is as the title of this introduction notes: the end of the world simply will not end.

All of this gloom and doom suggests pessimism about the future of humanity, whether that pessimism is found in the pages of a study on apocalyptic television series or in the more comfortable confines of our living rooms, where we are fed—feed ourselves—a steady diet of such nihilistic narratives. This was the question posed to, and by, the essays in this collection. What does it mean to be in the middle of the end? What does it mean when the end of the world will not end? And if these questions seem to speak only to doom and defeat and despair, well, it may very well be that all we have to offer—all that being in the middle of such events offers—is doom and defeat and despair.

Not every scholar of the apocalypse believes that it is as bad as all that. Heather Urbanski suggests that these series show "us our nightmares, and therefore contribute[s] to our efforts to avoid them" (1). Mary Pharr, Leisa Clark, and Amanda Firestone, in the introduction to their book *The Last Midnight: Essays on Apocalyptic Narratives in Millennial Media*, speak of apocalyptic narratives as harbingers, and not reflectors, of doom:

> It seems too much to bear—but as warnings, apocalyptic narratives also signify our species' growing awareness of danger, of the need both to recognize and react to what does not have to be inevitable. Humans still have the choice to work for the world's survival. It's not quite midnight yet [23].

It may not yet be midnight, but it is pretty darn close. *The Bulletin of Atomic Scientists* gave its annual presentation on January 24, 2019, pronouncing that the Doomsday Clock is set at two minutes until the "symbolic apocalyptic midnight," the closest to midnight the clock has been since its inception in 1947 (tied with 1953). Many cultural and philosophical scholars are indicating that these truly are the end times. As the journalist Holly Yan wryly observed, in her response to the adjusted Doomsday Clock setting, "If you have anything left on your bucket list, do it now, because the world is close to annihilation." Wheeler Winston Dixon echoes Yan's belief: "time is running out. I can feel it. The romance of Armageddon is being replaced by the spectre of inevitable destruction" (ch. 3).

Dixon laments that "thoughtfulness" is missing from contemporary films about the end: "All that matters is destruction, with a continual wave of fresh victims as scenery" (ch. 3). We are those victims, and the tattered remnants of our living rooms are that scenery. We have surrendered the apocalyptic narrative of rebirth—the *end* of the end—for Deleuze's interminable middle of the end. This suggests not the evolution of humanity as the result of cataclysm, as apocalyptic eschatology contends, but rather constant continuation, not only of the apocalyptic narrative, but of all that led up to it. As Barbara Gurr observes:

> Post-apocalyptic narratives, necessarily set after the world ends and the work of rebuilding something new begins, frequently fail to imagine new experiences of race, gender, and sexuality. Instead, the stories created for us in film and television all too often reproduce conservative ideologies which shape how we "read" social constructions of race, gender, and sexuality as natural and inevitable, perhaps even necessary for survival. Many of these post-apocalyptic films and TV shows … feature survivors scrambling to reestablish the previous order of things, uncritically reinstalling previous hierarchies and … expectations [1–2].

Gurr suggests that simply surviving may take more energy than the imagination needed to envision something new and different, a very pessimistic view of what is to come indeed.

And yet, as the contributors to this collection have noted, the apocalypse does not seem fated to bring out the best in us. William S. Allen's essay "Apocalyptic Television, Hobbes's Moral Psychology and the Tenuous Nature of Liberal Democratic Values" notes that moral philosophers, such as Thomas Hobbes, acknowledge that humans are amoral, egotistic, and power-hungry, and act in their own best interests even in good times. If the end of the world merely produces only the end of *our* world as we know it, is that not enough to be labeled truly apocalyptic?

Sherry Ginn's essay "Post-Apocalyptic Competition and Cooperation in *The Handmaid's Tale* and *The Walking Dead*" continues this line of thought by discussing evolutionary forces that dictate sexuality and reproduction, noting that conflict seems to be inherent to such efforts. This is especially true of events as depicted within the Republic of Gilead in *The Handmaid's Tale*. Selfish acts and selfish actors will dominate the apocalypse—as much, or perhaps more, as they dominate the present. Or maybe not? Perhaps there is some hope? Ginn's essay also argues that cooperation would be a beneficial strategy for survivors of an apocalyptic event. Cooperation would allow for sufficient resources for the survival of many people rather than a few. History records that conflict *and* cooperation have been necessary for humankind to survive the natural and human-made disasters of the past. Survivors following the apocalypse will have to compete for scant resources and then cooperate so that any type of societal grouping, whether intra-familial or extra-familial, will survive. And yet, how successful will such endeavors be?

Fernando-Gabriel Pagnoni Berns, Juan Ignacio Juvé, and Emiliano Aguilar's "The Long Winter of Discontent: The Changing Society of *Survivors*" concludes that perhaps the best one can hope from cooperation is a reversion to the status quo, the same status quo that resulted in the cataclysm to begin with. Another essay in this collection by Sebastian Müller ("Risk Without End? The Seriality of Risk, the Outbreak Narrative and Serial Post-Apocalypse in Guillermo del Toro and Chuck Hogan's *The Strain*") also explores scenarios where, when given a choice to act selfishly or for the greater good, characters often act in their own self-interests, further dooming the species as a whole. There does exist cooperation in these texts—usually among small bands of heroic actors/main characters—but this cooperation is often undermined by figures from within who sabotage the actions of others for their own needs, extending the apocalyptic middle and ensuring that the world's end will not come anytime soon.

And yet, heroes may emerge in these series. Heroes are important to the myth culture of humanity, as Joseph Campbell explained in his landmark study *The Hero with a Thousand Faces*, and may act as moral or physical loci of heroic activity. Tony Perrello and C. Anne Engert's essay "Driven to Extinction, Again: *Cadillacs and Dinosaurs* and the Irresistible Apocalypse" notes how the protagonist figure of Jack Tenrec in *Cadillacs and Dinosaurs* strives to achieve balanced, moral outcomes in his post-apocalyptic world. E. Leigh McKagen applies Campbell's theories on heroism directly to *Battlestar Galactica* in "The End of Everything: Survival Narratives and Everyday Heroism in *Battlestar Galactica*." She notes that Campbell's discussion of compassion and suffering coupled with the challenge of living in the present is more indicative of events on *Battlestar Galactica*, though the fate of those on the series is also strongly impacted by the actions of independent, heroic actors. And yet McKagen notes that these heroic actions are problematic unto themselves, and relying on heroes in apocalyptic times may only be for legends, and not for real life.

As Urbanski observed, perhaps one reason we watch post-apocalyptic television series is as a means of preparation. We speculate about the types of disasters that are theoretically possible given the current geopolitical climate—plagues, economic collapse, seismic events, or nuclear detonation—and observe the response generated as a result of this destruction. JZ Long's essay "Apocalypse(s) Already: Doomsday Preppers at the End of The(ir) Worlds" both reflects this concept as well as the notion that that belief, that global pessimism, may be all that is truly necessary to declare this epoch an apocalyptic period. These doomsday preppers, symptomatic of society as a whole, may not be reacting to an imagined apocalypse, but causing the very real one.

For good and for ill, the individual actors in narratives like *The Strain* and *Doomsday Preppers* reiterate a recurrent theme in these essays—the desire to save one's self, if only for the immediate future, rather than to save humanity, and create an enduring future for the whole. Yet what if the "whole" is never truly threatened? The next four essays in this collection examine apocalyptic texts where the apocalypse is far more personal or metaphysical than global.

In separate essays Christina Wilkins ("Reinvesting in the Rapture: Apocalypse and Faith in *The Leftovers*") and Derek R. Sweet ("Social Life and Death in *The Leftovers*: Surviving the Personal Apocalypse") explore the series *The Leftovers*, where the apocalyptic-like event does not have disastrous ramifications for society as a whole (after all, the world itself is not destroyed in *The Leftovers*; people are simply "left behind" when a small percentage of the world's population disappears). Yet the world is still left broken and shattered, and even those not directly impacted by the event face each day with the enormous burden of "survivor's guilt." Since the event is never explained, and since the fate of those who disappeared remains unknown, the series reflects a different type of never-ending end, a middle that is psychological and not physical, that is damning to the soul but that leaves life relatively intact. This series, the only one discussed in this book to do so, argues that faith may be all that stands between us and our understanding of how everything works. The series also affirms that simple communication—being with others—may be all that is necessary for survival in the personal apocalypse.

On the other hand, as Michael G. Cornelius observes in his essay "'How many times have I died?': Time Loops, Post-Human Reversion and the Editable Self in *The Magicians*," the loss of magical ability for the characters in the series reveals that life is mundane—boring even. Without magic the protagonists of the series realize that they are just like everyone else. Like those left behind in *The Leftovers*, the characters in *The Magicians* have nothing with which to define themselves following events in the series. The loss of family and the loss of identity are quite serious indeed. But do they truly rise to the level of apocalypse? Or do we only perceive it to be so?

Adam Ellerbrock's essay, "*Westworld* and the Apocalyptic Cycle," explores a series where shifts in identity actually trigger an apocalyptic event. In a world where loss is artificial and yet extremely heartfelt, the author may be hinting that it will be these personal apocalypses that will ultimately doom us all.

Marenko and Brassett, writing about Deleuze's concept of the "middle" and another form of narrative artifact, the book, note that

> when Deleuze and Guattari write that the rhizome "has neither a beginning nor an end, but always a middle (milieu) from which it grows and which it overspills" (1987: 21), it transforms how we might think of the relationality of the book. It is not a question of an essential quality of the book, how "open" it is for example, it is rather an issue of what the book activates and is activated by. Thinking of the book as a rhizome, as a middle and medium, at once both removes from the "book" the sentimentality it has as a cultural artefact, and makes us consider the milieu in which it roams, connects and animates [200].

Deleuze's interminable middle and the never-ending end of the world scenarios explored in the essays in this collection seem to offer no hope, no optimism, no relational means through which humanity may survive the myriad apocalypses that challenge our psyches and souls every time we tune them in. We are cognizant that our own sense of pessimism about this world pervades the argument(s) broached in this introduction. And yet we cannot help but remember a particularly revealing moment from *The Magicians*. During the third season of the show, the main characters embark on a quest to revert the apocalyptic disaster that has drastically impacted their world (again) and eliminated the wholesale use of magic. In the ninth episode of the season, the group of eight central magicians find themselves separated into four distinct planes of dimensional existence, though—momentarily—their thoughts are united by a magical object. One of their group, Josh (Trevor Einhorn), is being threatened with death, and another member, Quentin (Jason

Ralph), pleads for the aid of everyone to help rescue him. When one of the other questers responds to Quentin's call with, "We've got some life-and-death stakes of our own over here," Quentin replies, "Yes! We're all fucked in our own way, like always! But if we do not do this, then the quest is done" ("All That Josh"). He unites the group and manages to save Josh, preserving the quest for at least one more moment in time.

Quentin achieves this feat through a rather unorthodox manner: by combining forces with the group in a sing-along to Queen and David Bowie's "Under Pressure." Though his observation that the individual members of the group are "fucked ... like always" is correct, their unified voices result in outcomes where the peril each faces is thwarted. Though the song itself lasts less than four minutes, the group is left energized by this turn of events. Their immediate crises are averted, and their quest can continue. As viewers, we, too, are uplifted—perhaps the day can be saved. Perhaps, just this once, everything will be all right. Ultimately, though, the magicians' quest will fail. While the group does restore magic to the world, they are betrayed (not once, but twice), and the end result is a totalitarian, dystopian regime heading the world of magic—like always, they swap one apocalypse for another.

What is the purpose of such a scene, then? And what lesson does Deleuze hold for us at the end of all/some things? If these apocalyptic saturations are both "middle and medium," as Marenko and Brassett suggest, and that what is essential is what these apocalyptic visions "activate" and are "activated by," then it may be that perdition is our only future (200). If the genre that defines our contemporary milieu is indeed apocalyptic, that suggests it activates feelings of hopelessness and nihilism, and that these visions are activated by all that is around us. Deleuze's middle seems to offer us no hope—and yet, as John Elia suggests in the final essay in this collection, "Postnatural Comedy in *The Last Man on Earth*," hope may be found in the most unlikely of places— the face of a clown. Elia suggests that this broadly farcical series indicates that it is not a matter of living through the apocalypse, or seeing it to its end. Perhaps, as human beings, our apocalypses are as inevitable as our demises. Perhaps we should just accept this fate, and smile. As Elia observes, living in and through a time of trial and tribulation may be easier to swallow if one can find something inherent in all of it to simply laugh about.

If there is one conclusion the essays in this collection reach about living through these end times, it may be that the heroic narratives of earlier apocalyptic television series—where the day is saved—have shifted, from broadly heroic gestures to facets of crisis management, saving not the day, but perhaps just one moment in time. Pitetti notes that "any present status quo must be understood as temporary" (449). This seems to contradict Deleuze's construct that we are "always in the middle of a path." Or perhaps the middle shifts, in ways both subtle and grand, and we do not perceive these shifts until it is too late to truly note their origin, and we only notice social, cultural, and personal movement after it has happened. Does this mean that this moment, too, shall pass, that our apocalyptic present is only here for a while? Will this belief that we are living in an apocalyptic period elapse? Will we re-embrace optimism and the singular hero(es) who can stave off the apocalypse in lieu of the wholesale destruction of post- and intra-apocalyptic narratives? Perhaps.

All we can say for sure is that living in, living with, and living within the end times—this is what serialized versions of the apocalypse are really all about. They are about us, who we are now, who we fear we may become, or how we may even find a little hope or laughter at the end of the world. Perhaps these narratives suggest how desperately we long for change, even if we cannot conceive of the world changing without a bloody, protracted period of tribulation, terror, and fear. Or perhaps these narratives suggest that we fear we may never change, and that we are simply doomed to experience only small moments of triumph, like Quentin and his friends or the main characters on *The Walking Dead* or the inhabitants of any number of apocalyptic televisual worlds, moments of elation that will soon be subsumed by the ever-grinding nature of the apocalypse itself. Yet, as *The Magicians* wryly notes, we may all be "fucked ... like always," but for fleeting moments we—like Quentin and his magical cohorts—can sing; we, too, can come together, and remind ourselves that any genre that purports to examine how we die truly explores how we live, and that perhaps these apocalyptic saturations best remind us to live for the moment, to live in the now, since tomorrow is never guaranteed, not for any of us.

Notes

1. We should note that catastrophic events are not necessarily singular. As noted, the Spanish Flu decimated an already overstressed population following World War I. The Fukushima Daiichi nuclear disaster followed a cascading sequence of catastrophes. Active nuclear reactors at the plant reacted automatically following the Tōhoku earthquake; however, a subsequent tsunami disabled the generators, which would have provided electricity to power the pumps cooling the radioactive cores. And while over 1,000 deaths are attributable to the nuclear incident, almost 16,000 deaths are the result of the earthquake and tsunami.

2. Sources note the difficulty in tracking illnesses and stress-related deaths that can be directly linked to the event, and even differ on the definition of event-related deaths. Even official, government documents differ on these totals. An editorial from March 1, 2014, edition of *The Japan Times* noted, "The latest report from Fukushima revealed that more people have died from stress-related illnesses and other maladies after the disaster than from injuries directly linked to the disaster. The report compiled by prefectural authorities and local police found that the deaths of 1,656 people in Fukushima Prefecture fall into the former category. That figure surpasses the 1,607 people who died from disaster-related injuries. Another 434 people have died since 3/11 in Iwate Prefecture and 879 in Miyagi Prefecture" ("Fukushima's Appalling Death Toll"). David Guiterrez, a staff writer for *Natural News*, wrote, "According to data collected by the Fukushima Prefecture, 2014 saw 1,232 nuclear-related deaths" ("Fukushima

Disaster Caused at Least 1,232 Fatalities Last Year as Radiation Death Rate Accelerates"). The newspaper *The Tokyo Shimbum* (March 6, 2016) listed 1,368 deaths as "related to the nuclear power plant" (the original is available only in Japanese; this translation was found through Wikipedia "Fukushima Daiichi Nuclear Disaster Casualties").

    3. For those who want to know what the first seven are, they are heart disease, all cancers, chronic lower respiratory diseases (e.g., chronic bronchitis, emphysema, COPD), accidents, stroke, Alzheimer's disease, and diabetes.

    4. One reason it is difficult to know exact figures is because of the many people who were displaced, killed, or missing following World War I.

    5. This is not to suggest that the universe created in the Star Trek franchise or its presentment is wholly utopian, though elements are presented as such; rather, the *genre* of the varying series in the franchise are largely utopian, though more recent series (including *Deep Space Nine*, *Enterprise*, and *Discovery*) have pushed the franchise into more dystopian-leaning realms, though the overall generic structure remains intact. Hassler-Forest revisits the utopian model of Star Trek in his book *Science Fiction, Fantasy, and Politics*, while other scholars identifying the Star Trek franchise as a utopian model include Katrina Boyd, Patrick Brereton, David Golumbia, and Michael Jindra, to name but a few. To be fair, many of these same scholars suggests that the series (often inadvertently) complicates the nature of its utopian presentment, but most scholars of science fiction television firmly place Star Trek into the utopian genre model.

    6. For a listing of apocalyptic television series, please see Appendix 1 of this collection.

Works Cited

Benedictow, Ole J. "The Black Death: The Greatest Catastrophe Ever." *History Today*, vol. 55, no. 3, 2005, pp. 42–49. www.historytoday.com/ole-j-benedictow/black-death-greatest-catastrophe-ever. Accessed 15 January 2019.

Boyd, Katrina G. "Cyborgs in Utopia: The Problem of Radical Difference in *Star Trek: The Next Generation*." *Enterprise Zones: Critical Positions on Star Trek*, edited by Taylor Harrison, Sarah Projansky, Kent A. Ono, and Elyce Rae Helford. Westview, 1996, pp. 95–113.

Brereton, Patrick. *Hollywood Utopia: Ecology in Contemporary American Cinema*. Intellect, 2004.

Campbell, Joseph. *The Hero with a Thousand Faces*. New World Library, 2008.

Cousin de Grainville, Jean-Baptiste. *Le Dernier Homme (The Last Man)*. 1805. Translated by I.F. Clarke and M. Clarke, Wesleyan UP, 2003.

Deleuze, Gilles, and Claire Parnet. *Dialogues*. Translated by Hugh Tomlinson and Barbara Habberjam, Columbia UP, 1977.

Dixon, Wheeler Winston. *Visions of the Apocalypse: Spectacles of Destruction in American Cinema*. Wallflower, 2003, Kindle edition. dx.doi.org/10.3998/fc.13761232.0041.102.

Florea, Maria. "Media Violence and the Cathartic Effect." *Procedia: Social and Behavioral Sciences*, vol. 92, 2013, pp. 349–353. doi.org/10.1016/j.sbspro.2013.08.683

"Fukushima Daiichi Nuclear Disaster Casualties." Wikipedia, en.wikipedia.org/wiki/Fukushima_Daiichi_nuclear_disaster_casualties#cite_note-22, Accessed 14 Aug. 2019.

"Fukushima's Appalling Death Toll." *The Japan Times*, 1 Mar 2014, www.japantimes.co.jp/opinion/2014/03/01/editorials/fukushimas-appalling-death-toll/, Accessed 14 Aug. 2019.

Gilgamesh. Translated and edited by Herbert Mason, Penguin, 1972.

Golumbia, David. "Black and White World: Race, Ideology, and Utopia in 'Triton' and 'Star Trek.'" *Cultural Critique*, no. 32, 1995–1996, pp. 75–95.

Gurr, Barbara. "Introduction: After the World Ends, Again." *Race, Gender, and Sexuality in Post-Apocalyptic TV and Film*, edited by Barbara Gurr, Palgrave Macmillan, 2015, Kindle edition.

Gutierrez, David. "Fukushima Disaster Caused at Least 1,232 Fatalities Last Year as Radiation Death Rate Accelerates." *Natural News*, 7 Apr. 2015, www.naturalnews.com/049277_Fukushima_disaster_radiation_deaths_thyroid_cancer.html. Accessed 14 Aug. 2019.

Hagberg, Garry L. "Apocalypse Within: The War Epic as Crisis of Self-Identity." *The Philosophy of War Films*, edited by David LaRocca. UP of Kentucky, 2014, pp. 205–245.
Haines, Andy, and Kristie Ebi. "The Imperative for Climate Action to Protect Health." *New England Journal of Medicine*, vol. 380, 2019, pp. 263–273.
Hassler-Forest, Dan. *Science Fiction, Fantasy, and Politics: Transmedia World-Building Beyond Capitalism*. Rowman and Littlefield, 2016.
_____. "*Star Trek*, Global Capitalism, and Immaterial Labour." *Science Fiction Film and Television*, vol. 9, no. 3, 2016, pp. 371–391.
Heffernan, Teresa. *Post-Apocalyptic Culture: Modernism, Postmodernism, and the Twentieth-Century Novel*. U of Toronto P, 2008.
Hunter, Brad. "Next Pandemic Could Kill a Billion People: Researchers." *Toronto Sun*, 30 July 2018, torontosun.com/news/world/next-pandemic-could-kill-a-billion-people-researchers. Accessed 15 January 2019.
Jeffries, Richard. *After London*. 1885. Dover, 2015.
Jindra, Michael. "Star Trek Fandom as a Religious Phenomenon." *Sociology of Religion*, vol. 55, no. 1, 1994, pp. 27–51.
Kermode, Frank. *The Sense of an Ending: Studies in the Theory of Fiction*. 1966. Oxford UP, 2000.
Kreuziger, Frederick. *The Religion of Science Fiction*. Popular Press, 1986.
Lord Byron (Gordon, George). "Darkness," *Poetry Foundation*, www.poetryfoundation.org/poems/43825/darkness-56d222aeeee1b. Accessed 1 November 2018.
Marenko, Betti, and Jamie Brassett. *Deleuze and Design*. Edinburgh UP, 2015.
Matheson, Richard. *I Am Legend*. 1954. Tor Books, 2007.
Moya, Ana, and Gemma López. "Looking Back: Versions of the Post-Apocalypse in Contemporary North-American Cinema." *Film Criticism*, vol. 41, no. 1, 2017. Doi.org/10.3998/fc.13761232.0041.102.
Newitz, Annalee. *Scatter, Adapt, and Remember: How Humans Will Survive a Mass Extinction*. Anchor Books, 2013.
Pannaraj, Pia. "US Measles Outbreaks Catalyzed by Vaccine Hesitancy." Healio, N.d., *Healio.com*, www.healio.com/pediatrics/vaccine-preventable-diseases/news/print/infectious-diseases-in-children/%7B8073077c-43e9-407a-8766-4752884bb162%7D/us-measles-outbreaks-catalyzed-by-vaccine-hesitancy, Accessed 31 January 2019.
Pharr, Mary F., Leisa A. Clark, and Amanda Firestone. "Introduction." *The Last Midnight: Essays on Apocalyptic Narratives in Millennial Media*, edited by Leisa A. Clark, Amanda Firestone, and Mary F. Pharr. McFarland, 2016, pp. 4–24.
Pitetti, Connor. "Uses of the End of the World: Apocalypse and Postapocalypse as Narrative Modes." *Science Fiction Studies*, vol. 44, no, 3, 2017, 437–454.
Rickel, Jennifer. "Practice Reading for the Apocalypse: David Mitchell's *Cloud Atlas* as Warning Text." *South Atlantic Review*, vol. 80, no. 1–2, 2016, pp. 159–177.
Ritzenhoff, Karen A., and Angela Krewani. "Introduction." *The Apocalypse in Film: Dystopias, Disasters, and Other Visions About the End of the World*, edited by Ritzenhoff and Krewani. Rowman and Littlefield, 2015, xi–xxi.
Santhanam, Laura. "CDC Says More People Die of Influenza Worldwide Than Some Experts Have Estimated." PBS News Hours, 13 Dec 2017, www.pbs.org/newshour/health/cdc-says-more-people-die-of-influenza-worldwide-than-who-estimated. Accessed 19 Oct. 2018.
Scheff, Thomas J. "Catharsis and Other Heresies: A Theory of Emotion." *Journal of Social, Evolutionary, and Cultural Psychology*, vol. 1, no. 3, 2007, pp. 98–113. dx.doi.org/10.1037/h0099826.
Shelley, Mary. *The Last Man*. 1826. The Floating Press, 2009.
Urbanski, Heather. *Plagues, Apocalypses and Bug-Eyed Monsters: How Speculative Fiction Shows Us Our Nightmares*. McFarland, 2007.
Vera, Amir. "Washington Is Under a State of Emergency as Measles Cases Rise." *CNN*, 29 January 2019, www.cnn.com/2019/01/26/health/washington-state-measles-state-of-emergency/index.html. Accessed 31 January 2019.
Wells, H.G. *The War of the Worlds*. 1898. Heritage Press, 1964.
Yan, Holly. "The Doomsday Clock Says It's Almost the End of the World as We Know It.

(And That's Not Fine.)" *CNN*, 24 January 2019, cnn.com/2019/01/24/world/doomsday-clock-2019/index.html. Accessed 25 January 2019.

Young, Jessie. "Australia's Deadly Wildfires Are Showing No Signs of Stopping. Here's What You Need to Know." CNN, 13 January 2020, cnn.com/2020/01/01/australia/australia-fires-explainer-intl-hnk-scli/index.html. Accessed 15 January 2020.

Filmography

"All Good Things..." *Star Trek: The Next Generation*, season 7, episodes 25 and 26, syndicated, 23 May 1994.

"All That Josh." *The Magicians*, season 3, episode 9, SyFy, 7 Mar. 2018.

Angel, created by Joss Whedon, The WB / CW, 1999–2004.

Buffy the Vampire Slayer, created by Joss Whedon, The WB / CW, 1997–2003.

The Day After Tomorrow, directed by Roland Emmerich, Twentieth Century Fox, 2004.

Doctor Who, created by Sydney Newman, C.E. Webber, and Donald Wilson, BBC, 1963–present.

"Encounter at Farpoint." *Star Trek: The Next Generation*, season 1, episode 1, syndicated, 28 Sept 1987.

Fantastic Four, directed by Josh Trank, Twentieth Century Fox, 2016.

"The Gift." *Buffy the Vampire Slayer*, season 5, episode 22, The WB, 22 May 2001.

Independence Day, directed by Roland Emmerich, Twentieth Century Fox, 1996.

The Leftovers, created by Damon Lindelof and Tom Perrotta, HBO, 2014–2017.

The Magicians, created by Sera Gamble and John McNamara, SyFy, 2015-present.

"A New Man." *Buffy the Vampire Slayer*, season 4, episode 12, The WB, 25 Jan 2000.

Star Trek: Deep Space Nine, created by Rick Berman and Michael Piller, syndicated, 1993–1999.

Star Trek: Discovery, created by Bryan Fuller and Alex Kurtzman, CBS All Access, 2017–present.

Star Trek: Enterprise, created by Rick Berman and Brannon Braga, UPN, 2001–2005.

Star Trek: The Next Generation, created by Gene Roddenberry, syndicated, 1987–1994.

The Strain, created by Guillermo del Toro and Chuck Hogan, FX, 2014–2017.

Suicide Squad, directed by David Ayer, Warner Bros. Pictures, 2016.

2012, directed by Roland Emmerich, Columbia Pictures, 2009.

The Walking Dead, created by Frank Darabont, AMC, 2010–present.

X-Men: Apocalypse, directed by Bryan Singer, Twentieth Century Fox, 2016.

Apocalyptic Television, Hobbes's Moral Psychology and the Tenuous Nature of Liberal Democratic Values

WILLIAM S. ALLEN

In a pivotal scene in the apocalyptic television series *The Strain* (2014–2017), the series' protagonists find it necessary to drive through Queens, despite the fact that this part of New York has been deemed a "no-man's land" due to the inability of the local authorities to protect its residents from an outbreak of vampirism. The borough resembles a ravaged, war-torn city, and the armed residents shout threats at the series' heroes as they attempt to reach their destination. Surveying the scene, Dr. Ephraim Goodweather (Corey Stoll), a CDC scientist, comments, "I was in South Sudan once. It was like war and disease had a contest to see who could create more suffering. I never thought it could happen here." Mr. Quinlan (Rupert Penry-Jones), a centuries-old vampire-human hybrid, replies, "Civility is an illusion. Savagery is the default state of humanity" ("Collaborators"). As if to prove this point, the scene ends with the protagonists witnessing a family being robbed by armed men; though they endeavor to dissuade the thieves from their course of action, they ultimately kill the thieves in self-defense.

Mr. Quinlan's assessment of human beings in such an imagined environment is consistent with the description of humans in the "state of nature" as proposed by 17th century philosopher Thomas Hobbes (1588–1679). Generally, the state of nature is a hypothetical environment in which no sovereign power is present to enforce laws and provide protection. Although accounts of the state of nature vary according to the philosopher, the purpose of it is to display the fundamental features of the human psyche unaffected by civil society. Hobbes's account claims that when there is no common authority to protect the well-being of people, humans are characteristically distrustful, competitive, amoral, and power-seeking for the sake of self-preservation. Due to such a nature, people in the state of nature will choose to harm each other, if they deem such action serves to fulfill their desires and meet their interests.

In the scene from *The Strain,* the rest of the city and the federal government have abandoned Queens; hence there is no common power to enforce the law and protect its inhabitants. When strangers appear, the residents display distrust and exercise power through their threatening behavior. The self-interested thieves display a lack of respect for the well-being of others. Mr. Quinlan's assessment of humanity echoes Hobbes's description of life in the state of nature: "when government is absent, civility, respect and morality in general is non-existent.... Every man is enemy to every man" (76).

The setting of people living in a survivalist environment where government is absent is common in apocalyptic, post-societal television series. I define an apocalyptic, post-societal television series as one in which society has broken down internally due to an apocalyptic event, where no common ruling force exists that subjects or attempts to subject all inhabitants, and where characters are forced to function in a survivalist environment. Generally, the main plot of such series is the protagonists attempting to establish a safe community while combating others who seek to kill or dominate them. These characters always value freedom, cooperation, and respect for others (although they may struggle to act upon such values). In *The Walking Dead* (2010–present), for example, characters live in the aftermath of a zombie apocalypse. The main plot since season 3 has not focused on combating walkers (the series name for zombies), but rather on battles between the series protagonists and people who threaten the protagonists' attempts to establish a safe community. *The 100* (2014–present) is set 97 years after a nuclear apocalypse. The protagonists are the descendants of survivors who fled to a space station during the apocalypse. The main plot point of the series features the descendants' attempt to establish a safe community on Earth while combating the Grounders, the descendants of the survivors who remained behind. Similar plots can be found in *The Last Ship* (2014–2018), which is set after a global viral pandemic, and *Revolution* (2012–2014), a series set in the near future where electricity has been disabled and the United States is ruled by warring militias, to name but a few.

All the series mentioned present a Hobbesian state of nature-like environment in which humans are distrustful of each other, compete for resources, and engage in inhumane behavior for the sake of survival and/or control. Although Hobbes presents a bleak and pessimistic view of human nature in the state of nature, I will argue here that apocalyptic, post-societal television series present an even more pessimistic view of humans than Hobbes. Hobbes proposes that, as creatures of reason, people in the state of nature will eventually realize that, for the sake of self-preservation, they should seek peace, cooperate, and agree to the establishment of a common ruler. Although hypothetical, Hobbes's state of nature ultimately serves to argue that civil society and government are the logical outcome of human nature. I will demonstrate that apocalyptic, post-societal television series challenge Hobbes's account of the human psyche. Such series seem to argue that in an anarchic environment, most humans will be directed by their base desires coupled with self-interest, and that peace is not possible. This argument has further philosophical import in that it challenges the commitment of people in liberal democratic societies to fundamental liberal values such as respect for rights to life, liberty, and property, the value of civility, and collective political cooperation. Apocalyptic, post-societal television series challenge whether the commitment to such values would survive the dissolution of civil society and government.

The Egoistic Nature of Humans and the Genesis of Morality

In Western philosophy, the characterization of humans as primarily self-interested, amoral, and uncivil begins with the ancient Greek philosopher Plato (429–348 BCE). Plato's *Republic*, a dialogue about the nature of justice and the formation of a just city-state, starts with an argument against justice having intrinsic value. The setting is the home of an acquaintance of Socrates, and present are Socrates' brothers and other guests. One guest, Thrasymachus, argues that justice is an artifice created by those with power who use it to serve their own advantage; thus, those with power are the only ones who truly benefit from justice. Socrates quickly refutes this argument by noting that those with power are not infallible, and sometimes their use of power does not serve toward their advantage. However, Socrates's brother, Glaucon, revisits Thrasymachus's argument and argues that humans do not value justice in and of itself but rather as a means to some other end. His argument, known as Glaucon's Challenge, concludes that justice is a social artifice and is only valued because it serves the human interest to be protected from people who would do us harm.

Glaucon begins with the ontological claim that humans are primarily self-interested and amoral. Naturally people have no qualms about committing unjust acts if it serves their interest. People only deter from performing such acts when it is not in their interest (e.g., there is a chance of being caught and punished). In philosophy, Glaucon's argument is a form of psychological egoism, a theory which claims that, fundamentally, people always act according to what they deem as their self-interest. Glaucon supports his position with a couple of illustrations, the most famous being The Ring of Gyges. In this myth a peasant named Gyges finds a magical ring that makes him invisible. While invisible he can do whatever he wishes without anyone knowing. He has the choice to use the ring justly or unjustly. Gyges chooses to use the ring for his own interest and thereafter seduces the queen of the kingdom, kills the king, and takes over as ruler.

Glaucon argues that we are all like Gyges in that if we could get away with doing injustice without punishment, we would do so if we deemed it conducive to our interests. However, even though we would like to commit injustice with impunity, we hate having injustice done to us even more. Hence the value of justice is to provide security against having injustice done to us. Plato writes,

> To commit injustice is, they say, in its nature a good thing, and to suffer it a bad thing; but the bad of suffering injustice exceeds the good of doing injustice; and so, after the two-fold experience of both doing and suffering injustice, those who cannot avoid the latter and choose the former find it expedient to make a contract of neither doing nor suffering injustice [*Republic* 359e–359a].

Justice is essentially a compromise between having the freedom to harm others and the desire not to be harmed by others. The belief that justice has value or existence independent from its instrumental use is a false belief according to Glaucon. Justice only comes into existence in the form of the artificial laws and moral codes created by human beings, which serves the primary human interest of self-preservation.

Although Plato gives a compelling argument for psychological egoism, he disagrees with the theory. Glaucon's Challenge is merely a frame for Plato's actual argument that justice *does* have intrinsic value, and that it is not advantageous for the individual or city-state to be unjust. The rest of the *Republic* serves as a response to Glaucon in which the character Socrates argues that the individual is designed, and the ideal city-state should be designed, according to a natural order. Justice is not a social construct but a natural part of the order of all things.

In respect to the individual, Plato argues that humans possess a soul which is naturally designed such that reason rules over other parts of the soul, like the appetites. The appetites are non-rational impulses such as hunger, thirst, lust, violence, and other physical desires. When reason controls the appetites, the soul is in harmony. When the soul is in harmony, justice is manifest within the individual, and the individual is happy. When the appetites rule over reason, the result is immoral behavior, the soul is in disharmony, and the individual is unjust and unhappy. Ultimately, Plato argues for a teleological account of human nature in which humans are designed to strive to cultivate a well-ordered soul.[1] However, his account of psychological egoism serves as a precursor to arguments made by subsequent philosophers such as Hobbes.

Hobbes is traditionally considered a psychological egoist although, upon closer analysis, his account of the human psyche is more complex. One can find excerpts in *Leviathan* that support psychological egoism: "For no man giveth but with intention of good to himself, because gift is voluntary, and of all voluntary acts the object is to every man his own good" (94). In this passage "gift" is broadly construed as performing an act for the benefit of another. The implication of this quote is that humans are incapable of altruistic behavior without the fundamental motive being self-interest. This is consistent with psychological egoism, for the theory does not imply people are incapable of helping others, but that they do so with the root motive being self-interest.

To fully understand Hobbes's psychological theory, one must begin with his materialist metaphysics. Hobbes believes that everything in existence is made of matter and all phenomena can be explained in terms of mechanistic material interactions. This includes mental processes and consciousness itself. Fundamentally, all human thought is a direct or indirect response to sense stimuli, according to Hobbes. His account of the psyche begins with the claim that all human acts are motivated by desires toward that which serves the well-being of the individual and aversion toward that which does not. Naturally, without the influence of society and government (living in the state of nature), people call that which they desire good and that which they have an aversion to bad. Morality in this natural state is non-existent. Hobbes writes:

> But whatsoever is the object of any man's appetite or desire that is it which he for his part calleth good; and the object of his hate and aversion, evil; and of his contempt, vile and inconsiderable. For these words of good, evil and contemptible are ever used with relation to the person that useth them, there being nothing simply and absolutely so, nor any common rule of good and evil to be taken from the nature of the objects themselves, but from the person of the man (where there is no commonwealth), or (in a commonwealth) from the person that representeth it… [29].

The claims about moral psychology in this quote are consistent with Glaucon's argument. In absence of a ruling power, morality is subjective (or non-existent in any robust sense) and people are primarily motivated by satisfying their own interests.

Hobbes reiterates this position specifically in relation to the state of nature. He writes, "To this war of every man against every man, this also is consequent: that nothing can be unjust. The notions of right and wrong, justice and injustice, have there no place. Where there is no common power, there is no law; where no law, no injustice" (78). Without a common power to restrain people in the state of nature, people will do whatever they deem necessary to survive. However, because the state of nature is a continual state of war and thus conflicts with self-preservation, Hobbes argues that no reasonable person would wish to live under such conditions in perpetuity. Eventually, people in the state of nature conclude they should seek peace in the form of Hobbes's first two laws of nature:

   1. Every human ought to seek peace and defend themselves when peace cannot be obtained.

2. For the sake of peace, humans should be willing to give up the freedom/liberty they have in the state of nature and this agreement requires the reciprocation of all parties.

The laws of nature are not natural in the sense of being inherent properties of the psyche. They are not instinctual akin to self-preservation, but are the result of using reason for the sake of self-preservation. The desire for self-preservation and the aversion to fear eventually leads individuals to use reason to conclude the laws of nature. Additionally, Hobbes states that the laws are not "laws" in a proper sense, since there is no one to enforce them.

The realization of the first two laws of nature is analogous to the realization found in Glaucon's Challenge. Glaucon argues that, for the sake of self-preservation, people must give up the freedom to do injustice with impunity. Similarly, Hobbes argues that for the sake of self-preservation people must seek peace and give up the complete freedom to do whatever they wish (which includes injustice) in the state of nature. Once people realize the first two laws of nature collectively, they come together to form a contract in which they give their freedom to a common power who maintains peace. According to Hobbes, this contract is as follows: "I authorize and give up my right of governing myself to this man, or to this assembly of men, on this condition, that thou give up thy right to him, and authorize all his actions in like manner" (109). This agreement to establish government and law is what is known in philosophy as the Social Contract. At this point morality comes into existence, with the first moral edict—and third law of nature—being: heed all contracts made. However, keeping contracts is not merely for the sake of self-interest but is a sign of moral virtue. Hobbes states that abiding by contracts is the first instance of expressing the virtue of justice, which co-extensively includes nobleness and courage.

Philosopher David Rutherford provides a bolder account of the role virtue plays in Hobbes's moral psychology. Rutherford argues that the laws of nature in their entirety should be understood as logical conclusions aimed at maintaining peace in which the moral virtues are a means to such an end. Furthermore, he argues that the moral virtues are present in Hobbes's state of nature. To support his argument, he refers to the following passage: "For the laws of nature, which consist in equity, justice, gratitude, and other moral virtues on these depending, in the condition of mere nature are not properly laws, but qualities that dispose men to peace and obedience" (Hobbes 174). According to Rutherford, "mere nature" refers to the state of nature and the quote essentially states that humans are disposed to the moral virtues in the state of nature. Additionally, the fact that people in the state of nature are disposed to seek peace infers the virtue of prudence.

Ultimately, Rutherford argues that the traditional view of Hobbes's moral psychology is correct in that morality does not exist in the state of nature in the sense that there is no common code of conduct; however, it is possible for individual actors to possess moral virtues. Rutherford writes, "I submit, it is Hobbes's position that the virtue of justice can exist in the state of nature and that it is not explicable as a habituated tendency to perform actions. Just actions do not exist in the state of nature, but a just person can" (8).

Philosopher Bernard Gert's assessment of Hobbes seems to concur with Rutherford. Gert provides his own evidence of reference to moral virtues in Hobbes's work. Gert acknowledges that there is evidence in support of Hobbes as a psychological egoist; however, he concludes,

> Hobbes's political theory is often thought to require an egoistic psychology, whereas what it actually requires is only that all men be concerned with their own self-interest. That is, though Hobbes's political theory requires that all men be concerned with their own self-interest, especially their own preservation, it does not mean that they cannot be concerned with anything else [512].

Ultimately, whether Hobbes is a psychological egoist is a matter of debate among philosophers. Although I fall into the category of people who believe Hobbes's moral psychology is more complex than psychological egoism, my argument here is not contingent upon resolving this debate. Since my focus is on Hobbes's state of nature, I do not think it is too controversial to say that self-interest as self-preservation is the fundamental motive in Hobbes's state of nature. Even if self-interest, power-seeking, distrust, etc., are not representative of the totality of Hobbes's human psychology, there is enough evidence to accept that such traits are at least representative of most humans in his account of the state of nature.

The importance of Rutherford and Gert's analyses are that they present a problem for the traditional account of Hobbes's moral psychology. If humans are amoral, asocial, self-interested, and power-seeking in the state of nature—as the traditional view claims—how is it possible for people in the state of nature to collectively reach the conclusion they should seek peace? Even if people are compelled by fear to end the state of nature, it does not necessarily lead to the conclusion that they should seek to establish a social agreement that requires trust, cooperation, and submission to the will of another. An equally probable conclusion is finding a more efficient way to dominate others and secure power over them. It seems more probable that if, collectively, people in the state of nature had the propensity to be virtuous and overcome their baser desires (as Rutherford argues) that the transition to the Social Contract would occur. This is where apocalyptic, post-societal television series present a challenge to the traditional account of Hobbes's moral psychology and Rutherford. Such series seem to argue that, in a survivalist environment akin to Hobbes's state of nature, most people will act according to the traditional Hobbesian egoistic account of human nature. However, because most people in this environment will be incapable of transcending their egoistic tendencies, collectively they will not choose a social agreement as a solution to their predicament.

Skepticism of Reason in Apocalyptic, Post-Societal Television Series

Although the traditional account of Hobbes's state of nature is consistent with the moral psychology and portrayal of life in apocalyptic, post-societal television series, such series present a challenge to Hobbes's proposal of how people exit the state of nature. Hobbes's implication that people in a survivalist environment would conclude that cooperation and living in peace serve the mutual interest of self-preservation seems plausible in the case of reasonable people. However, Hobbes fails to recognize that—given his account of the human psyche—it is also plausible that people could have a response other than cooperation or respond irrationally. It is possible people will conclude that the only way to establish peace is through the conquest of others—to "win the war," so to speak. Alternately, there is no guarantee that reason will prevail over irrational desires for most people. It is possible that self-interest combined with irrational desires such as greed, lust for power, and vengeance may keep people in the state of nature indefinitely. Both responses are common in apocalyptic, post-societal television shows.

Arguably since season 3 of *The Walking Dead*, the zombie walkers have become the secondary threat in the series. Plots now largely focus on the attempts of Rick Grimes (Andrew Lincoln) and his group to establish a safe community while combating others who wish to destroy or exploit their efforts. The primary antagonists embody the worst of human nature as described by Hobbes. They are self-interested, distrustful, competitive, power-hungry, and willing to commit atrocious acts for the sake of maintaining power.

The Governor (David Morissey), who appears in the third and fourth seasons, is a power-hungry, cruel sociopath. Any group he encounters, who has resources or poses a threat, he attempts to eliminate. Among the inhumane acts he commits are torture, attempted rape, and murder, all for the sake of his goal of domination. However, the most revealing act he commits is his final attack on Rick and company in the episode "Too Far Gone." Through deception The Governor has convinced a group of survivors to attack the prison where Rick's group lives. At this point, The Governor is not only motivated by his lust for power, but vengeance due to his previously unsuccessful attempt to take the prison. After presenting his hostages, Michonne (Danai Guirra) and Hershel (Scott Wilson), The Governor demands Rick and his people abandon the prison. Rick responds with an impassioned speech to The Governor's followers offering to share the prison:

> Look, I fought him [The Governor] before. And after, we took in his old friends. They've become leaders in what we have here. Now you put down your weapons, walk through those gates and you're one of us. We let go of all of it, and nobody dies. Everyone who's alive right now. Everyone who's made it this far. We've all done the worst kinds of things to just stay alive. But we can still come back. We're not too far gone. We get to come back. I know we all can change ["Too Far Gone"].

Rick's plea essentially embodies Hobbes's two laws of nature. Rick infers that everyone is tired of being at war with each other and wants peace. He offers a compromise in which everyone agrees to disarm and become part of a cooperative group. Based on Rutherford's reading of Hobbes, Rick is one of the virtuous people in the state of nature. His willingness to prevent war and allow strangers to share his resources is a display of courage and wisdom. The Governor, however, is too far gone and unable to transcend his base desires. In response to Rick's speech, he mutters "Liar," then beheads Hershel and starts a firefight which eventually leads to his death.

Rick's plea initially may seem to support Hobbes's claim that people will eventually recognize that they must cooperate for the sake of peace, as well as Rutherford's claim that virtuous people exist in the state of nature. However, Rick and his group are the exception rather than the norm in the world of *The Walking Dead*. Very few people they encounter possess the enlightened self-interest and virtues of Rick. Most people they meet are various degrees of The Governor. In season 7 the primary antagonist, Negan (Jeffrey Dean Morgan), is essentially a more lethal version of The Governor. Negan's group, the Saviors, condone Negan's philosophy of domination and exploitation and are, in most instances, as ruthless and inhumane as Negan.

Protagonists in conflict with people who wish to kill, dominate, or exploit them are a common theme in apocalyptic, post-societal television series. In *The 100* the Sky People return to Earth from a space station only to find they must fight for survival against the Grounders, who are the majority of Earth's inhabitants. A continuing theme throughout the series is the Sky People's attempt to establish peace with the Grounders, who only wish to kill or dominate them. As usual for such series, the protagonists value peace, cooperation, freedom, and respect for human beings, and the antagonists are violent, antisocial, and inhumane. As a warrior culture, the Grounders value strength and power; the leaders of each Grounder clan only hold their positions if they display such characteristics. Peace, cooperation, and sympathy are viewed as weaknesses, which is why the Grounders view the Sky People as weak and a target. In season 2, for the sake of fighting a common enemy, the Sky People and various Grounder clans agree to form an alliance. The alliance is precarious at best as each subsequent leader of the alliance, the Commander, is challenged by other members, and the different clans secretly plot against one another. The Grounders do not want peace in any robust sense. Any alliance ultimately serves as an opportunity to assume leadership over all the clans.

The serialized nature of televisual media is key to this reading. After several seasons of antagonist figures being replaced by new ones who espouse similar goals and motivations, the viewer begins to believe that there will never be a time of peace for the series protagonists. Rick and his group will continually encounter new groups of humans they will have to combat for survival, and the Sky People will always have to contend with some faction of the Grounders or a new enemy seeking to destroy or dominate them.

Hobbes does not provide a time limit for how long people can remain in the state of nature. Hobbes is also aware that government and civil society can be established by conquest. He states there are two ways the sovereign can come into power: when people collectively agree to establish the sovereign or by force. Both, he claims, require submission to the will of another and are the product of fear. Regardless of the accuracy of Hobbes's claims, the state of nature is meant to highlight the uncivil characteristics of human nature and hence provide for the basis that government and civil society are necessary. The Social Contract, in its various iterations, ultimately serves as models for government based on the consent of the people. The import of the Social Contract tradition is not in its historical accuracy but in the principles and values which inform the liberal democratic societies that subsequently resulted from such thought.

Apocalyptic, post-societal television series challenge the commitment of liberal peoples to the principles and values they profess to hold. The inhabitants in such series are the product of a liberal society. They are familiar (if not habituated to) Western conceptions of democratic government, human rights, and general rules of civility. The inference from such series is that once liberal people are placed in a survivalist environment without a common government, they will abandon liberal values and culture. Ultimately, such series not only confront the viewer with some unsettling implications about the moral agency of humans, but the tenability of liberal democratic society as well.

The Fragility of Liberal Values

The apocalyptic, post-societal television series challenge to liberal people's commitment to liberal values extends beyond Hobbes. It is consistent with a criticism of liberal philosophy in general. Philosopher John Gray, for example, argues that the liberal project (in which Hobbes is a central figure) is outdated; it is unable to sufficiently provide a solution to how peace can be established among people with conflicting worldviews. Gray writes,

> The liberal problem—which is that of specifying terms of peaceful coexistence among exponents of rival, and perhaps rationally incommensurable, world-views—is no less

pressing than in early modern times, when it appeared in Hobbes's thought with a clarity and starkness that was never to be surpassed; but the hope of resolving it by refounding morality on a universally compelling basis of reason, which animated Hobbes's project of a moral geometry, his individualist philosophical anthropology and the conception of rational choice as the generator of political order which these Enlightenment beliefs supported, has faded irrecoverably [86].

The reliance on reason to resolve conflicts of interest and beliefs is a central feature of traditional liberal thought and can be found throughout its history.

Succeeding Hobbes, the golden age of liberal thought occurs during the Enlightenment Period, with English philosophers such as John Locke (1632–1704), Scottish philosophers David Hume (1711–1776) and Adam Smith (1723–1790), and French philosophers such as Jean-Jacques Rousseau (1712–1778). They serve as the architects of liberal democratic thought, which continues to inform the political culture and understanding of rights, government, and citizenship for liberal societies. For example, Thomas Jefferson's statement in the Declaration of Independence that all men are due "life, liberty and the pursuit of happiness" was influenced by Locke's statement that all men are due "life, liberty and property" (Locke 271). Similarly, Rousseau's idea that government should be based on the general will of the people influenced political thought that led to the French Revolution.

Gray argues that all variants of traditional liberalism share four characteristics that originate with early liberal thinkers such as Hobbes and the Enlightenment period thinkers. First, moral primacy is given to the individual above any group or collective. Second, all humans are morally equal. Third, liberal moral values are claimed to be right for all humans regardless of culture (universalism). Finally, the proper use of reason is espoused to be reflected in liberal institutions and such institutions lead to the continual improvement of human well-being (meliorism). Gray states that the last two characteristics are particularly central to a liberal political outlook and are definitive of liberal political philosophy.

However, according to Gray, analysis of world history in the 20th century belies the universalism and meliorism of traditional liberal thought. The rise of nationalism, authoritarianism, fundamentalism, and tribalism throughout the 20th century counter the notion of a liberal destiny for humanity. Ultimately, Gray is skeptical about the efficacy of traditional liberalism domestically in the United States and internationally. He argues that a postliberal thought should be developed which discards universalism and the reliance on rational choice to establish peace. Instead, liberal people should learn to live in harmony with non-liberal people and create institutions that allow a diversity of political thought. The liberal project now should be finding a *modus vivendi* for diverse cultural forms.

Gray does not give a complete account of what a postliberal government entails, but he states that it should be minimalistic, though strong in terms of its capability to enforce law and protect its citizens. He compares it to a Hobbesian state in which the primary duty of government is to ensure peace among various groups. Rather than groups keeping a *modus vivendi* among themselves, the government deters conflict. My criticism of Gray (which apocalyptic, post-societal television series seem to imply) is that given traditional Hobbesian moral psychology, how is it ensured that all groups will respect the state's authority in perpetuity (particularly if there is no unifying moral, religious, or political belief)? What prevents one group from assuming political power and using government for their own interests or the sovereign becoming corrupt? Gray recognizes this as a problem and responds that hopefully citizens would find it is in their interest to maintain such a government to avoid totalitarianism. His response, however, seems to rely on the same faith in the reasonableness of humans that he criticizes.

However, Gray's account of the liberal problem is consistent with themes in some apocalyptic, post-societal television series in which the basis for conflict is not merely differences in moral character, but worldviews. In such series, the antagonists are not one-dimensional villains but have a worldview motivating their actions. In *The Walking Dead*, Negan sees the world as in need of saving. Negan's group calls themselves "the Saviors," and Negan believes that, through conquering other communities, he is saving humanity. Only through the establishment of a totalitarian authority can humanity have peace and security. He is puzzled by the defiance of Rick's alliance. Negan believes everyone is better off under the rule of the Saviors. Negan, in one sense, is Hobbesian in that he believes the sole role of the ruler is to prevent internal conflict and protect people from external threats. The idea of liberal human rights and freedom is absent from his ideology. At its root, the conflict between Rick's alliance and the Saviors is ideology, one being liberal and the other totalitarian.

Negan's totalitarianism is most evident in the requirement that the Saviors show their loyalty to Negan and unity by stating, "I am Negan." Such a statement is similar to Nazi German officers saluting and saying "Heil Hitler"; it displays loyalty and unity of thought. Additionally, "I am Negan" is a display of extreme collectivism in which individuality and self-identity are symbolically erased. It can be inferred that Negan's solution to the problem of liberalism is to eliminate differences in beliefs, interests, and identity by having them all subjugated to one belief system, identity, and worldview. However, Negan's ideology is flawed in that he cannot guarantee everyone (internal or external to his group) will subscribe to his ideology indefinitely. Not only does Negan have to contend with Rick and his allies, but he must also struggle with dissidents within the Saviors who disagree with his ideology and seek to subvert it in various ways (in season 8, Negan's downfall is partly due to the acts of people within his group).

Even in those series in which there are attempts to reinstitute the government, skepticism of the commitment to liberal democratic values abounds. A common plot device in apocalyptic, post-societal series is the appearance of a group claiming they wish to reinstitute the United States' government, for example, when they secretly aim to institute a non-liberal form of rule. In season 3 of *The Last Ship*, the cure for the pandemic has been distributed throughout the United States, and the office of the president has been reinstituted. However, parts of the country are controlled by regional leaders who (along with people within the president's cabinet) plot to establish an autocratic oligarchy. Self-interest and difference in political views motivate the actions of the regional leaders. The regional leaders believe their residents would be better off retaining their autonomy as independent states rather than under a centralized government. Additionally, they oppose the president's egalitarian economic policy which includes the distribution of resources from advantaged communities to disadvantaged communities. The regional leaders eventually stage a coup in which they assassinate the president and replace him with a puppet leader.

In the second season of *Revolution* a similar plot device is used in which the remnants of the American government return to the mainland from Guantanamo Bay, Cuba. Calling themselves The Patriots, their goal is to eliminate the various Republics (regions ruled by militias) and unify the country under a neo-fascist totalitarian dictatorship. The Patriots' president, Jack Davis (Cotter Smith), proclaims in a speech to his followers that he wishes to establish a "new order of ages" to correct the ruin of the United States before an apocalypse by "perverts and parasites" ("Exposition Boulevard"). His speech and the form of government he wishes to institute indicate that he believes liberal democratic government and liberal values led to the ruin of the country. The solution he implements involves brainwashing potential soldiers at reeducation camps, killing people with "undesirable" physical and mental disorders, and murdering anyone that is a threat or defies his rule.

Although apocalyptic, post-societal television series provide a good critique of human rationality and the commitment to liberal values, such series are flawed in their portrayal of tribalism. Most series do not realistically portray the racial, gender, religious, and ethnic divisions reflective of contemporary America. Whether in respect to the main protagonists or antagonists, the members of disparate groups in such series are diverse in terms of race, gender, and age (and in some cases religious and sexual orientation). For example, from the start of the first season of *The Walking Dead*, Rick's group has been racially and gender diverse. As the series progressed it became more diverse with the inclusion of gay and lesbian members and a Muslim character. The Governor's community and the Saviors are similarly diverse. Considering that the series setting is in the deep south, where racial stratification is particularly prevalent, such in-group diversity seems odd and unrealistic. Indeed, the post-apocalyptic world of *The Walking Dead* seems to be more racially integrated than the United States as a whole.

Considering the asocial and self-interested nature of humans in Hobbes's state of nature, in an anarchic post-apocalyptic world, people generally would form groups based on familial, communal, racial, and religious ties and commonalities. Additionally, conflicts between groups would partly be motivated by such differences in addition to competition for resources. I suspect the form of diversity in apocalyptic, post-societal television series is motivated by a general trend in contemporary television and film toward diverse casting. My argument here is not against diversity in casting, but in how said diversity is portrayed. By portraying diversity unrealistically, it limits discussion of racial, gender, and religious relationships that such series could address.

There are two notable exceptions. In season 3 of *The Walking Dead* spin-off *Fear the Walking Dead* (2015–present), the plot focuses on conflict between a survivalist group with racist beliefs and a neighboring Native American community. Before the apocalypse, the survivalist group's founders acquired land from the indigenous Native Americans through both legal and nefarious means. The Native Americans claim the land was stolen from them. After the apocalypse, the dispute over land rights exacerbates to armed conflict. The main core group of series protagonists (who are a racially diverse group) arrive at the survivalist group's ranch and must contend with the conflict between the two groups. The plot, on the surface, is like other apocalyptic, post-societal television series, but the fact that it explicitly addresses some of the racial and cultural tensions that underly contemporary American society adds depth, realism, and relevance to the series' presentation of these issues.

Another example can be found in the episode "Sisters of Mercy" of the campier zombie apocalypse show *Z Nation* (2014–present). The protagonists (again, a racially diverse group) arrive at a sanctuary for women and children. The community, Sisters of Mercy, only allow women to enter their grounds and have no qualms killing intruders. Their leader, Helen (Kelly McGillis), divulges that she was in an abusive relationship with her husband that extended after the apocalypse and, upon his death, she founded the sanctuary. Additionally, most of the women in the community experienced abuse by men after the apocalypse. Such experience leads Helen to have a bleak outlook on men, made explicit by her statement, "Man. He can't help himself. The animal instinct takes over. Kill, destroy, rape. Now this disease, this virus. Testosterone is the most toxic chemical on Earth" ("Sisters of Mercy"). Eventually a more sinister side of Helen and the sanctuary is revealed when it is discovered that Helen murdered her husband, adolescent boys are exiled from the community (ensuring their death), and men who harm women are imprisoned with a zombie bear.

Conclusion

Ultimately, apocalyptic, post-societal television series raise four interrelated, unsettling implications about liberal people and liberal societies. First, such series seem to imply that regardless of people's political, moral, and religious convictions, most are like the various antagonists rather than protagonists. As a viewer, we identify with the protagonists because they respect liberal values and have a moral compass. We would like to think that if we were in such a scenario we would be one of the "good guys," the Ricks of the world. However, given that the good guys are few in such shows and that even the good guys struggle with being faithful to their values, the implication is that most of us would likely be people who abandon or compromise moral, religious, and political values in the name of self-preservation.

A second implication is that liberal democratic society is very fragile. In these series the adherence to such values disappears quickly, and it is extremely difficult (if not impossible) to restore liberal democratic society. At best, the viewer hopes the protagonists win and establish a defensible community or establish an alliance with other groups to secure safety. In season 8 of *The Walking Dead*, the latter seems to be the direction the show is moving toward with Alexandria forming an alliance with The Hilltop and The Kingdom. *The 100* as well has moved in this direction with the alliance between the Sky People and the Grounders. However, there is no indication in either show that any form of central governance will return to what it once was, or even that these alliances will persist for more than a few episodes.

Third, such series imply that conflict cannot be avoided when parties have incompatible worldviews or interests. Resolving conflicts through dialog and overcoming differences is improbable. Even a *modus vivendi* is precarious. The Grounders' warrior culture and the liberal democracy of the Sky People are incompatible. In the last episode of *The Walking Dead*'s eighth season ("Wrath"), it is foreshadowed that Rick's alliance will disintegrate due to a disagreement over the fate of the defeated Negan and The Saviors.

Lastly, liberal democratic people place a high value on protecting liberty and rights and limiting the power of government to infringe upon them. Apocalyptic, post-societal television series suggest that without common government, we easily lose freedoms and rights and hence humans need to be controlled by a dominant force to enjoy such freedoms. The anarchist position that people are capable of self-government and do not need hierarchical political institutions to live in peace is not tenable in such series. The implication is that humans cannot handle the complete freedom the state of nature offers. We can only live in peace and hopefully enjoy liberal rights by living under the constraint of government and law.

Hobbes and Rousseau recognize that a sacrifice must be made for peace.

After providing the verbiage for the Social Contract, Hobbes writes, "This done, the multitude so united in one person is called a commonwealth.... This is the generation of that great Leviathan, or rather (to speak more reverently) of that Mortal God to which we owe, under the Immortal God, our peace and defence" (109). Government is a great monster or god that constrains the freedom of the public. Rousseau famously writes, "Man is born free, and everywhere he is in chains" (141).[2] We are naturally born to enjoy the complete freedom found in the state of nature, but, for human well-being, our freedom must be constrained by living under governance. Even though living under the rule of government is better than living in the environment presented in apocalyptic, post-societal television series, if we accept the account of human psyche presented in such series, we must accept a disconcerting social ontology in which our nature must be suppressed by a powerful authority.

Although I do not think the aftermath of an apocalypse would necessarily be as hellish as apocalyptic, post-societal television series portray, I think such series do reveal a darker side of the human psyche that we should be concerned about. We do not have to turn to a fictional future to question whether human beings are self-interested and amoral or whether average citizens truly believe the liberal values they espouse. Social issues such as rising nativism, religious intolerance, racial divisions, income inequality, and the persistence of poverty are arguably manifestations of Hobbesian moral psychology and evidence of our lack of commitment to liberal values. From this standpoint the apocalyptic, post-societal television series is clearly not a warning of human nature in some possible future, but rather a critique of humanity itself in our very real present.

NOTES

1. This is a very general account of Plato's teleology in relation to humans. A full account entails discussion of the Realm of Forms, a nonmaterial realm of perfect entities which includes the "Form of Man," the ideal which mortal humans are designed to strive to become. Discussion of the Form of the Good is also necessary in that it is the primary form from which all other forms are derived. Discussion of the forms can be found in book six of *Republic*.

2. In *Of the Social Contract* Rousseau attempts to solve the problem of maintaining complete freedom while being governed by introducing the concept of the "general will." He argues that proper governance is when the will of the public is expressed in the laws and policies of political institutions. The actions of government are then claimed to be that which a reasonable individual would make and thus the individual is not constrained by an external authority but are constraining themselves. This position is problematic in terms of how to assess the general will, accounting for the will of groups with minority positions, and the requirement that citizens are reasonable people.

WORKS CITED

Gert, Bernard. "Hobbes and Psychological Egoism." *Journal of the History of Ideas*, vol. 28, no. 4, 1967, pp. 503–520.

Gray, John. *Liberalism*. University of Minnesota Press, 2nd ed., 2003.
Hobbes, Thomas. *Leviathan*, edited by Edwin Curley. Hackett, 1994.
Locke, John. *Two Treatises of Government*, edited by Peter Laslett. Cambridge UP, 2004.
Plato, *The Republic of Plato*, translated by Allan Bloom. Basic Books, 2nd ed., 1991.
Rousseau, Jean-Jacques. *The Basic Political Writings*, translated by Donald A. Cress. Hackett, 1987.
Rutherford, David. *Hobbes on Moral Virtue and the Laws of Nature*. Accessed 10 October 2018. philosophyfaculty.ucsd.edu/faculty/rutherford/papers/Hobbesvirtue.pdf.

Filmography

"Collaborators," *The Strain*, season 3, episode 7, FX, 9 Oct. 2016.
"Exposition Boulevard," *Revolution*, season 2, episode 16, NBC, 12 Mar. 2014.
Fear the Walking Dead, created by Frank Darabont and Dave Erickson, AMC, 2015–present.
The Last Ship, created by Hank Stein and Steven L. Kane, TNT, 2014–present.
The 100, created by Jason Rothenberg, The CW, 2014–present.
Revolution, created by Eric Kripke, NBC, 2012–2014.
"Sisters of Mercy," *Z Nation*, season 1, episode 11, SyFy, 21 Nov. 2014.
The Strain, created by Guillermo del Toro and Chuck Hogan, FX, 2014–2017.
"Too Far Gone," *The Walking Dead*, season 4, episode 8, AMC, 1 Dec. 2013.
The Walking Dead, created by Frank Darabont, AMC, 2010–present.
"Wrath," *The Walking Dead*, season 8, episode 16, AMC, 15 April 2018.
Z Nation, created by Karl Schaefer and Craig Engler, Syfy, 2014–present.

Post-Apocalyptic Competition and Cooperation in *The Handmaid's Tale* and *The Walking Dead*

Sherry Ginn

> "This is the valley of death. And there's a fuck-ton of evil to fear."
> —Offred, *The Handmaid's Tale*, "Night"

Survivors of apocalyptic events must ultimately decide whether there is security in numbers or whether they would rather rely upon only themselves for protection. Safety in numbers—banding together with other survivors—comes with the realization that one person alone may not have the requisite skills to ensure survival. This type of collective cooperation, of working with others to achieve a goal, increases the probability that any given person within a community will survive. Nevertheless, some survivors will eschew cooperation, unwilling to share scant resources with other people or even trust others with their individual safety. For these survivors, competition over resources is of paramount importance, and this competition can often have violent and devastating consequences. While it may seem counter-intuitive to focus on individual competition when the survival of the entire species is at stake, instances of those who choose competition over cooperation are frequently depicted in apocalyptic and post-apocalyptic media, though for the sake of this essay I discuss two popular televisual examples, both based upon written source material: *The Walking Dead* (2010–present) and *The Handmaid's Tale* (2017–present). Each of these series touches upon exactly what human beings will do to survive an apocalyptic event, with the former providing a more "cooperative" portrayal of the human response to adversity than the second. Although there are multiple psychological theories that can explain the actions of the survivors illustrated in these two series, evolutionary psychology provides powerful and disturbing insight into the actions of human beings faced with circumstances beyond any one person's control.

At its most basic, evolution refers to genetic changes that occur in a species over many generations due to natural selection, which is the process whereby organisms better adapted to their environments tend to survive and produce more offspring. The theory of evolution proposes that all species are related and gradually change over time. Evolution happens because of an interaction between biological and environmental factors, and it affects not only biology, but psychology as well. Hence, psychological processes that help individuals adapt to their environments also help them survive, reproduce, and pass advantageous traits and abilities on to their offspring. Many psychologists and biologists propose that species evolve via a process Charles Darwin referred to as sexual selection. Simply stated, sexual selection is natural selection arising through preference by one sex for certain characteristics in individuals of the other sex. Thus, female birds prefer male birds with bright plumage or that sing specific songs; consequently, they mate with those males that possess the desired trait. Sexual selection of this nature has long been the dominant theoretical perspective of scientists, and as such its influence can manifest in many aspects of contemporary life, including film and television.

It is this influence that I examine in this essay. I plan to demonstrate that many post-apocalyptic television programs indicate that human behavior, especially human sexual and reproductive behavior, reflects sexual selection theory, which is based upon competition. Yet I also argue that *social* selection, which is another system of natural selection, though one based on reproductive transactions and a two-tiered approach to evolution and the development of social behavior, is also illustrated in post-apocalyptic television. Reproductive transactions refer to situations where one organism offers assistance to another in exchange for access to reproductive opportunity. If sexual selection emphasizes competition, then after the apocalypse both men and women will be competing for the resources necessary to sustain life for themselves and their offspring. Social selection, on the other hand, emphasizes cooperation, suggesting that a better strategy for survival comes through associating with others. Cooperation includes actions that benefit everyone, not those done specifically for oneself or only a few. Cooperation increases the probability that a majority, and not a minority, of people may survive an apocalyptic event.

These differing manifestations of post-apocalyptic competition and cooperation can perhaps best be illustrated through the ways in which these media illustrate sex, mating, and reproduction. Apocalyptic television series such as *The Walking Dead* feature, as an undercurrent to survival, the need for reproduction and re-population. *The Handmaid's Tale*, on the other hand, depicts an apocalyptic scenario whereby reproduction and re-population are the essence of society's existence. These series allow for the scrutiny of both sexual and social selection, demonstrating that while sexual selection and its emphasis on competition may still be a default assumption in contemporary film and television depictions of the apocalypse, the notion of social selection—of cooperation—may, indeed, hold a key to humanity's survival in a post-apocalyptic world.

Sexual Selection, Competition and Cooperation in The Handmaid's Tale

In September 2018 thousands and thousands of women and men in the United States rallied to the support of Dr. Christine Blasey Ford upon her testimony before the Senate Judiciary Committee regarding an alleged sexual assault that happened when she was in high school. Many women shared their own experiences being sexually assaulted with the public. Some of these survivors detailed horrific rapes and assaults occurring many years prior to their revelations, which frequently resulted in a too-often heard pushback query as to why they had not come forward at the time to divulge the attack.[1] These Congressional hearings came hard upon the heels of the #MeToo movement, which has served as a clarion call revealing the breadth and depth of the crisis of harassment, sexual assault, and the rape of women and men in the United States.[2] People have expressed shock at the extent of this problem and have actively wondered what causes such horrific behavior on the part of the perpetrators.

One common explanation involves power: men such as comedian Bill Cosby and producer Harvey Weinstein held positions of power within the entertainment industry, allowing them to determine whether or not particular women and men could work in the industry. Because these were such powerful men, those who were allegedly assaulted by them were afraid to come forward for fear of reprisal. Some were coerced into signing non-disclosure agreements, receiving pay-offs in return for their silence. Such differentials in status and authority have commonly been markers for abuse throughout recorded history; our current era is certainly no exception.

However, a more insidious explanation of this behavior, one purported to express fundamental nature or biology, ultimately emerged as a type of counterpoint to the #MeToo movement. This is the "boys will be boys" argument, which implies that aggression leading to sexual violence is an integral part of male behavior. This type of argument was a strong part of the narrative surrounding Brett Kavanaugh, the man accused of assaulting Ford (see, for example, Akpan). Such an explanation implies that men cannot help themselves; they are programmed by their genetic make-up to act this way. The reason men are programmed this way, according to an evolutionary psychology approach, is that violence is justified: it incurs an evolutionary advantage on such men, with more violent men having power over their less violent counterparts. This evolutionary advantage occurs whenever the more violent men subdue their rivals and assume control of resources, which may include property, wealth, and, more insidiously, women and children, very much a scenario played out in post-apocalyptic narratives time and again.[3]

According to evolutionary psychology, behaviors and mental processes that increase the probability of an organism's survival will be selected, meaning that the organism will survive to reproduce and the psychological traits that aided in that survival will be transmitted to the next generation.[4] Men can (theoretically) father thousands of children in their lifetimes, assuming a limitless supply of fertile women (Buss). Men reach the age of sexual maturity at approximately 14 and are generally fertile their entire lives. Women, on the other hand, have a limited time within their life-spans when they can produce children: roughly from 12 years until 50, although most women become less and less able to bear children as they enter their fourth and fifth decades. Thus, evolutionary psychologists propose that men and women have different strategies with respect to reproduction. Because men produce millions of sperm cells in each ejaculate, but only one is necessary for fertilization, it is in a man's evolutionary interests to impregnate as many females as possible. This ensures that some of his offspring will reach the age of maturity and his genes will be transmitted to future generations. Men have little "energy" invested in their offspring. Women, on the other hand, generally only carry one offspring at a time, and it is in their best interests to ensure that this one offspring survives to maturity so that it can transmit its mother's genes to future generations. Because women invest more "energy" in their offspring's survival, women are motivated by different forces than men. Men want to mate with as many women as possible, but women want to mate with one man who will help them raise and protect their offspring, to optimize the chances of their offspring reaching maturity. Although any given woman might not know who the father of her child is, she will always know that her offspring is her own; before the development of DNA testing, men could never reliably know that a woman's children were his (hence different reasons for jealousy). If a woman is sexually unfaithful, then her offspring might not belong to her mate, and he is left raising a child not his own. If the man is emotionally unfaithful, he might abandon her, which would leave her and her child undefended, rendering them unsafe in an unsafe environment. She will also lose her mate's resources and his paternal investment (Buss).

Although this is a very brief description of evolutionary psychology and its theories on human mate selection and reproduction (and does not take into account cultural components of human reproduction that also clearly influence human mating behavior), the theory can be used to illuminate many of the sexual selection-type relations depicted in science fiction, both literary and cinematic. This is especially true of post-apocalyptic science fiction that envisions a dystopian future. In these nightmarish visions, the strongest people, usually men, control valuable resources, such as food, water, territory, and weapons. The strong also control sexual access to both female and male subordinates and slaves. Sexual access may be consensual, if one can consider the powerless able to give consent, or it may not, with rape being a common occurrence for women, men, and children in these dystopian worlds. Reading or viewing this type of speculative fiction can be disturbing, as in many cases sexual violence occurs as a means of control rather than as a means of reproduction. Rape has always been about violence and control and usually not considered directly connected to sexuality or reproduction. And yet, in post-apocalyptic scenarios, these lines often blur tremendously, as the need to "repopulate" becomes both an impetus and excuse for the sexual exploitation of others. This rather grim variation on sexual selection can perhaps best be illustrated by Hulu's recent serial adaptation of Margaret Atwood's dystopian novel *The Handmaid's Tale*.

First published in 1986, *The Handmaid's Tale* can be considered a response to what Susan Faludi called the conservative, antifeminist backlash occurring during the Reagan administration (Neuman). Bruce Miller's television adaptation informs its 21st century audience that this backlash is clearly not over. Set in the post–United States Republic of Gilead, the series depicts women with limited roles in the state: wife, handmaid, servant (Martha), aunt, prostitute (Jezebel), econowife ("normal" married women), or unwoman (undesirable). Handmaids are assigned to a married couple and serve as sexual surrogates for infertile wives.[5] They have sexual relations with the husband during a sanctified Ceremony, and the wife's role in the process is passively holding the handmaid's hands as she reclines in the wife's lap. The story is narrated by a woman named June (Elisabeth Moss), who has been assigned to the Waterford household, composed of a wife named Serena Joy (Yvonne Strahovski) and a high-status husband named Fred (Joseph Fiennes), whose title is commander. Handmaids are not allowed to use their own names in Gilead—they have no personal identity—and are referred to only by the name of the commander to whom they are assigned, with the prefix "of" preceding the name. Hence, June is referred to as "Offred."

Gilead illustrates a conservative religious culture in which women are not allowed to read or write; they are only allowed to fulfill their religiously sanctioned role of reproduction. Although men in this society are also only supposed to copulate for procreative purposes, the evolving story exposes the hypocrisy of the commanders in Gilead by showing them frequenting prostitutes and even engaging in sexual relations with their handmaids outside of the Ceremony, sometimes clandestinely, and sometimes with their wives' consent ("The Bridge"). Commanders are complicit in their violation of the rules, speaking of their handmaids in ways that are not indicative of the "sanctified" role these women play in bearing children. In the second season episode "The Last Ceremony," June is believed to be in labor. As the wives gather to join Serena in the "birth" of her baby, the commanders gather in Fred's study to smoke cigars and drink various alcoholic beverages. Commander Grinnell enters the room and speaks to Fred:

> **GRINNELL:** My handmaid is about to reach her expiration date. And she wasn't that much fun to begin with. How's yours?
> **FRED:** Well, she has proven fruitful.
> **GRINNELL:** Hmm. And not bad looking, either?

While Fred's cautious reply reflects the male biblical role to "Be fruitful and multiply," Grinnell's remarks here demonstrate his evaluation of his handmaid's sexual prowess and not her fruitfulness. Though their society structures the male role in sex as focusing on procreation, for most men of influence in Gilead, this is simply not the case; many of them frequent brothels in order to have sexual relations outside of the Ceremony—and away from the watchful eyes of their wives, with whom they do not have sex.

It is not just the men who are sexual actors in the series; some handmaids also have sexual relations with men to whom they are not "assigned." In fact, the actions of both the women and the men can be read as an example of the sexual strategies employed by men and women in terms of sexual selection. The men in the book/series wish to copulate with a variety of women. Indeed, in the novel Offred's commander states that nature made men that way, hence the need for prostitutes who are readily available for sexual congress whenever the male wishes. He tells Offred: "It means you can't cheat Nature. Nature demands variety, for men. It stands to reason, it's part of the procreational strategy. It's Nature's plan. Women know that instinctively" (Atwood 236). For her part, Offred either has sex with, or is offered sex with, several men in the novel; in the series she has sex with Fred and Nick Blaine (Max Minghella), Fred's chauffeur. Her fertility is not in question, as she had a child prior to events in the story. Knowing that she is fertile prompts these offers; Serena Joy seems perfectly willing to have Offred impregnated by any man as long as the child can be passed off as her husband's. In terms of evolutionary psychology, this strategy would serve Offred and Serena's reproductive future; however, it undermines the commander's, as he would be nurturing a child who is probably not his own biological child. In this dystopian society everyone is willing to "cheat" in order to have children, as social success for commanders and their wives depends upon fertility.

The first episode of the television series, entitled "Offred," illustrates how the women of Gilead have been subjugated for the purposes of reproduction.

June informs us that the majority of women are infertile in Gilead. As such, drastic measures were taken to ensure the survival of the human race. Versions of these measures have been used throughout history and are here instated to assure that only certain men have access to women for the purposes of procreation. Wives are placed on pedestals in Gilead, much as Southern plantation owners' wives were prior to the American Civil War, or the landed gentry and nobility in Victorian and Edwardian Great Britain. Such women managed the household—usually supervising a large contingent of slaves or servants (depending upon time and location)—bearing children until a sufficient number of heirs had been produced and those duties were no longer required of them. Many of these women happily turned a blind eye to their husbands' escapades with the slaves or servants or with mistresses discreetly hidden "in town." Gilead reprises these so-called "genteel" times, with wives having little to do other than supervise their "Marthas" (servants) and pray that their "handmaid" will get pregnant and bear them a child. In the Republic of Gilead, the Book of Genesis is used to justify the actions of the commanders: just as a barren Rachel gave her handmaid Bilhah to Jacob in order to bear him children, so, too, must the handmaids provide such a service to the commanders and their wives.

The handmaids' lives are completely ritualized and scrutinized. They are first programmed and brainwashed into accepting their new lot in life. This is epitomized by the violent control and indoctrination they must endure at the Red Center. For example, Janine (Madeline Brewer), a defiant new handmaid, is forced to relive her violent past. She is told that her gang rape was her fault and is shamed by her fellow handmaids. This powerful psychological ordeal, compounding her past traumatic experiences, "breaks" Janine, which is key to the Republic's control over the handmaids. This indoctrination is ultimately designed to convince these women that they must accept their new lives; one way to do this is to let them know what horrible, shameful creatures they actually are.

As noted, handmaids do not own their own names in Gilead. Handmaid names are impermanent, changing whenever the handmaid is assigned to a new commander. That the handmaids might not be willing to accept their fate in such a society is clear. Handmaids are not allowed to leave their commanders' homes except in pairs. They are continually told that they are being watched, and they can never trust anyone because that someone might be an "Eye." This tactic, used by every totalitarian state in history, keeps its citizens compliant. In addition, men with guns not only patrol the streets of the city in which Offred lives, they are also posted every few feet. Violence is not unknown. As Offred and her shopping companion Ofglen (Alexis Bledel) return from the market, they pass by the corpses of three hanged men: someone who worked in an abortion clinic, a priest, and a homosexual. The latter is particularly disturbing for both women, first because Ofglen is a lesbian, and second because Offred's best friend from the past, Moira (Samira Wiley), is also a lesbian.

Envisioning a future such as that depicted in *The Handmaid's Tale* is deeply disturbing, and many critics have noted its connectivity to the political climate of the Trump-era United States. For example, Matthew d'Ancona in *The Guardian* scathingly noted,

> What seemed a cautionary tale then feels more like a deafening klaxon now. Why? Because the world of Offred, though still notionally a fiction, has migrated from creative construct to the realm of the thinkable. Gilead's use of technology to subordinate women overnight seemed all too close to the bone in the year in which the power of digital manipulation and cyberwarfare to distort the democratic process became chillingly apparent. If the roots of pluralism, minority rights and constitutionalism were as shallow as Trump clearly believed, then anything was possible [n.p.].

He continues by saying, "And that is not all: just as the series acted as a mythic commentary upon the culture wars of the Trump era, it also prefigured the fightback of the #MeToo movement" (n.p.). Yet dystopian, post-apocalyptic narratives have long abounded with illustrations of female endangerment and disempowerment. Atwood herself contends that

> Without women capable of giving birth, human populations would die out. That is why the mass rape and murder of women, girls and children has long been a feature of genocidal wars, and of other campaigns meant to subdue and exploit a population. Kill their babies and replace their babies with yours, as cats do; make women have babies they can't afford to raise, or babies you will then remove from them for your own purposes, steal babies—it's been a widespread, age-old motif. The control of women and babies has been a feature of every repressive regime on the planet ["Atwood on What"].

Indeed, a common motif in post-apocalyptic tales is the sexual endangerment of the populace, especially women. For example, in the first season episode "The Armory" of TNT's *Falling Skies* (2011–2015), survivors of an alien invasion chance upon a group of marauders, led by a man named Pope (Colin Cunningham). At the end of the episode a young woman named Maggie (Sarah Carter), who is perceived to be a member of Pope's gang, kills two male gang members, intimating they had repeatedly been forcing themselves upon her. Believing their brutality had left her reconciled to a life of bondage and violence, the gang had begun to trust her with weapons. Killing her tormentors can be read as a woman's unwillingness to surrender to those who would treat her as a thing to be used at will, but the storyline's existence demonstrates the fragility of women's independence from the fear of sexual aggression, assault, and rape; in this instance, though society is threatened by an alien invasion, Maggie—like so many of her ilk—discovers that, all too often, the most dangerous creatures are fellow human beings.

Similar scenes abound in post-apocalyptic worlds. On AMC's *The Walking Dead*, the characters of Michonne (Danai Gurira) and Carl (Chandler Riggs) are both threatened with rape in the same episode ("A").[6] The people who inhabit the community Terminus became cannibals—preying on fellow survivors who seek shelter in their community—following horrific, repeated assaults upon the women of the community by outsiders (directly connecting sexual assault with the disintegration of society as a whole). Later, when the series protagonist Rick Grimes (Andrew Lincoln) and his companions are captured by the ruthless antagonist figure Negan (Jeffrey Dean Morgan) and forced to submit to his demands, they learn that Negan has multiple "wives," although not by their choice. Negan's "harem" is indicative of his brutality and totalitarianism as a leader; an avatar for sexual selection, he utilizes his "wives" as a symbol of his authority and his willingness to do what it takes to maintain control over his followers.

Sex is obviously used as a means of control in many of these examples, with men competing against one another for access to both willing and unwilling sexual partners. Nevertheless, issues revolving around reproduction are also apparent, and instances of both competition between and cooperation with other people can be observed. Human beings will continue to have children, even in the worst of times; for example, Lori (Sarah Wayne Callies) gives birth to Judith and Maggie (Lauren Cohan) to Hershel on *The Walking Dead*, and Anne Glass (Moon Bloodgood) gets pregnant twice on *Falling Skies*.

Sometimes the issue of reproduction is seen as an act of patriotic duty to the future of the human race, as occurs in *Battlestar Galactica* (2004–2009), when President Laura Roslin (Mary McDonnell) tells Commander William Adama (Edward James Olmos), "I'm going to be straight with you here. The human race is about to be wiped out. We have fifty thousand people left and that's it. Now, if we are even going to survive as a species, then we need to get the hell out of here and we need to start having babies!" ("Miniseries, Part 2"). Although Roslin's statement does not suggest that the surviving women of the 12 colonies will be forced to bear children, she does issue an executive order banning abortion, thereby removing the right of choice from the survivors ("The Captain's Hand"). *Battlestar Galactica* also illustrates an overwhelming urge to procreate among the Cylons, who realize that their desire to "become" their creators is impossible because they cannot reproduce themselves physically. The Cylons hypothesize that they need humans in order to reproduce and eventually kidnap human women and force them to breed ("The Farm").

Sexual and reproductive strategies such as those mentioned above are disturbing to viewers of these series. Indeed, the mechanisms of sexual selection can be disturbing and revolting, especially when one considers that both competition and cooperation figure into such acts. Men compete with each other for access to sexual subordinates and for access to women for the sake of reproduction, with the strongest and most powerful man "winning" in each category. However, cooperation, of a decidedly perverse sort, can also be observed in these scenarios. Subordinate men might help more powerful men in their quest for dominance. Once the most powerful man triumphs, he can dole out favors to those who helped him on his rise to power.

One example of this can be seen in the second season episode "Seeds" of *The Handmaid's Tale*. Guardians are men who serve commanders; they may act as escorts to wives or as drivers to commanders. In "Seeds" a number of guardians are rewarded for their service to Gilead, including Nick, Fred's chauffeur and the (supposed) father of Offred's daughter. Each guardian is "gifted" with a wife and a communal wedding takes place. These new wives are very young; Nick's wife Eden (Sydney Sweeney) is only 15 years old. Here is another instance of the hypocrisy shown by the commanders. They are unwilling to follow the strictures they placed upon the populace of Gilead; they understand what men "need." Hence they reward what they consider to be appropriate male behavior which serves as a means of keeping power unto themselves and ensuring compliance in everyone else. Indeed, it becomes readily apparent in season 2 of *The Handmaid's Tale* that everyone in the Waterford household, including Fred, is aware that Nick is the father of Offred's baby. They are all complicit in their silence. June and Nick are powerless to claim the child and Fred and Serena are perfectly willing to allow everyone in Gilead to believe that Fred is fertile. Actions such as these illustrate how cooperation can be a completely selfish act, meant to benefit only a few, to keep those with power in power.

Plotlines in *Battlestar Galactica* and *The Handmaid's Tale* illustrate the near-extinction of humanity following apocalyptic events and indicate that drastic measures might be needed to repopulate the planet. They highlight the violence of sexual selection and the imperative biological drive to replicate one's genetic material. Ultimately, these narratives seem to suggest that post-apocalyptic worlds must be dominated by such violent forms of reproduction if the human race has any chance to survive, and that the success of violent, aggressive males may be crucial for rebuilding a population forced to exist in such harsh, unforgiving environments.

The Handmaid's Tale provides a chilling example of society following apocalyptic events. Formed to limit the power of women and rebuild America as a religiously conservative society, this series depicts an extreme example of sexual selection, with its emphasis on competition for scant resources—in this case, fertile women—necessary to repopulate the country and retain control of a population complicit in the effort. The series also illustrates a form of perverse cooperation, one that is forced on the society by design. Women either comply with the new strictures on their behavior or they are punished.

Likewise, Maggie in *Falling Skies* and Negan's wives in *The Walking Dead* depict post-apocalyptic worlds where men seem to believe that women will exchange the rights to their bodies—even against their will—in return for a semblance of safety. The powerful need for a feeling of safety may thus force men and women to cooperate in ways beneficial to any given individual but harmful to the group at large. Turning a "blind eye" to the rape and torture of the handmaids gives everyone else a sense of safety, even though this makes them complicit in those same barbaric crimes.

Social Selection, Competition and Cooperation in The Walking Dead

While instances of unselfish cooperation can be observed in *The Handmaid's Tale*—such as among the unwomen of the Colonies—it is evident that the forms of sexual cooperation in the series are perverted adaptations of sexual cooperation and really extensions of violent forms of sexual selection. *The Walking Dead*, on the other hand, is much more illustrative of unselfish cooperation and social sexual selection. Joan Roughgarden purports that sexual selection "tells a story of selfishness, deceit, and coercion" (236). As such, sexual selection emphasizes competition and renders cooperation as simply another means of "conquest" and "victory." Indeed, viewers of post-apocalyptic television have become so inured to sexual violence in these series that, all too frequently, such scenes seem to pass by without much comment or notice by the audience. It has simply become part of the fabric of these narratives. For example, the handmaids' rape during the Ceremony is presented in such a sterilized fashion that one almost forgets that these women did not give consent for their bodies to be used in such a way. The audience is jolted back to "reality" when Offred is forcibly raped by Fred, ostensibly to induce labor, while Serena holds her down. Offred begs him to stop and says to herself: "You treat it like a job. One detaches oneself.... No more to you than a bee is to a flower. Not me. Not my flesh. I am not here" ("The Last Ceremony"). In similar fashion the letters given to June, and eventually smuggled out of Gilead, convey the horror of life as a handmaid in Gilead to the people of the world ("Smart Power").

If we can assume that post-apocalyptic scenarios are exaggerations of existing cultural conditions—that these texts are humanity taken to one extreme—what does this emphasis on sexual selection, on competition, violence, and the perverse cooperation of confederates, indicate about us? Yet there is perhaps an even more intriguing question to consider here: what does the recent trend of post-apocalyptic series spotlighting social selection, with its emphasis on cooperation, likewise say about us? This last question may be especially germane, because post-apocalyptic television is one of the only places one can see the auspices of social selection play out in popular culture. Could this indicate a palpable shift in the manner in which we envision how the world must be rebuilt? Are we moving toward more ethical, more cooperative "end times" scenarios?

In an examination of social selection, Roughgarden proposes that cooperation can explain most of the actions observed in non-human and human animals with respect to both sexuality and reproduction. As she observes,

> the elements of social selection derive from an alternative view of biological nature, a view predicated on teamwork, honesty, and genetic equality. The fact that conflict and deception certainly occur in nature, too, does not alter the possible truth of the alternative view because conflict and deception can be understood as secondary imperfections of processes that promote cooperative behavior and evolutionary outcomes [247].

In other words, organisms may compete for access to the opposite sex for purposes of procreation; however, they may also cooperate for the same reason. Providing a safe environment in which to rear offspring is one of the many ways in which organisms may cooperate to ensure the survival of the species, even if any given individual does not survive. Mass spawning is another, where a group of organisms provides security for one another during a process that often lessens their ability to survey their surroundings (there is safety in numbers). Whereas sexual selection seems to focus more on the competition for a mate in order to reproduce, competition does not necessarily ensure that the offspring of any given mating will reach the age of maturity and continue the genetic mandate to evolve. Cooperation is more likely to ensure a future for any species, even and especially humankind, rather than the competition so often depicted in post-apocalyptic media.

Some post-apocalyptic narratives are mirroring the principles of social selection in their depiction of post-apocalyptic reproductive practices, emphasizing cooperation and community in their depictions of sexual relationships and reproduction. For example, although *Falling Skies* presented one female character victimized by men, other women in the series were presented in myriad roles; the main female character in the series, Anne Glass, a physician, bonds with the series protagonist Tom Mason (Noah Wyle) and has children with him. In this series, the Second Mass (the moniker given to the local militia), along with their families, conduct a guerrilla war against a race of alien invaders. These people have banded together, believing that there is strength in numbers, and every member of the group—even the children— have jobs to do that will help with the fight to reclaim the United States. Their entire society is founded upon a principle of cooperation.[7] In this instance the series presents evidence of the theory of social selection rather than sexual selection. Cooperation extends even into mating and child-rearing; when

Anne's daughter Alexis (Scarlett Byrne) disappears in the fourth season of the series, several members of the community aid Anne in her search for Alexis and care for her on her journey.

Rather than emphasizing strategies that male and female animals exhibit in order to maximize their chances of mating, as sexual selection proposes, Roughgarden says we should be examining the strategies that males and females exhibit in order to maximize the chances of their offspring surviving. In *Falling Skies*, members of the larger community undertake a perilous journey in order to preserve a single member of their community; Roughgarden would note the connection here not to successful mating, but to successful child-rearing. Though somewhat uneven in tone, *The Walking Dead* provides another good example of a current post-apocalyptic series with respect to its emphasis on cooperation.

Rick Grimes, a former police officer, leads a group of survivors (whom I will refer to as the main group) looking for a safe place to live following a zombie apocalypse. Membership in this main group changes as the series progresses because, as one would expect of life in a post-apocalyptic world, people die. Rick and his companions welcome those who wish to join them, giving all newcomers—except those prisoners still living at the prison—the benefit of the doubt with respect to their motives for doing so. The main group's willingness to add new members—reinforcing the belief that there is strength in numbers—is apparent when Rick invites citizens of Woodbury to join the community they are attempting to build at an abandoned prison ("Welcome to the Tombs"). Unfortunately this invitation infuriates Woodbury's leader, the Governor, and he declares war on Rick and his group, with the result that the prison is overrun by walkers and everyone is forced to flee ("Too Far Gone"). Rick's group is eventually invited to live at a gated and walled community called Alexandria, populated by multiple individuals and families who have managed to remain untouched by the reality of life outside their walls. Threatened by walkers and by marauders who call themselves "Wolves," Rick and the others help the Alexandrians defend themselves ("First Time Again"; "JSS"). Rick's actions illustrate cooperation rather than competition; although not directly related to reproduction and repopulation, his actions are based upon his desire to provide a home for people whereby they can survive these new "end times." One could argue that these actions are selfish in the sense that each member of the group wishes to survive, but fighting to help strangers—because that is essentially what the people of Alexandria are when first encountered—illustrates selflessness on the part of the main group. Of course, they have their own motivation for helping besides being asked to do so, and that is so they, too, can find a community where they can put down roots and be safe. Rick, after all, is father to Carl and Judith and wants his children to be secure as well as the other members of the group with whom he has bonded. Even Daryl (Norman Reedus), the prototypical loner, begins to advocate for searching for additional people to invite into Alexandria.

Because there are so few people left in the world, especially those who have not abandoned any sense of community, everyone who is left has a purpose and a place rebuilding society, with little to no restrictions upon one's role in the new order. For example, after Rick's wife Lori dies in childbirth, everyone, including Daryl, pitches in to help care for baby Judith and keep her safe. The main group's primary goal is to find a safe haven for themselves and anyone who wishes to join them, and to forge a community whereby everyone will be safe, especially the children. In addition, women are not assumed to be helpless; they have a place that is very egalitarian, with women assuming leadership roles without becoming "masculinized" women.[8]

The roles that women play in the post-apocalyptic communities of *The Walking Dead* are often highly indicative of the community's reflection of social versus sexual selection values. Negan's "harem" suggests that his group, the Saviors, are organized on principles of sexual selection—the strongest male gets the most "mates." The main group's egalitarian principles and communal sharing is more indicative of social selection, although it was not always this way. For instance, in the first two seasons of *The Walking Dead*, the women were generally observed in various domestic duties, such as washing clothes and preparing meals. One of them, Andrea (Laurie Holden), rebels against this insistence that women occupy traditional gender roles and duties; she demands instead to have a gun to work defending the others.[9] This desire creates conflict in the group when Lori accuses Andrea of shirking her "duties":

> **ANDREA:** I contribute. I help keep this place safe.
> **LORI:** The men can handle this on their own. They don't need your help.
> **ANDREA:** I'm sorry. What would you have me do?
> **LORI:** Oh, there's plenty of work to go around.
> **ANDREA:** Are you serious? Everything falls apart. You're in my face over skipping laundry?
> **LORI:** Puts a burden on the rest of us ["18 Miles Out"].

Lori's reinforcement of gendered roles and domestic stereotypes suggests a reversion to an earlier time, a time well before the apocalyptic events of the series. As Barbara Gurr indicates, "these stories tell us there is enough challenge in simply surviving, and the human imagination cannot extend beyond the terror of constantly fighting off zombies... to create a new society with new social mores and rules of engagement" (2). It may be that Lori finds comfort in the reinforcement of such strictly gendered structures in the aftermath of a cataclysmic event. Yet the series gradually but purposefully leaves behind these stereotypical roles, and the men and women grow to be much more egalitarian in their gender roles (Lavin and Lowe). It becomes commonplace to see Carol (Melissa McBride), Maggie, and Michonne defending the group against human and zombie threats while Rick and Tyreese (Chad L. Coleman) care for baby Judith, a complete inversion of the series' early presentment of gender. Indeed, baby Judith is probably the best example of social selection in the entire series. Judith's paternity is unknown. Lori had a sexual relationship with Rick's best friend Shane (Jon Bernthal) following the apocalypse and prior to discovering that Rick was still alive. Shane is convinced the child is his. Lori is unsure which man impregnated her. However, Rick claims the baby, stating that Judith is his, and he treats her accordingly. One can argue that Offred's baby (Holly/Nichole) is also illustrative of this same construct, given that apparently everyone knows Nick is the father of the baby but that Fred and Serena will claim her. I would argue, however, that Rick's is the selfless act. He is not claiming Judith for any reason other than that he loved her mother and has grown to love her as she grew in Lori's womb. Fred and Serena want a baby to solidify his power within Gilead and her status as a commander's wife. Serena acknowledges that all she ever wanted was to have a child and apparently is willing to do whatever is necessary to get one ("Holly").

Rick's actions toward Judith are incompatible with the notion that humans are motivated mainly to perpetuate their genes into future generations and that they are not altruistic enough to "waste" energy on the survival of unrelated offspring. In some ways, this may seem as "odd" a gender role inversion as the women defending the group and the men tending to childcare. Yet the apocalypse is nothing if not the violent disestablishment of society itself. In such instances, it may only seem logical that cooperation is the key to humanity's survival.

There are other examples of cooperation in *The Walking Dead*, especially in the name of creating community so that some sense of stability and safety can be established. Seasons 2 and 3 saw such an establishment at Hershel Greene's (Scott Wilson) farm while seasons 3 and 4 saw the main group, including the survivors of Hershel's farm community, create a safe-haven at the West Georgia Correctional Facility. Each location provided a short-term place of settlement wherein the members of the main group were able to establish a semblance of normality, with crops growing in the fields and livestock providing fresh meat. After Negan claims sovereignty over Alexandria in season 7, Rick pays tribute to Negan in order to maintain some semblance of normality within the walls of Alexandria. However, season 8 sees several different groups of survivors cooperate with one another in order to destroy Negan and his followers. Unlike *Falling Skies*, in which the major goal of the Second Mass is to repel the alien invaders and rebuild the United States, people depicted in other series are content to settle in small communities which are perhaps more manageable and (sometimes) democratic than larger ones.[10] Even so, the various groups in *The Walking Dead*'s season 8—the Alexandria Safe-Zone, the Kingdom, and the Hilltop—unite to defeat Negan and the Saviors. Building community with like-minded individuals who share a common goal—one that is beneficial for everyone in the community—sets *The Walking Dead* apart from *The Handmaid's Tale* with its emphasis on placing power in the hands of a select few at the expense of everyone else.

Conclusion

Whatever the cause of the apocalypse, many post-apocalyptic series will have us believe that human beings will revert to savagery to save themselves, even if it means everyone else dies. These series also suggest that society will devolve into small competitive units. With apparently little incentive to unite, humankind will compete for the scant resources still available following the end. In such scenarios, women and their bodies become "resources" and, as such, are competed over, often violently. Competition may ensure that any given individual will be able to claim enough resources to live and reproduce, thus ensuring a type of immortality, even in the face of mass destruction. Evolutionary theorists would say that this drive is in our own best interests; after all, if we do not survive, we die not only in the present but in the future as well.

Yet some series have begun to embrace an ethos of cooperation instead of competition. In *The Walking Dead*, it is evident which strategy is more effective. Factions like Terminus and the Saviors are ultimately destroyed, while the main group lives on. Though it has lost most of its original members, the group and its ethos—and offspring—survive. Many scholars have argued the purpose of post-apocalyptic television is to provide thought experiments about the collapse of society, to prepare us for the worst, to allow us to practice and prepare for the eventuality of doom. Perhaps. Or, perhaps, we are living in the end times now, and shows like *The Walking Dead* are urging us to come together, to unite—in short, to cooperate—if we wish to have any chance of surviving.

Notes

1. On September 21, 2018, President of the United States Donald J. Trump tweeted this about Dr. Ford: "I have no doubt that, if the attack on Dr. Ford was as bad as she says, charges would have been immediately filed with local Law Enforcement Authorities by either her or her loving parents. I ask that she bring those filings forward so that we can learn date, time, and place!" Considering this reaction from the highest elected official in the land, and considering the endless hostile questions, enmity, and threats Dr. Ford fielded about her sexual assault, one could reasonably wonder why any person, regardless of age, would report such an incident (for more, see Petula Dvorak).

2. Statistics on the extent of sexual violence in the United States can be found at www.nsvrc.org/node/4737, the website of the National Sexual Violence Resource Center. The numbers are staggering. For instance, one in four girls and one in six boys will be sexually assaulted before they are eighteen. Sixty-three percent of rapes are *not* reported to the police. About 80 percent of victims knew the perpetuator.

3. I would be remiss if I did not point out that the vast majority of men, regardless of their status, do not engage in or condone such behavior, and that such a simplification as the one presented here neither qualifies nor endeavors to explain this phenomenon.

4. Portions of this section were previously published in *Foundation, the International Review of Science Fiction* (pages 28–29); see Works Cited for complete citation.

5. The assumption made is that only women have become infertile. Male infertility is apparently not considered to be possible.

6. *The Walking Dead* television series rarely shows sexual violence, which is commendable. However, the graphic novels on which the series is based do not shy away from such violence, nor did Robert Kirkman's novelization about the Governor, which was quite graphic in its description of Michonne's sexual brutalization at his hands and her subsequent revenge (for more, see Kirkman and Bonansinga).

7. I am certainly aware that *Falling Skies* reinforces patriarchal hierarchies, particularly those of a post–9/11 United States, and I find it problematic that the major characters in the series are men. See Lavigne for more on this issue as well as Faludi for a discussion of post–9/11 America (*Terror*).

8. Lavigne's argument for the patriarchal aspects of the "Ricktatorship" on *The Walking Dead* is acknowledged. I argue that this series is much better in its portrayal of women and their various leadership and non-leadership roles than other post–9/11 series (such as *The Last Ship*, 2014–2018). For more, see Lavin and Lowe.

9. According to Lavigne, Andrea's eventual death at the hands of the Governor illustrates what happens to women who rebel against their place in a patriarchal society ("Welcome to the Tombs"). However, I argue that Andrea's insistence upon having a choice—whatever the result—is a right demanded of what we now call second-wave feminism.

10. Aspects of cooperation can be observed in other post-apocalyptic series discussed in this book, such as in *Survivors*, *Cadillacs and Dinosaurs*, and *The Leftovers*.

Works Cited

Akpan, Nsikan. "In Kavanaugh Debate, 'Boys Will Be Boys' Is an Unscientific Excuse for Assault." *PBS News Hour*, 21 Sept. 2018, www.pbs.org/newshour/science/why-boys-will-be-boys-is-an-unscientific-excuse-for-assault. Accessed 1 October 2019.

Atwood, Margaret. *The Handmaid's Tale*. Houghton Mifflin, 1986, Kindle edition.

_____. "Margaret Atwood on What 'The Handmaid's Tale' Means in the Age of Trump." The New York Times, 10 March 2017, www.nytimes.com/2017/03/10/books/review/margaret-atwood-handmaids-tale-age-of-trump.html. Accessed 11 Nov. 2018.

Buss, David M. *The Evolution of Desire: Strategies of Human Mating*. BasicBooks, 1994.

d'Ancona, Matthew. "The Handmaid's Tale Held a Mirror Up to a Year of Trump." *The Guardian*, 26 December 2017, n.p. www.theguardian.com/commentisfree/2017/dec/26/the-handmaids-tale-year-trump-misogyny-metoo. Accessed 11 Nov. 2018.

Darwin, Charles. *The Descent of Man and Selection in Relation to Sex*. Murray, 1871.

Dvorak, Petula. "Millions of Women Understand Christine Blasey Ford's Decades of Silence." *The Washington Post*, 20 September 2018, www.washingtonpost.com/local/but-why-did-kavanaughs-accuser-wait-37-years-to-say-something/2018/09/20/04118d42-bcdd-11e8-be70-52bd11fe18af_story.html?noredirect=on&utm_term=.6446ec52c72d. Accessed 11 Nov. 2018.

Faludi, Susan. *Backlash: The Undeclared War Against American Women*. Knopf Doubleday, 1992.

_____. *The Terror Dream: Myth and Misogyny in an Insecure America*. Picador, 2007.

Ginn, Sherry. "For Women It's Love, for Men It's Sex: Evolutionary Psychology Meets Science Fiction." *Foundation, the International Review of Science Fiction*, vol. 39, no. 108, 2010, pp. 28–38.

Gurr, Barbara. *Race, Gender, and Sexuality in Post-Apocalyptic TV and Film*. Palgrave Macmillan, 2015. Kindle edition.
Kirkman, Robert, and Jay Bonansinga. *The Walking Dead: The Fall of the Governor*, parts 1 and 2, St. Martin's Press, 2014.
Lavigne, Carlen. *Post-Apocalyptic Patriarchy: American Television and Gendered Visions of Survival*. McFarland, 2018.
Lavin, Melissa F., and Brian M. Lowe. "Cops and Zombies: Hierarchy and Social Location in *The Walking Dead*." *Race, Gender, and Sexuality in Post-Apocalyptic TV and Film*, Barbara Gurr, editor. Palgrave Macmillan, 2015. Kindle edition.
Neuman, Shirley. "'Just a Backlash': Margaret Atwood, Feminism, and *The Handmaid's Tale*." *University of Toronto Quarterly*, vol. 75, no. 3, 2006, n.p. dystopiaandgender.files.wordpress.com/2016/09/just-a-backlash.pdf. Accessed 27 August 2019.
NSVRC. "Get Statistics: Sexual Violence in the United States." National Sexual Violence Resource Center. www.nsvrc.org/node/4737. Accessed 10 November 2018.
Roughgarden, Joan. *The Genial Gene: Deconstructing Darwinian Selfishness*. U of California P, 2009.

Filmography

"A." *The Walking Dead*, season 4, episode 16, AMC, 30 Mar. 2014.
"The Armory." *Falling Skies*, season 1, episode 2, TNT, 19 June 2011.
Battlestar Galactica, created by Glen A. Larson and Ronald D. Moore, Sci-Fi, 2004–2009.
"The Bridge." *The Handmaid's Tale*, season 1, episode 9, Hulu, 7 June 2017.
"The Captain's Hand." *Battlestar Galactica*, season 2, episode 17, Sci Fi, 17 Feb. 2006.
"18 Miles Out." *The Walking Dead*, season 2, episode 10, AMC, 26 Feb. 2012.
Falling Skies, created by Robert Rodat, TNT, 2011–2015.
"The Farm." *Battlestar Galactica*, season 2, episode 5, Sci-Fi, 12 Aug. 2005.
"First Time Again." *The Walking Dead*, season 6, episode 1, AMC, 11 Oct. 2015.
The Handmaid's Tale, created by Bruce Miller, Hulu, 2017–present.
"Holly." *The Handmaid's Tale*, season 2, episode 11, Hulu, 27 June 2018.
"JSS." *The Walking Dead*, season 6, episode 2, AMC, 18 Oct. 2015.
"The Last Ceremony." *The Handmaid's Tale*, season 2, episode 10, Hulu, 20 June 2018.
The Last Ship, created by Steven Kane and Hank Steinberg, TNT, 2014–2018.
"Miniseries, Part 2." *Battlestar Galactica*, Sci-Fi, 9 Dec. 2003.
"Night." *The Handmaid's Tale*, season 1, episode 10, Hulu, 14 June 2017.
"Offred." *The Handmaid's Tale*, season 1, episode 1, Hulu, 26 Apr. 2017.
"Seeds." *The Handmaid's Tale*, season 2, episode 5, Hulu, 16 May 2018.
"Smart Power." *The Handmaid's Tale*, season 2, episode 9, Hulu, 13 June 2018.
"Too Far Gone." *The Walking Dead*, season 4, episode 8, AMC, 1 Dec. 2013.
The Walking Dead, created by Frank Darabont, AMC, 2010–present.
"Welcome to the Tombs." *The Walking Dead*, season 3, episode 16, AMC, 31 Mar. 2013.

The Long Winter of Discontent
The Changing Society of Survivors

FERNANDO-GABRIEL PAGNONI BERNS,
JUAN IGNACIO JUVÉ *and* EMILIANO AGUILAR

This essay analyzes the British television show *Survivors* (BBC, 1975–1977), a series illustrating all the complexities framing the UK in the 1970s. *Survivors* connects with the study of complex issues such as social unrest, class, and gender by opening onto the question of post-apocalyptic scenarios represented by a plague pandemic and its effects upon the UK and its citizens. However, the way in which this is brought about—through the viewer's ability to assume an uncomplicated empathy with the "leaders" of the survivors—is problematic. Each of these leaders—Abby (Carolyn Seymour), a happy, upper-class housewife; Jenny Richards (Lucy Fleming), a young career woman in London; and Greg Preston (Ian McCulloch), the show's male hero—represent a status and social class that must be considered as narrative factors. The serial narrative allows the viewer to empathize with each of them, investing in their different adventures and the decisions they must make as the series progresses. The serial format, however, also allows "complex plotlines and more in-depth character studies across a broader storytelling canvas," so the representation of these characters, especially Abby, continually oscillates between opposite ideological poles (Griggs 73).

Survivors itself repeatedly fluctuates between potential progressive and reactionary readings which seemingly negotiate against the real changes taking place in the UK in the 1970s. Dubbed "the Winter of Discontent," the Britain of the late 1970s was a place of moral panics, strikes, and power cuts (O'Farrell 190). *Survivors* thus tapped into a Britain framed by a sense of decline and bleak mood.

This "Winter of Discontent" hypothesis, however, is "riddled with inaccuracies" and myth (Martín López 11). As Dominic Sandbrook argues, "the point is not that Britain was a stagnant or unchanging society, but that the overall picture was so messy, diverse and variegated that any generalization is bound to be risky" (46). This contradictory climate, which unites progressive momentum with conservative attitudes, is negotiated and represented through different subplots in the television series. Since science fiction taps into social and cultural anxieties, and seriality grants the illustration of complex narrative arcs, *Survivors* constructed its stories allegorizing the many upheavals of a turbulent era while ensuring that existing power structures of right-wing ideology and male power are confirmed rather than radically challenged, as both the show and British politics come close(r) to the ideologies of Margaret Thatcher. Only two years after the closing episode of *Survivors* aired, Thatcher became Prime Minister after winning the 1979 general election, thereby changing the history of the country from that point forward.

The Mythical World of the "Winter of Discontent"

Survivors' title sequences illustrate the events that transpired prior to the first episode of the series. An Asian scientist accidentally drops a glass tube containing a new virus seemingly designed in a laboratory. The scene cuts to a scientist (maybe the same one) collapsing at an airport while the camera focuses on close-up shots of passports from Moscow, Madrid, Paris, and London. The action begins immediately after the title's sequence. Focusing on London, audiences see the effects of the viral pandemic as millions die and civilization disintegrates as a result.

The story revolves around a group of emotionally wounded survivors who come together and attempt the laborious re-construction of a new society no longer able to depend on the commodities produced by technology and electricity. The survivors seem to live under a perpetual state of "strike," as nothing works properly anymore. Neither do they know if the new society should be a replica of the lost one or something entirely and radically new.

This basic plot, however, was not wholly born in a vacuum; it may have answered to the social and cultural concerns of the "Winter of Discontent." The phrase, first applied to the events by Robin Chater, a writer working at *Incomes Data Report*, was later used by Larry Lamb, editor of the *Sun* and quickly translated into common usage (Shepherd 126). The denomination "Winter of Discontent" parallels, to some extent, the mindset of the American "Me Decade," as Tom Wolfe (1976) labeled the 1970s in the United States. That American decade saw the decline of the countercultural ideological drive of the 1960s, as the "flower power" culture and its sexual liberation slowly transformed into hedonism and commoditization. What unites the "Me Decade" with the "Winter of Discontent" are not paralleling circumstances but a sense of decline, as the ideal of a gentle consensus and the altruistic rebellion of youth dominating swinging London came to an end. It seemed that there was little space for progressive ethics in an unstable world traversed by a severe crisis on oil prices that put under the microscope the position of dominant geographies such as the United States and the United Kingdom. It was time for Britain to "snap out of its hangover from the '60s" (Turner 23).

With recession, a high rate of annual inflation (Matthijs 118) and recurrent battles between the government and trade unions, the British 1970s left behind an imprint of constant crisis—hence, the "Winter of Discontent." The label suggests a decade traversed by crisis and a very freezing winter, the last nail in the coffin of a social unrest which began years earlier, even as early as the 1950s. This was a bleak scenario, one rife with protest. In the midst of 1978–79, strikes erupted across Britain as workers rejected the Labour Government's attempts to curtail wage increases with an income policy. Media reported that "powerful militant unions had paralyzed Britain by striking to get colossal and inflationary pay claims, showing a total disregard for the general public" (Shepherd 126). Furthermore, citizens felt that the government of James Callaghan was "out of touch" with the feeling of "mounting chaos that the strikes were supposedly causing in Britain" (Martin López 97). The idea of a "mounting chaos" can be seen, in retrospect, as exaggerated and misleading, but it must be stated that the latter half of the 1970s can be read as a decade of (quasi-)apocalyptic landscapes (Sayer 190). Alwyn Turner's history of the critical 1970s even uses the word "apocalyptic" to describe the ordeals that Britain faced in the latter half of the decade (xiii). Strikes paralyzed industries (now working a three-day week) and, along with recession and the bitter cold, put citizens in a bad mood, while recurrent blackouts took place across the city and power cuts took away a significant diversion from these dire situations: escapism through television. In November 1973 the Conservative government introduced the three-day work week to save electricity, along with television broadcasts ending at 10:30 p.m. The dramatic and almost surreal effects of these strikes could be seen clearly on 21 February of that year, when *Blue Peter* presenters Peter Purves and John Noakes demonstrated how to use layers of newspaper to keep the elderly warm if they were affected by power cuts (Martin López 40). Dustmen stopped collecting garbage and the rubbish piled up in the streets, while trains stopped running. Children's hospitals, schools, and geriatric nurseries suffered due to strike action. Even "bodies piling up in morgues (because grave-diggers were on strike)" produced a scenario of wasteland close to those depicted in apocalyptic science fiction scenarios, with streets cloaked in darkness and people illuminating their homes using petrol (Sayer 190).

In this scenario, Britain in the 1970s was ready for a television apocalypse in the form of *Survivors*. Indeed, for many citizens, living in Britain was a question of surviving in a world that had seemingly suddenly become more primitive than before. However, the 1970s were also years of political commitment and visibility of collectives such as feminism and gay liberation (visibility that began in the 1960s). Chris Megson cites conservative and progressive points of view when she states that the "popular metaphor of the 1960s as a wild party and the 1970s as the hangover" is "too simplistic" (178). Much of the political and cultural activity of the era was sustained by a progressive thinking despite blatant inequalities and living standards decreasing through the decade. Laurel Forster and Sue Harper state that this decade, "with swings to the political Right and Left," has been "a sort of 'Bermuda Triangle' of historical analysis" (5).

Survivors very much swings between the apocalyptic imagination, telling about the end of the world and its social interests. The latter tapped into an acute political and social awareness which stages, on one hand, feminist consciousness and class mobility while, on the other hand, marking a slow progress to the right-wing mentality that would prevail at the end of the decade. Like the survivors of the show, the British were caught at the crossroads of an uncertain future, while progressive measures, such as the availability of the contraceptive pill, needed to be protected from conservative mentalities. Britain had to be rebuilt, but there was little consensus on how or what the new country should be.

Survivors: *Negotiating with a Bleak Era*

Throughout its three seasons,[1] *Survivors* played with shock, awe, and ethics as the remnants of humanity fought to recapture some sense of community and, most importantly, a sense of citizenship as a way to survive. Two recurrent situations, however, are strikingly noticeable throughout the episodes and different seasons: first, the fact that the many survivors, rather than group together in larger social structures to better face the myriad challenges ahead, prefer to form small groups separate from each other. The different groups know that there are other bands of survivors living nearby, but still they prefer to keep their small communities isolated from each other. Arguably, this sense of isolation echoed the lack of ideological union and general distrust permeating Britain since the late 1960s. The lack of a common political and national vision caused British author Francis Wheen to describe the 1970s as "the golden age of paranoia" and the times of "the paranoia blues" (1). For example, the episode "A Friend in Need" opens with a reunion promoted by Greg. Leaders of many communities meet at the reunion, with the goal of organizing some kind of protection from external attack, if needed. The reunion, however, fails due to the mutual distrust circulating between the participants. They all prefer to live in separate communities.

The second interesting narrative point, also recurring throughout the three seasons, concerns the weightier sense of futility at the notion of creating community at all. In each episode, new members join the little group of four or five people (among them, the three main characters of Abby, Jenny, and Greg). Thus, the small group seems weighted to grow incrementally. At the same time, however, other characters die or leave the group, with the number diminishing again. Thus in spite of the concerted efforts of the characters, *Survivors* rejects the concept of rebuild and the common goal. For example, the second season's opening episode "Birth of a Hope" begins with the main group's living space burning down, killing several people. While this plot device was used as a way to reset the series after the first season incrementally increased the size of the main group, the fire and resulting reduction in group numbers manages to enhance the sense of futility that marks all the efforts undertaken by the survivors. There is no time to remember the past, much less the victims who fall by the wayside. The latter is especially marked by the absence of leading characters who disappear from the show for different reasons—as Abby does in season 2, and as Greg does in season 3.

The regular lack of mention in regard to past characters that apparently just disappeared enhances the sense of ephemerality framing the series, as the leaders are unable to sustain their presence and project a sense of commonality among the survivors. This lack of a communal goal mirrors the absence of a clear objective in 1970s Britain, with only the third season depicting a slight resurgence of society re-establishing itself after two seasons focused on isolated communities. This new nation depicted in season 3, however, offers contradictory readings: on one hand, "civility" is on the rise again, especially after electricity is restored in the last episode. On the other hand, everything seems to be falling back to previous patterns, as there is no indication of any radical reconstruction of the country. In the penultimate episode of season 3 ("Long Live the King," also the penultimate episode of the series), Alec (William Dysart), a specialist in electronics, warns Jenny against the return of capitalism. He claims "Your Greg Preston wants to bring back money," to which Jenny, who is in love with Greg, quickly retorts "Well, it had its uses, I reckon." Their dialogue continues:

> ALEC: Money was the cause of everything that destroyed us.
> JENNY: It was the plague that destroyed us.
> ALEC: Society was rotten long before that.
> JENNY: Not in everyone's eyes.
> ALEC: Not in yours, maybe. Two cars, nice house, holidays abroad, hairdresser once a week. You were one of the Haves with the big H.
> JENNY: And you, so inadequate you had to become a junkie. One of the great unwashed Have Nots. No wonder you're jealous of money.

Alec is actually a good man. Thus, his left-wing words can gain sympathy from viewers. Jenny, however, is the true heroine of *Survivors* and the only member of the cast to have been in the series from episode 1, so it is she who, presumably, carries the audience's sympathy. As the decade was coming to a close, Jenny's advocacy for money to return suggests the right-wing's hostility toward socialism and the embrace of a conservative way of life detrimental to any possibility of change.

A Lawless Nation: Democracy at the Crossroads

The collapse of the social order and any system of law enforcement is one of the more important topics explored throughout the series. The possibilities of the reconstruction of Britain in the series are in some ways infinite, since the epidemic caused the obliteration of any type of governmental or military control. In consequence, after electric power is cut off, the streets are taken over by the marginal. After her roommate dies, Jenny is told to run away from London. She tries to do so; however, a group of delinquents attack her, taking advantage of the darkness. The second person Jenny meets after running from the robbers is Tom Price (Talfryn Thomas), a homeless man sleeping outside. The whole situation mirrors the social context of the British 1970s, in which people were made to feel that anomie was gaining ground, with a weak government not strong enough to face the social crises shaking the country.

In this new apocalyptic reality, however, there were some characters who tried to constitute some kind of authority and state of legality. In "Genesis," the first attempt to generate a primitive governmental organization appears; while all the characters are still wandering around trying to figure out how to survive in this new context, Abby arrives at a castle where she meets Arthur Wormley (George Baker), a former union leader who plans to re-establish the state. He wants to use a group of armed men to create a feudalistic system in which he sees himself as the center. Despite his initial cordiality, it quickly becomes clear that Wormley is a ruthless man, executing anyone who disagrees with his law. The fact that Wormley was a former union leader is not accidental, especially if one keeps in mind that, during the 1970s, the unions emerged as one of the great powers in the country, with an important influence on the Labour government. Further, many calls to strikes were considered politically motivated or extremist (Dorey 149). Clearly, with Wormley the series is reflecting what it deems the natural evolution of such methods, especially in the absence of a hierarchical, governmental authority to curb such violent tendencies.

In "Gone Away," Wormley's men fight when they try to prevent Greg and Abby from taking food from an abandoned supermarket without prior authorization. Wormley's men work as a kind of parastatal group, attuned, perhaps, to the anxieties of 1970s Britain: "With a collapse in confidence in the mainstream, the 1970s did indeed prove fertile ground for fringe groups, both in politics and beyond," such as the skinheads (Turner 160). The skinheads were one of several working-class youth subcultures to emerge in Great Britain in the late 1960s/earlier 1970s. They "were ardently nationalist in political orientation and fervently opposed to foreign immigration" (Simi and Brents 189). Like Wormley's men, skinheads' favorite pastimes were the bashing of "enemies." Wormley's men's favorite pastime is burning to ashes the different hideouts sheltering the survivors.

There is another attempt at governmental organization in the second season of the series, in the double episode "Lights of London." Ruth (Celia Gregory), a community doctor, is taken by deception to London. This new settlement in the city still has services such as electricity, hot water, and radio. The leader is Manny (Sydney Tafler), who wants Ruth to collaborate in the development of health services and the creation of a medical school. Greg learns that Ruth has been taken to London and goes to rescue her. He finds Ruth, and both realize that Manny wants to be a monarchical ruler. Ruth decides to return to the country with Greg, and they try to make an escape with Manny in pursuit. The episode ends with Manny shot by an inhabitant of his own community who had been condemned to death.

The representations that signal authority and the state throughout the show are quite negative. Both Manny and Wormley try to regenerate a kind of state authority in this new world where all the old democratic institutions no longer have any weight. These attempts are characterized by trying to revive the most repressive face of the state—absolute control of, and by, force. Here, force is exercised in the most violent way possible, since both rulers-to-be use their strength to apply capital punishment in cases where their orders are disobeyed.

In opposition, the protagonists of the series live in a community where the important decisions are made through scrupulous voting. It seems, however, that the show's advocacy for democracy masks the fact that the "old order" that must be erased is either fascism or feudalism. Capitalist democracy, on the other hand, is slowly recuperated through the series. Jenny and Greg's attempts to bring money back reveal an ideological ethos that presupposes that all the chaos assaulting the UK will end with the recuperation of both capitalism (in the form of money and electricity) and the taming of the union leaders, turned feral in this post-apocalyptic scenario. Still, even democracy can fail: in "Law and Order," the community decides, after voting, to apply the death penalty to a man with a mental disability (John Hallet), who apparently has committed a murder. After killing him, the community discovers his innocence. This was a shocking moment for *Survivors*, one that dares to point to the fallibility of both old institutions of order and heroes. It is Abby, the main heroine of season 1, who weights the decision with her final vote: she chooses to kill the man. The completely innocent man is taken outside and shot down by the "heroic" Greg. The ideological and political complications of this choice are diluted, however, as the show progresses without further mention of this episode and the killing. Thus while the series seems to illustrate the infeasibility of British policy during these years, it also demonstrates a palpable lack of reflection, on the part of those in charge, whether they be governmental-type authority figures or even the citizen-rulers of *Survivors*.

A Time of Social Changes in a Post-Apocalyptic Scenario: Feminism and Class Mobility

Cultural theorist Stuart Hall and his colleagues commented that the first half of the 1970s were years of sustained and open class conflict of a kind unparalleled since the end of World War II (293). He claimed that the postwar boom saw a break with traditional ideologies that produced a sense of loss of "familiar landmarks and thus provided the basis for growing social anxiety" (155). The feminist collective was giving women increasing visibility, British imperialist ideology was a relic of the past, and traditional values were starting to evaporate. Like the fictional society of *Survivors*, Britain was another country entirely.

One of the show's imperative concerns was theorizing about class struggles and the new roles of women within the UK in the 1970s. The tone of the series is clearly observed in the pilot episode. "The Fourth Horseman" opens with Abby playing on her own tennis court against a ball machine at her large country house, a clear reference to her social status. When she enters the house, Abby asks her housekeeper, Mrs. Transon (Margaret Anderson), for a drink, rather than fetching it for herself. Abby stands for the bourgeois class, oblivious to what is taking place "out there." In fact, the bad news about something going wrong in the world comes from Mrs. Transon; it is she who tells Abby about the strange silence of her sister, who has remained quiet for the last several days. Abby, on the other hand, remains calm: everything will be fine, she states. The worries of the working class, however, are confirmed to be true. The world outside the bourgeois countryside is starting to collapse. After leaving Mrs. Transon at the train station (and while waiting for her husband to return from London), Abby receives bad news on the radio about a new kind of flu, affecting many. The camera pans to a poster on the wall claiming "High Speed Trains: Speed for the Seventies." It is this new kind of mobility that allows for a rapid spread of the sickness throughout the world, and thus the technological advances of the new decade are depicted as somewhat culpable in the spread of the pandemic. When Grant (Peter Bowles), Abby's husband, arrives from London, he is upset by the long delays on the trains. This may be read as the first of many "strikes" that will put the country as a whole under strained circumstances. Issues such as non-working telephones or delayed trains were not exactly unusual in the mid–1970s. As Abby enumerates the many problems that come with the flu, the episode strongly resembles a common day in the "Winter of Discontent": "There's no power, no lighting or cooking. And food, even if you get it into the city you can't distribute it. And there's water, sewage. Things like that." Her husband, reassuring her, says, "We will manage" ("The Fourth Horseman"). Immediately afterward, the electricity goes off.

The scene then cuts to the first victim depicted in London, Patricia (Elisabeth Sinclair), Jenny's roommate, who is in an advanced state of sickness. Little information is given about Jenny and Patricia, but both live in a small apartment decorated by a profusion of "mod" objects, marking them both as "flower power" children. While Abby remains isolated in the countryside, urbanity is already brewing the collapse of society. When Jenny arrives at the hospital looking for help for Patricia, she finds the building overrun with patients and a severe shortage of doctors. It is in the hospital where Jenny learns about the "panic" running amok through the country.

When Abby learns about the strange flu taking London by storm, the city is already overridden with sick people, but the news comes late for her and her world. After her husband dies in the first episode, Abby's first action is to pray to God for some kind of solution. This passive action is in sharp contrast with the end of the episode. After accepting that humanity faces a return to more primitive times, Abby takes a more proactive approach: she returns to her home, takes a bath, cuts her hair short, and sets the house afire to avoid spreading the virus. The last shot of the first episode reveals a new Abby, now far removed from the bourgeois woman playing tennis against a machine shown at the beginning of the episode.

Abby becomes a kind of conscience to the group of survivors. Until halfway through the first season, she is adamant about working together with other people, but her major goal is to find her lost son, Peter. Her maternal role, if subdued, is still an issue for her character. For the last half of the season, however, she decides to abandon her maternal interest to instead focus on the reformation of the new democracy. This decision is based on the responsibilities that the other characters have placed on her due to her qualities as a leader. Abby is the first one in the series to tell people that they should preserve natural gas, food, and petrol as a way to shore up against shortages, and the one who suggests a collective body for making decisions through consensus. Despite its shortfalls in terms of falling into the stereotype of the short-haired (i.e., masculine) female leader, *Survivors* remains a step in the right direction in its representation of more nuanced portrayals of women. This characterization, however, is complicated after season 1. The loss of Abby robs *Survivors* of its strong female leader, since Jenny, albeit a "mod" working-class girl, plays a more passive, traditional role, as she becomes Greg's girlfriend and mother of his child.

The rise of feminism "was one of the more far-reaching developments of the early 1970s, though inevitably it was one that attracted a great deal of suspicion in a society that was still male-dominated" (Turner 85). One of the ways this manifests in *Survivors* is through the series' depiction of contraception. In the 1970s, "there was a significant increase in the proportions of married women using the pill" (Kiernan et al. 32). This was also the decade in which the pill became easily available. In the episode "Corn Dolly," Charles (Denis Lill), the leader of a small community, claims that repopulation is the only hope for the future of UK. In his opinion, all women of child-bearing age need to be in a constant state of pregnancy to repopulate Britain: the identity of the father, love, sexual desire, marriage, stability, and even consent were of no importance. Abby finds the idea of women becoming cattle unpleasant, so she leaves the community. Interestingly, Charles will return in season 2 and will become a leading character in season 3. With his return, his misogynistic views are downplayed; he now practices monogamy, suggesting a return to (or embrace of) older and yet (for him) more progressive, equality-based values.

Still, Charles is happy when, in the episode "Over the Hills," he discovers that one of the new girls, Sally (June Page), is pregnant. His interest in more of the women having children is re-ignited. The community doctor Ruth, however, is trying to concoct natural contraceptives for the group, creating tension with Charles. Her ideological posture is explicit: she does not want to sacrifice the right of women to make decisions about their own bodies and return to a pre-feminist era of enforced nurturing.

If the role of women in the 1970s was an important issue for the series, class mobility was another point of tension. One strong difference between the 1960s and the 1970s was, according to Sandbrook, "disappearance of that supremely fashionable media catchphrase" that coded the UK as a "classless society" (48). The idea of a society without class struggles "was utter nonsense, of course. British politics and culture in the 1970s were saturated in class-consciousness" (Sandbrook 49). Class background informs many of the characters and actions shaping *Survivors* even if, at first, social mobility seems a new norm in this apocalyptic arena. During the 1970s, changes in the social structure of the UK and a lack of confidence in traditional political parties resulted in increased social mobility and "dealignment," which refers "to the erosion of the historical identification between a voter and a particular social class" (Joyce 5). In this scenario of social mobility, Abby leaves behind any trace of her bourgeois upbringing to become one with the group of survivors. In fact, Abby finds leadership a tiresome and thankless task; she prefers to pass her time alone in her bedroom. Still, Abby's leadership comes parallel with her class privileges, as she is a woman who, as the first episode reveals, was nurtured to command others. She sharply contrasts with working-class Jenny, the latter slowly situating herself within the traditional roles of mother and wife, almost an extension of her previous life as secretary in a world dominated by men.

Whereas Abby "sinks" to the working-class while keeping her privileges as a leader, Tom Price, the derelict, moves up. In "Gone Away," Tom explores a deserted farmhouse in search of anything useful. There, he finds a shotgun (which provides him with some authority), costly cigars, and clean, expensive clothing. Later in the episode, he chases a chicken and claims it as his property when another family, which has not eaten in days, wants the animal. This deviation to "private property" seemingly marks Tom's desire (and envy) for a bourgeois lifestyle. It is interesting to note that Tom's first appearance in the pilot delineates him as a form of comic relief. However, as the series progresses, Tom becomes a dark character, adamant about gaining status and power, a desire that ultimately leads him to sexual assault and murder ("Law and Order").

Conclusions

Survivors' long-reaching narrative arcs and complex sub-plots, together with a large cast of characters, favored an exploration of the complexities of an era associated with a bleak mood but also with a progressive agenda and ideological crisis. Rather than being a passive "reflection" of the era, the show negotiated with the moral and political shifts taking place throughout this particular and complex era in British history. Neither entirely progressive nor conservative, *Survivors* depicted an era rife with contradictions and oscillations.

The series ended with the promise of some return to the status quo in the form of electricity. Indeed, the last episode revolved around the return of electrical power to London, a considerable feat given the circumstances. Ironically, the end of the series in 1977 was closer to the proper beginning of the "Winter of Discontent," a time of rationing of energy. The return of electricity and, with it, industry, prophesized the return of the capitalist structures and the labor division, the latter resulting from the continuous failure of the "alternative" options essayed through the series. (Ironically, Britain's economy based on industry was abandoned through the 1980s in favor of finance capital and consumerism.)

Labour's consequent electoral defeat at the hands of the Conservative Party headed by Margaret Thatcher ushered in an era of new social changes for Britain after a decade of turmoil and political fragility. Indeed, the economy appeared to be enjoying a boom and the summer defrosted the long "Winter of Discontent." The United Kingdom slowly redirected its attention to a new force, Thatcherism, which may be understood as a complete break from the politics and policies of the 1970s. Thatcher herself paralleled some apocalyptic concerns established by *Survivors*: in a speech regarding the strikes and the Winter of Discontent, she commented, "Unless we change our ways and our direction ... our greatness as a nation will soon be a footnote in the history books" (cited in Fallon 60). This same statement could easily have been said by Abby or any other character within the world of *Survivors*. With more than a subtle nod toward the social anxieties of the age, *Survivors*' unnerving reality and distinct social context demonstrates the power of post-apocalyptic television to depict not only our fears, but also ourselves.

Notes

1. Unlike American serialized television shows, "Britain, traditionally with a more regulated public service system, commissions a relatively high number of series with shorter runs" (Freedman 214). In the 1970s, an American season comprised more than twenty episodes (generally, ranging from 22 to 26), while *Survivors*' seasons are short: 13 episodes each in seasons 1 and 2 and 12 in season 3. This shorter format usually allows a high capital investment (*Survivors* contains many locations, both interior and exterior). Furthermore, each season may be read as a self-contained story: season 1 is about the pandemic and people trying to cope with a new world; season 2 revolves around the main characters discussing a potential reconstruction of the nation; and, season 3 provides the first steps in the reconstruction of a new social order. What distinguishes *Survivors* (and British serialized fiction in general) from American serialized forms the most, however, is its "literariness" (Newcomb 1500), which emphasizes more character studies, philosophical/sociological reflection, and mood over action.

Works Cited

Dorey, Peter. "Industrial Relations Policy." *Developments in British Public Policy*, edited by Peter Dorey, SAGE, 2005, pp. 133–160.
Fallon, Janet. *A Communication Perspective on Margaret Thatcher: Stateswoman of the Twentieth Century*. Lexington, 2017.
Forster, Laurel, and Sue Harper. "Introduction." *British Culture and Society in the 1970s: The Lost Decade*, edited by Laurel Forster and Sue Harper. Cambridge Scholars, 2010, pp. 1–12.
Freedman, Des. *The Politics of Media Policy*. Polity, 2008.
Griggs, Yvonne. *Adaptable TV: Rewiring the Text*. Palgrave Macmillan, 2018.
Hall, Stuart, Chas Critcher, Tony Jefferson, John Clarke, and Brian Roberts. *Policing the Crisis: Mugging, the State and Law and Order*. Palgrave Macmillan, 2013.
Joyce, Peter. *The Politics of Protest: Extra-Parliamentary Politics in Britain Since 1970*. Palgrave Macmillan, 2002.
Kiernan, Kathleen, Hilary Land, and Jane Lewis. *Lone Motherhood in Twentieth-century Britain: From Footnote to Front Page*. Clarendon Press, 1998.
Martín López, Tara. *The Winter of Discontent: Myth, Memory, and History*. Liverpool UP, 2014.
Matthijs, Matthias. *Ideas and Economic Crises in Britain from Attlee to Blair (1945–2005)*. Routledge, 2011.
Megson, Chris. *Modern British Playwriting: The 1970s: Voices, Documents, New Interpretations*. Methuen Drama, 2012.
Newcomb, Horace, editor. *Encyclopedia of Television*. Routledge, 2004.

O'Farrell, John. *An Utterly Exasperated History of Modern Britain: Or Sixty Years of Making the Same Stupid Mistakes as Always*. Black Swan, 2009.
Sandbrook, Dominic. *State of Emergency. the Way We Were: Britain 1970–1974*. Penguin Books, 2011.
Sayer, Andrew. *Why We Can't Afford the Rich*. Policy Press, 2016.
Shepherd, John. "The Fall of the Callaghan Government, 1979." *How Labour Governments Fall: From Ramsay Macdonald to Gordon Brown*, edited by Timothy Heppell and Kevin Theakston, Palgrave Macmillan, 2013, pp. 113-140.
Simi, Pete and Barbara Brents. "An Extreme Response to Globalization: The Case of Racist Skinhead Youth." *Globalizing the Streets: Cross-Cultural Perspectives on Youth, Social Control and Empowerment*, edited by Michael Flynn and David Brotherton, Columbia UP, 2008, pp. 185–202.
Turner, Alwyn. *Crisis, What Crisis? Britain in the 1970s*. Aurum, 2013.
Wheen, Francis. *Strange Days Indeed: The Golden Age of Paranoia*. Fourth Estate, 2009.
Wolfe, Tom. *Mauve Gloves & Madmen, Clutter & Vine*. Farrar Straus Giroux, 1976.

Filmography

"Birth of a Hope." *Survivors*, created by Terry Nation, season 2, episode 1, BBC, 31 March 1976.
"Corn Dolly." *Survivors*, created by Terry Nation, season 1, episode 4, BBC, 7 May 1975.
"The Fourth Horseman." *Survivors*, created by Terry Nation, season 1, episode 1, BBC, 16 April 1975.
"A Friend in Need." *Survivors*, created by Terry Nation, season 2, episode 7, BBC, 12 May 1976.
"Genesis." *Survivors*, created by Terry Nation, season 1, episode 2, BBC, 23 April 1975.
"Gone Away." *Survivors*, created by Terry Nation, season 1, episode 3, BBC, 30 April 1975.
"Law and Order." *Survivors*, created by Terry Nation, season 1, episode 9, BBC, 18 June 1975.
"Lights of London, Part 1." *Survivors*, created by Terry Nation, season 2, episode 3, BBC, 14 April 1976.
"Lights of London, Part 2." *Survivors*, created by Terry Nation, season 2, episode 4, BBC, 21 April 1976.
"Long Live the King." *Survivors*, created by Terry Nation, season 3, episode 11, BBC, 1 June 1977.
"Over the Hills." *Survivors*, created by Terry Nation, season 2, episode 12, BBC, 16 June 1976.

Risk Without End?
The Seriality of Risk, the Outbreak Narrative and Serial Post-Apocalypse in Guillermo del Toro and Chuck Hogan's The Strain

SEBASTIAN MÜLLER

The postmodern apocalypse in U.S. popular culture is an ending without an end. Although the original apocalypse envisioned by St. John in the Book of Revelation (Rosen xiii–xiv) promises to be the "end of everything" (Abbott 5) and the absolute destruction of the world, Elizabeth Rosen and James Berger have separately highlighted the paradox of the apocalypse—namely that the apocalypse in postmodern fiction promises absolute closure but delivers a continuing post-apocalyptic world *after the end* (Rosen xxi, Berger 5–6). Instead of closing, the post-apocalypse continues, effectively making the post-apocalypse serial. This serialization—the lack of an end due to a continuous deferral of narrative closure—seems especially fitting for contemporary television storytelling (Allen and van den Berg 2). Contemporary television is, according to Jason Mittell, marked by "a particular model of narrative complexity" (4). This narrative complexity is based on serial storytelling: it combines a "cumulative narrative that builds over time, rather than resetting back to a steady-state equilibrium at the end of every episode" with "accumulative sequential storyworlds" which allows for longer and more complex narrative arcs (18, 12).

Science fiction television series have often been discussed in terms of a broad range of apocalyptic topics, including the changing figure of the vampire/zombie, the role of science, the question of post-apocalyptic genders, societal breakdown and effects on the community—most recently in the essay collection *The Last Midnight: Apocalyptic Narratives in Millennial Fiction* (2016), edited by Leisa A. Clark, Amanda Firestone and Mary F. Pharr, and Stacey Abbott's monograph *Undead Apocalypse: Vampires and Zombies in the Twenty-First Century* (2016). Yet, the serial nature of the post-apocalypse on television remains somewhat underexplored. This aspect merits scholarly attention, especially as the post-apocalypse in complex television is in fact propelled by a serialization of risk(s).

One of the most important risks in contemporary post-apocalyptic science fiction television has become the biological risk of infection and the ensuing threat of a global epidemic, as evidenced by series such as *The Walking Dead* (2010–present), *Fear the Walking Dead* (2015–present), *The Last Ship* (2014–2018), *Z Nation* (2014–2018), and *The Strain* (2014–2017). This dominance of the risk of viral infection can be read as a response to real-world epidemics such as SARS, Avian Flu, H1N1, Ebola, and AIDS, which all carry with them the specter of global catastrophe and apocalyptic "end of the world" fears and rhetoric (Abbott 6). By taking one specific example, the science fiction/horror television series *The Strain* (created by Guillermo del Toro and Chuck Hogan), this article explores how the biological risk of infection becomes a means for serializing what Priscilla Wald calls the "outbreak narrative" as well as serializing the post-apocalyptic world this form of narrative is usually set in (i.e., the risk of infection "maintains" an ongoing post-apocalyptic world in crisis) (1). Examining this serialization of the outbreak narrative and post-apocalyptic worlds through the risk of infection in *The Strain* not only sheds a new light on how risk and seriality become intertwined in contemporary complex post-apocalyptic television series but also on how these series reflect on the implications of the seriality of risk in the real world of the 21st century.

The Seriality of Risk, Carriers and the Outbreak Narrative

The approach to risk most useful for reading the threat of infection in *The Strain* is German sociologist Ulrich Beck's definition of risk. This particular approach to reading contemporary fiction through Beck's theory on (global) catastrophic risk emerges from recent work on risk in literature and popular fiction pioneered by Ursula Heise in her monograph *Sense of Place and Sense of Planet: The Environmental Imagination of the Global*, in which she links global and local imaginations in "risk-related narrative genres" and Beck's notion of risk (12). Heise's work has been followed up on by Sylvia Mayer, who argues for what she calls a "risk narrative" (495). Mayer proposes, using Beck's idea of the "staging" of risk, that literature (and fiction in general) becomes an important means in the process of risk communication as literature can make risks more intelligible and graspable (in contrast to scientific reports) and can explore risks and their implications through speculative and imaginative practices (501–508).

Beck argues that risk has become Western society's dominant "perceptual and cognitive schema" since the beginnings of modernization (accelerated by industrialization and urbanization processes in the 19th century), as modern society had and still has to take into account that the future is uncertain and demands preemptive decision-making to prevent possible future global catastrophes from happening (*World at Risk* 4). He defines risk as "the anticipation of catastrophe" (9). Risk, hence, refers to a potential threat that might turn into a catastrophe in the future. This has a profound impact on politics and institutions, which not only have to identify risks, but also need to manage these risks preemptively before they turn into catastrophes. Although risk is to a certain extent unknowable and incalculable, it can still become a means for political action; risk "shapes our expectations, lodges in our heads and guides our actions, it becomes a political force that transforms the world" (Beck *World at Risk* 10).

According to Beck, one problem of risk management is that processes of management can lead to the creation of new risks (*World at Risk* 15), so there is an endless chain from risk to risk management, new risk to new risk management, and so on (Busby 73). Risk scholar Jerry Busby emphasizes that this recursivity of risk also transforms risk management processes into potentially infinite (serial*)* endeavors, as they are not a final "solution" to risk but risk management is "an unending and evolving process over time, not … a two-step solution exercise" (73).

This also has profound implications for the outbreak narrative structure of *The Strain* as a whole. According to Wald, the outbreak narrative is "an evolving story of disease emergence" that began to proliferate in American popular culture from the 1990s onwards (1). The outbreak narrative, according to Wald, "follows a formulaic plot that begins with the identification of a newly emerging infection, includes discussion of the global networks through which it travels and chronicles the epidemiological work that ends with its containment" (2). The serialization of the risk of infection in *The Strain* transforms the logic of the outbreak narrative from a three-step model to a potentially endless process.

The Strain interestingly already serializes the outbreak narrative through its representation of various open-ended routes to infection. The first episode of *The Strain*, "Night Zero," begins with the arrival of a plane at JFK airport which emergency lands on a service apron and does not respond to queries by the authorities. As they suspect either a terrorist assault or a viral outbreak, the authorities send a Homeland Security team and the response team of the Centers for Disease Control (CDC), headed by epidemiologists Dr. Ephraim "Eph" Goodweather (Corey Stoll) and Dr. Nora Martinez (Mía Maestro), to investigate the mysterious case of the silent plane. They discover that most of the plane's passengers are dead, except for four survivors. In the course of the series the CDC team learns that a deadly vampire outbreak has originated from a wooden cabinet that contains the "Master" (Robin Atkin Downes). The Master constitutes the "Patient Zero" of the infection, who has by now become a "superspreader"—an individual who carries and transmits the disease at a rapid pace and who additionally represents the risk of death (by feeding on victims) and enslavement (by a hive mind control over its victims) (Wald 4). The "Master" here becomes an agent for the ongoing spread of the infection: his existence and his state as a "superspreader" guarantee a serialization of the risk of infection, as the infection cannot be contained as long as the Master exists.

By centralizing the "Master" as a "superspreader," the series both personifies the anxiety of the virus itself and fundamentally changes the role of disease carriers in traditional outbreak narratives. As Wald notes, carriers (of which a "superspreader" is an extreme form) usually become unwilling agents who spread the disease further; they become the metaphor for the process of contagion themselves (21–22). The "Master" alters the role of the carrier in two ways. His "superspreader" status amplifies what Neeraja Sundaram has identified as a "crisis of reproduction," which is central to contemporary audiovisual disaster narratives (137). According to Sundaram, viruses transform human carriers into the locus for an "overproduction or hyperproduction of viral or pathogenic life," connoting that the infection is not containable by the boundaries of the human body and is even multiplied and spread by the body against the agency of the original infected host (137). Interestingly, *The Strain* shifts the focus from an unwilling carrier toward a fully volitional carrier, such as when the "Master" utilizes the infection to recruit his associate Thomas Eichorst (Richard Sammel) in his underground shelter in Poland in 1944 in the episode "The Disappeared." Later, he uses the four survivors of the plane incident in order to spread the virus to their families—as exemplified by little Emma Arnot (Isabelle Nélisse), who successfully infects her father in the episode "The Box"—and eventually throughout New York City. This reproduction of the virus is tailored toward increasing the power of the "Master," as he controls all infected via a hive mind, effectively turning him into a vampiric bioterrorist. This complex relationship between a volitional carrier and involuntary infected, who then become carriers in their own right, tweaks the logic of the outbreak narrative into a more serial form: the typical "crisis of reproduction" of the virus is complicated by encompassing the ongoing strategic interplay between the "Master" and the infected.

The role of the "Master" as a "superspreader" also visualizes the risk of infection and makes it perceivable in a concrete fashion. As Stacey Abbott points out, viruses constitute "invisible killers" which need to be visualized in order to be recognized and detected in the first place (49). Similar to the postmodern zombie, the vampire becomes a clearly perceivable metaphor for the invisible spread of a virus that usually remains hidden, except for a community of epidemiological experts, who manage to visualize the virus by means of microscopes (Abbott 45). In the case of the "Master," this visualization process not only enables the clear identification of the origin of the infection in a specific individual but also attributes agency to the disease by locating it as an instrument used by the "Master" for his own purposes. Professor Abraham Setrakian (David Bradley), an elderly vampire hunter and expert in vampire mythology and biology, explains to Goodweather that the "Master" spreads the disease according to a plan of maximizing the rate of infection and recruiting an undead army through the four survivors, and in consequence Goodweather recognizes that "[i]t's a disease, but it has an intelligence" ("Runaways").

Moreover, the "Master" functions as an "archetypal stranger" who simultaneously signifies the breakdown of national borders and represents the threat of the past invading the present (Wald 10). Wald emphasizes that outbreaks in popular fiction often lead to the stigmatization of individuals who carry the virus into the West, particularly the United States of America (10). The origin of the infection is often attributed to purportedly primitive geographical areas located in the global South (countries in Africa) or the East (countries in Asia), a process which she describes as a "thirdworldification" of the virus (45). In *The Strain*, the "Master" first appears to young Setrakian in a concentration camp in Poland in 1944 in the episode "Runaways" (shown in a series of flashbacks, which are continued in the following episodes). After he has witnessed how the "Master" feeds on other prisoners in the camp, Setrakian decides to kill the "Master" in order to prevent attacks on other people. Hunting the "Master" and his associate Thomas Eichorst becomes his life-long quest: despite marrying, he never stops tracking the "Master" and acquires fighting skills and knowledge about vampires and how to destroy them. He follows the "Master" to Albania in 1967 in order to finally exterminate him but is led into a trap by Eichorst, while the "Master" kills Setrakian's wife and escapes ("Last Rites"). This geographical localization of the origin of the risk of infection to Poland and Albania helps to construct "geographies of fear," which are—in the case of the "Master"—also tied to contemplating the infection itself as anachronistic (a part of the past entering the present) (Everts 95). As Jonathan Everts elaborates on the notion of imagined geographies of fear, "the interaction between ... different temporalities is imagined to be dangerous, because it is the modern and civilised world that encounters a forgotten and 'natural' past, that can no longer be coped with" (91). This anachronism of the infection does not only establish a connection between Eastern European countries and the U.S. but emphasizes the spread of the infection as having a serial history, covering a time period from the 1940s to the narrative present. Essentially, the flashbacks chart Setrakian's ongoing quest for closure by killing the "Master," yet he fails every time (both in 1944 and 1967) and closure is constantly deferred, a process which continues in the narrative present of the series.

In addition to the "Master" as a "superspreader" and "archetypal stranger," the series presents a variety of different ways of contagion, which ensures the ongoing serial spread of the infection and the intensification of an ongoing post-apocalyptic world in crisis. Already in the first episode "Night Zero," Goodweather and Martinez identify a second carrier of the virus: an organism that anatomically resembles a horse hair worm. This "blood worm" penetrates bodily boundaries, infects blood cells, and reprograms them into a worm-reproducing apparatus ("The Box")—a process not unlike the ordinary biological workings of a virus (Dibben 362). This means of infection is visually represented by the videographic use of extreme close-up shots (the hand of the coroner in "Night Zero," the eye of Kelly Goodweather in "Loved Ones"), which emphasize the penetrability of the body and spectacularize the moment of infection.

Another means of infection is constituted by the infected themselves. The infected experience the discoloring of the skin to a pale white and the loss of excreting organs, accompanied by shrill sounds and the sudden urge to consume blood ("The Box"). The viral transformation of their organs creates a new circulatory system throughout the body connected to a new organ: a plaque or cartilage that propels a tongue-like incisor or "stinger" ("It's Not for Everyone"). The infected latch this "stinger" onto the necks of their victims in order to feed and are therefore able to infect the host from a distance of about one to two meters. As Simon Bacon notes for the infected in the novel trilogy by del Toro and Hogan, the infected are a "hybrid, undead horde," a point that also applies to the representation of the infected in the television series (64). Abbott specifies this hybridity as a state in-between the vampire and the zombie (183). While the infected are driven by a primal need to feed on human beings and are reduced to growling and crawling beings similar to zombies, they also drink blood and become allergic to sunlight, established tropes of the vampire (183). This combination of vampire and zombie traits with the addition of a genetic mutation (the "stinger") not only turns them into a monstrous "Other" but also amplifies their potency for infecting a large number of victims (Abbott 183). Similar to the "Master," the infected constitute serial agents of infection: their complex in-between state (vampire/zombie/mutated beings) guarantees that the infection cannot be contained by conventional (epidemiological) means.

In addition to their ability to infect their victims rapidly, the infected are also drawn back to their families as they retain memories of their human hosts and the capacity for speech. For instance, the four surviving passengers experience flu-like symptoms during the period of incubation—defined by Chris Dibben as the time between infection and onset of illness—and therefore present an invisible risk to their families (362). Despite the already perceivable visual "otherness" of the infected in the early stages of their infection (the aforementioned pale skin), the four infected survivors of the plane manage to conceal the risk of infection they present by still acting and speaking like normal human beings, even though the virus is already rewriting their biology and influencing their brain chemistry. In contrast to the trope of the silenced monstrous "Other" often employed in science fiction that cannot speak or communicate with human beings, here the infected retain the ability to speak (Kerslake 11). This becomes especially important for the infected Emma Arnot. She gains entrance into her father's house by appealing to his emotions and stating that she is cold ("Night Zero" and "The Box"), implying that he should let her in and care for her. Essentially, this display of a faked familiarity which (initially) conceals the "Otherness" of the infected becomes another (narrative) means toward serializing the infection, as the infected are not recognizable as such during the incubation period.

Ultimately, the serialization of the risk of infection through presenting different ways of contagion/transmission, through the construction of a serial history of the outbreak, and through changing the role of traditional carriers serves to construct an ongoing post-apocalyptic world in crisis. Berger highlights that the post-apocalypse is a "study of what disappears and what remains and of how the remainder has been transformed" (7). The serialization of the risk of biological infection in *The Strain* here renegotiates traditional relationships between risk, the outbreak narrative, and post-apocalyptic worlds in audiovisual fiction: risk here becomes a continuing phenomenon that suffuses the post-apocalyptic world rather than a solvable problem (a vantage point on risk taken by the more traditional outbreak narrative explored by Wald).

(The Failure of) Risk Management and the (Serial) Implications of Contagious Spaces

In *The Strain*, the Centers for Disease Control (CDC) and later the U.S. government attempt to first assess and then manage the spread of the infection. The risk assessment and management process employed by Goodweather and the CDC follows the conventions of Wald's outbreak narrative in (initially) representing the medical work of the CDC as a two-step process: from risk assessment to risk management. In order to accurately assess the risk of infection, its danger to the biological workings of the human body, and its probability and velocity of spread, Goodweather and Martinez examine both the infected and the "blood worms" in biocontainment laboratory settings, first in sterilized and bordered tents at the airport ("Night Zero") and later at St. Sebastian's Hospital ("Gone Smooth"; "It's Not for Everyone"). Due to their scientific expertise, the two specialists on epidemics are deemed to be the appropriate authority figures to assess the gravity of the risk of an outbreak. Goodweather and Martinez begin their scientific examination of a dead vampire by performing a dissection. In contemporary outbreak narratives the vampire often becomes "the subject of the medical gaze" (Abbott 39), which Michel Foucault defines as a special type of looking: "the medical eye must see the illness spread before it, horizontally and vertically in graded depth, as it penetrates into a body, as it advances into its bulk, as it circumvents or lifts its masses, as it descends into its depths" (cited in Abbott 40).

The medical gaze in *The Strain* combines both visuals and rational scientific examination and analysis by Goodweather and Martinez in the episode "It's Not for Everyone." The camera even adopts the dissecting look of the medical gaze of the epidemiologists themselves by switching to a point-of-view, low-resolution handheld camera image recorded by CDC administrator Jim Kent (Sean Astin), who is asked by Goodweather to record the autopsy of the infected pilot Redfern (Jonathan Potts) with Goodweather's rather old-fashioned cell phone. In a series of dissolves and cuts to different camera angles, the extreme close-ups and alternating long shots of the body emphasize the abjectness of the infected body—putrefied and shriveled internal organs, necrotic arteries, a cartilage apparatus propelling the "stinger." At the same time, Goodweather's comments also express fascination as the virus is "rewriting human biology," a common ambiguity *vis-à-vis* the infection often expressed in outbreak narratives (Wald 43). While assessing the risk of infection, especially by the examination of the "stinger" as a means of infection, Goodweather also hints at potential "gains"—scientific and biological insights and knowledge—to be drawn from the mutation of the human body despite the risk it presents to the population of New York. At this point in the narrative, the detailed representation of Goodweather and Martinez's scientific analysis of the infected corpse and their reliance on the "medical gaze" seems to indicate a possibility for narrative closure: their thorough autopsy increases their knowledge about the spread of the virus, a necessary prerequisite for manufacturing a cure and eventually containing the outbreak.

In following the pattern of the outbreak narrative, Goodweather and Martinez ultimately propose quarantine as a risk management procedure in order to spatially contain the infected and prevent a further spread of the infection to other people in New York. A quarantine order accepts the fact that an outbreak constitutes a communication between people that serves to spread the virus (Wald 12). The notion of contagious space recognizes that space is, as geographer Doreen Massey stresses, a product of interrelations and interactions between people and other people and between people and objects (Massey 9–10). These interrelations become dangerous, which is why Goodweather and his team use the city's Emergency Alert System in "Last Rites" in order to broadcast images of their autopsy to the public: they warn the citizens of New York of the threat of a global pandemic, instruct them in how to avoid contact with infected loved ones, and advise the public to kill the infected by exposure to sunlight. They communicate the risk of infection to the population and suggest the enforcement of a voluntary quarantine by the healthy citizens in order to avoid infection. Again, their warning to the public—including specific countermeasures against the further spread of the outbreak—holds the potential for closure, for containing the outbreak before it can become pandemic.

Yet quarantines ultimately constitute an ineffective means of risk management, as the series constantly emphasizes their failure to contain the infection. For instance, Goodweather's CDC team establishes a perimeter around JFK airport in the beginning of the series, which initially seems to be effective, preventing the disease from spreading. As Bill Albertini notes for quarantine procedures in a bio-containment laboratory, a quarantine "controls space; it establishes a perimeter distinguishing inside from outside, clean from contaminated" (452). This model works by binaries and by the assumption that spaces can be separated and controlled by establishing fixed and policed borders. The problem with a viral infection, however, is that the virus does not acknowledge human-made borders in an increasingly borderless and interconnected world (Wald 34). A further complication arises from what Wald has called the "uncontrollable human factor," when human beings that carry the infection past the artificial borders created to contain it (21). In *The Strain*, Jim Kent unwillingly becomes such a "carrier" for the disease as he is blackmailed by Eldritch Palmer (Jonathan Hyde), a millionaire who collaborates with the "Master" in exchange for being healed from a fatal disease, and Thomas Eichorst to smuggle the wooden cabinet (containing the "Master" and blood worms in the soil) from JFK airport into Manhattan. A later attempt to quarantine Manhattan by the Secretary of Health and Human Services, Margaret Pierson (Maria Ricossa), is thwarted by Palmer's interference; he tries to persuade her not to establish a quarantine and kills her when she declines ("The Master"). Afterward, Palmer and Eichorst threaten CDC Director Barnes (Daniel Kash) into complying with their plan of spreading the infection. Scientific and political attempts at containment are therefore thwarted by individuals: the promise for closure/containment is shattered as actions by human individuals (and not so much the infection itself) become a means for the serialization of the risk of infection and the failure of (human) attempts at risk management.

Moreover, the ongoing serial spread of the infection and the impossibility to contain it through quarantines is explicitly tied to urban and globalized human transportation infrastructures throughout the first season of *The Strain*. As Wald notes, the outbreak narrative both "maps the spaces of global modernity" (33), which are marked by globalized transportation networks, and simultaneously problematizes the ambiguity of these systems

(37). While transportation networks facilitate human movement, they also provide means for the spreading of diseases across national borders, which in turn transforms these diseases into global threats. *The Strain* repeatedly emphasizes the negative consequences of such systems of transport: the "Master" arrives via a Regis Air plane from Berlin ("Night Zero"); the infection is carried into Manhattan by an SUV ("Night Zero"); and the infected spread throughout New York City by utilizing the urban sewer system ("Runaways"). All of these human-created networked infrastructures become risky; they counteract scientific risk management attempts (the CDC quarantine) as these networks are predicated on openness, the crossing of borders, and continuous movement and transfer of people and objects (including the Master's coffin) on a global scale. Setrakian points to the ongoing (serial) risk of these networks in the very last scene of "The Master" in a final voice-over comment which acknowledges the historical role humans have played in their own post-apocalyptic demise: "This planet, our host, once so wild and unknown—we've mapped it, paved it, arranged it on a grid never imagining that something else was watching us, a creature even more ruthless and predaceous than we are, eager to exploit the very infrastructure we so obligingly arranged" ("The Master").

The constant failure of risk management in *The Strain* demonstrates not only the impossibility of containing the infection spatially but also questions the position of power of institutions of scientific and political authority in general. In fact, institutions themselves are put at risk—public trust in these institutions dwindles as these institutions are no longer seen as capable risk managers and "saviors" but as actors who fail to manage risk or even contribute to perpetrating risks rather than managing them. As Albertini notes, the outbreak narrative promises that systems such as the state and public health institutions such as the CDC can protect the population from becoming infected (461). Yet, at the same time, narratives of the continuing spread of diseases ultimately prove "faith not in systems of containment, but faith in their failure" (461). This loss of faith in the ability of scientific institutions to manage risks in *The Strain* aligns with Beck's notion of a contemporary (world) risk society in which science and politics no longer operate as successful managers of risk; they must "not only [be seen as] a source of solutions to problems, but as a *cause of problems*" (*Risk Society* 156, italics original). Although Beck's point refers to risks that have been brought into existence by science itself, *The Strain* adds an important second dimension to contemporary (world) risk society here by highlighting how scientific and political institutions such as the CDC and the U.S. government can metaphorically be infected by the risks they attempt to manage; in *The Strain* these institutions become serial "carriers" themselves who distribute and spread risks instead of managing and containing them (155).

After Goodweather and his new team—Martinez; the pest control officer Vasily Fet (Kevin Durand); the hacker Dutch Velders (Ruta Gedmintas); vampire-hunter Abraham Setrakian; and Goodweather's son Zack (Ben Hyland)—realize that their attempt at managing risk through a quarantine is doomed to failure, they adopt Setrakian's plan to exterminate the infected vampires (also referred to by Setrakian as the *strigoi*) by exposing them to sunlight or killing them with silver weapons. They also make it their primary goal to locate and kill the Master. This way of risk management stands in the tradition of established tropes of killing vampires as Professor Abraham Setrakian bases his risk management procedure—just like Professor Abraham van Helsing in Bram Stoker's *Dracula*—on his knowledge of "tradition and superstition," which he has gathered through extensive, years-long research (Stoker 285):

> **SETRAKIAN:** It's far more likely to work. We kill the Master, and its spawn will die. I promise you.
> **DR. GOODWEATHER:** Okay, for convenience sake and strictly as a semantic term, we'll refer to him as "the Master." You're saying we kill the Master and that's somehow gonna stop this plague.
> **SETRAKIAN:** Yeah.
> **DR. GOODWEATHER:** That makes no biological sense! You destroy one creature, and somehow all the other ones die? How does that work?
> **SETRAKIAN:** I have verified the observations of these authors with my own experience. Those that are inaccurate, I have discarded. That is your scientific method, no? If you wish to defeat this evil, you must trust me. I understand this! You do not! At every turn, everything I have said has proven to be correct. Is that not true? ["For Services Rendered"]

Two points are noteworthy about this exchange. First, this dialogue seems to demonstrate a gradual shift from epidemiological risk management to mythical risk management. This seems to counter the contemporary trend in vampire film and television series in which there is an "increasing medicalisation of vampirism" (Abbott 41). According to Abbott, in recent television and film, vampire superstition and myth are left behind for a rational scientific explanation which works "to explain the cause of vampirism or reduce it to a set of familiar and rational concepts that make sense within our real world" (44). While *The Strain* does not abandon scientific risk management in favor of mythical and folkloric beliefs, it does integrate them. The series highlights the necessity for risk management processes to address the complexity of the serial spread of the infection and ongoing serial crisis through combining different ways of knowing how to deal with risk.

Second, Setrakian's words promise narrative closure as he indicates that the death of the "Master" will kill all vampires, thereby containing the outbreak. However, just as the plans of quarantine fail, so does the mythical extermination plan. Although the team manages to locate the Master in Vestry

Hall in Manhattan in the last episode of season 1, and they expose him to sunlight, the Master does not die. He manages to escape from them, which ensures a continuation of the narrative and the serial post-apocalyptic world in crisis (in seasons 2 to 4). The first season fittingly does not end with the containment of the infection—the successful managing of its risk to humanity—as a traditional outbreak narrative following Wald's pattern would. The ongoing threat of the infection conserves the power of seriality as "a multifaceted variable, with a range of potential storytelling possibilities" for the future seasons of the series as the risk of infection and a global pandemic still loom large (Mittell 22). The post-apocalyptic world in *The Strain* remains a world of risk, and the (preliminary) failure of risk management processes potentially opens up a crucial reflection on the notion of risk itself: the ongoing risk of infection here signals the limits of human agency and of the human possibility for mastery. Risk is transformed—both literally and imaginatively—into a serial, ongoing component of the post-apocalyptic world rather than a problem to be solved (as the traditional outbreak narrative would suggest).

Conclusion

Ultimately, the risk of infection in *The Strain* becomes a means for serializing the outbreak narrative and the post-apocalyptic world in which it is usually set. The representation of both (serial) ways of infection and the constant failure of scientific, political, and mythical attempts at containing the outbreak in *The Strain* breaks with the model of closure that defines the traditional outbreak narrative as defined by Wald. The traditional outbreak narrative basically follows a linear narrative (from the identification of a disease to an epidemiological analysis of the infection to the containment of the outbreak by finding a cure) that depends on closure. In contrast, *The Strain* and, by extension, other post-apocalyptic television series such as *The Walking Dead, Fear the Walking Dead, Z Nation*, and *The Last Ship* construct a serial form of the outbreak narrative which instead constantly defers closure through how it re-conceptualizes risk as an ongoing phenomenon of the post-apocalyptic world of the series rather than a problem that can be solved in three steps.

As this analysis has shown, the serialization of risk in *The Strain* reworks the conventions of the outbreak narrative and at the same time critically reflects upon contemporary scientific and political ways of risk management in the 21st century. *The Strain* serializes the outbreak narrative through representing a complex post-apocalyptic world in which risk has no end. The series constructs an interconnected web of serial carriers (the "Master," the blood worms, the infected); it presents the outbreak as an ongoing phenomenon which has a serial history (from 1944 to the narrative present); and it denies a resolution to the epidemiological crisis as all attempts at risk management through scientists and politicians inevitably fail, preventing the containment of the infection (and hence narrative closure). *The Strain* here becomes a paradigmatic example for how contemporary post-apocalyptic television series negotiate the relationship between risk, seriality, and the post-apocalypse—indeed, the ongoing crisis that defines the post-apocalyptic world is the seriality of risk. *The Strain* ultimately questions the very foundations of the outbreak narrative. If the risk of infection in recent contemporary complex television series is always presented as serial, and this serialization of risk in turn propels the serialization of (outbreak) narratives, then the model of closure which Wald identifies has lost its validity in contemporary television culture.

The series' representation of processes of managing risks also opens up a critical reflection on contemporary modes of (epidemiological and political) risk management in the 21st century. In particular, *The Strain* problematizes the position of power granted to scientific and political institutions in the risk management process and challenges traditional (epidemiological and political) ways of risk management *vis-à-vis* the constant breakdown of spatial borders in the 21st century. On the one hand, *The Strain* challenges the ability of institutions such as the CDC and the political government to contain the outbreak (as all attempts at quarantines fail) and critiques them for becoming a source of risk themselves (as they become serial carriers for the infection rather than saviors). On the other hand, *The Strain* also speculatively interrogates whether standard procedures of (epidemiological) risk management, particularly quarantines, can still master serially spreading risks in the interconnected world of the 21st century. The belief that infections can be contained by constructing clearly bordered spaces—a foundational assumption that structures both the outbreak narrative and real-world scientific risk management—is challenged in *The Strain*. Human individuals breach the borders of the quarantine, spreading the disease further, and both global and local transportation networks not only facilitate the movement of people and goods but are presented as dangerous contagion networks. Human beings and human-made global networks therefore are represented as interconnected elements within a risky, global serial web. This web becomes a source of fear for both the characters and the viewer because it is not just mere fiction, a product of post-apocalyptic speculation, but a (frightening) serial extrapolation of the contemporary world in the 21st century. Television series such as *The Strain* become a useful means for making this web and its risky interconnections visible. Ultimately, this series seems to suggest that in a post-apocalyptic world, and perhaps our own, risk is something that can no longer be managed or solved—just lived with and survived.

Works Cited

Abbott, Stacey. *Undead Apocalypse: Vampires and Zombies in the Twenty-First Century*. Edinburgh UP, 2016.
Albertini, Bill. "Contagion and the Necessary Accident." *Discourse*, no. 30, vol. 3, Fall 2008, Special Issue: Cinema and Accident, pp. 443–467.
Allen, Rob, and Thijs van den Berg. "Introduction." *Serialization in Popular Culture*, edited by Rob Allen and Thijs van den Berg, Routledge, 2014, pp. 1–7.
Bacon, Simon. "'This Is Something New … or—Something Very, Very Old': The Strain Trilogy in Context." *The Transnational Fantasies of Guillermo Del Toro*, edited by Ann Davies, Deborah Shaw, and Dolores Tierney, Palgrave Macmillan, 2014, pp. 63–82.
Beck, Ulrich. *Risk Society: Towards a New Modernity*. 1992. SAGE Publications, 2009.
_____. *World at Risk*. Translated by Ciaran Cronin. Polity, 2009.
Berger, James. *After the End: Representations of Post-Apocalypse*. U of Minnesota P, 1999.
Busby, Jerry. "Why Risk Is Recursive and What That Entails." *Routledge Handbook of Risk Studies*, edited by Adam Burgess, Alberto Alemanno and Jens O. Zinn, Routledge, 2016, pp. 73–80.
Clark, Leisa A., Amanda Firestone and Mary F. Pharr, editors. *The Last Midnight: Essays on Apocalyptic Narratives in Millenial Media*, McFarland, 2016.
del Toro, Guillermo, and Chuck Hogan. *The Strain*. William Morrow, 2009.
Dibben, Chris. "Human Epidemic." *The Routledge Handbook of Hazards and Disaster Risk Reduction*, edited by Ben Wisner, J.C. Gaillard, and Ilan Kelman, Routledge, 2012, pp. 361–371.
Everts, Jonathan. "Anxiety and Risk: Pandemics in the Twenty-First Century." *The Spatial Dimension of Risk: How Geography Shapes the Emergence of Riskscapes*, edited by Detlef Müller-Mahn, Routledge, 2013, pp. 82–96.
Heise, Ursula K. *Sense of Place and Sense of Planet: The Environmental Imagination of The Global*. Oxford UP, 2008.
Kerslake, Patricia. *Science Fiction and Empire*. Liverpool UP, 2007.
Massey, Doreen. *For Space*. SAGE Publications, 2005.
Mayer, Sylvia. "World Risk Society and Ecoglobalism: Risk, Literature, and the Anthropocene." *Handbook of Ecocriticism and Cultural Ecology*, edited by Hubert Zapf, De Gruyter, 2016, pp. 494–509.
Mittell, Jason. *Complex TV: The Poetics of Contemporary Television Storytelling*. New York UP, 2015.
Rosen, Elizabeth K. *Apocalyptic Transformation: Apocalypse and the Postmodern Imagination*, Lexington Books, 2008.
Stoker, Bram. *Dracula*. 1897. Penguin Books, 1994.
Sundaram, Neeraja. "Imagining Bio-disaster, Reproducing Social Order: Epidemics in Contemporary Hollywood." *Journal of Creative Communications*, vol. 7, no. 1 & 2, 2012, pp. 135–151. *SAGE*, www.journals.sagepub.com/doi/10.1177/0973258613501065.
Wald, Priscilla. *Contagious: Cultures, Carriers, and the Outbreak Narrative*. Duke UP, 2008.

Filmography

"The Box." *The Strain*, directed by David Semel, season 1, episode 2, FX, 20 July 2014.
"The Disappeared." *The Strain*, directed by Charlotte Sieling, season 1, episode 9, FX, 7 Sept. 2014.
Fear the Walking Dead. Created by Dave Erickson and Robert Kirkman, AMC, 2015–2018.
"For Services Rendered." *The Strain*, directed by Charlotte Sieling, season 1, episode 7, FX, 24 Aug. 2014.
"Gone Smooth." *The Strain*, directed by David Semel, season 1, episode 3, FX, 27 July 2014.
"It's Not for Everyone." *The Strain*, directed by Keith Gordon, season 1, episode 4, FX, 3 Aug. 2014.
"Last Rites." *The Strain*, directed by Peter Weller, season 1, episode 12, FX, 28 Sept. 2014.

The Last Ship. Created by Steven Kane and Hank Steinberg, TNT, 2014–2018.
"Loved Ones." *The Strain*, directed by John Dahl, season 1, episode 10, FX, 14 Sept. 2014.
"The Master." *The Strain*, directed by Phil Abraham, season 1, episode 13, FX, 5 Oct. 2014.
"Night Zero." *The Strain*, directed by Guillermo del Toro, season 1, episode 1, FX, 13 July 2014.
"Runaways." *The Strain*, directed by Peter Weller, season 1, episode 5, FX, 10 Aug. 2014.
The Walking Dead. Created by Frank Darabont, AMC, 2010–2018.
Z Nation. Created by Craig Engler and Karl Schaefer, SyFy, 2014–2018.

Driven to Extinction, Again
Cadillacs and Dinosaurs *and* the Irresistible Apocalypse

TONY PERRELLO *and* C. ANNE ENGERT

When an apocalypse of whatever origin arrives, immediate concerns generally center upon survival in a world crumbling into chaos. Once the dust settles, what is left of humanity attempts to find hope in creating culture anew. This project is often complicated and hampered by the twin preoccupations of reclaiming what was lost and avoiding repetition of the mistakes of the past. The difficulty usually lies in determining which is which. Such is the situation for the inhabitants of a post-apocalyptic America in *Cadillacs and Dinosaurs*, a 1993–94 animated television series adapted from Mark Schultz's acclaimed comic series *Xenozoic Tales*. Over the course of the series' 13 episodes viewers follow the protagonists' adventurous and heroic confrontations with bandits, corrupt politicians, and most notably, dinosaurs. However, in the long run, the forces that may thwart survivors' attempts to successfully reestablish culture and society reside not in these obvious opponents, but in toxic implications lurking within the reclaimed mythos and conceptualizing metaphors of the world of *Cadillacs and Dinosaurs*.

In their classic text *Metaphors We Live By*, George Lakoff and Mark Johnson explore the deeply influential ways that metaphors not only help us to describe our experiences in terms of creative correspondences, but also "provide coherent structure" to our understanding of the world (139). Through their power to shape our social perception of reality by "highlighting some things and hiding others," potent conceptualizing metaphors may be seen to "change what is real for us and affect how we perceive the world and act upon those perceptions" (139, 146). Lakoff and Johnson explain that a conceptualizing metaphor can become "a guide for future action" or even "a self-fulfilling prophecy" (156). Once a specific metaphor has become part of the social language around an issue, it "forces us to focus *only* on those aspects of our experience that it highlights, [and] leads us to view the entailments of the metaphor as being *true*" (156–7, italics original). Experience calls upon a metaphor for meaning; the metaphor, in turn, colonizes both the experience and the meaning with its own structure and truths. In this essay we will examine the two primary conceptualizing metaphors operating in the culture of *Cadillacs and Dinosaurs*—the world-as-frontier and nature-as-machine—setting them in conversation with their real world effects in our own history and exploring the perilous potential of uninterrogated cultural mythology in both this fictional world and in reality.

The stories in *Cadillacs and Dinosaurs* exploit both the popular obsessions and the environmental angst of late 20th and early 21st century America. The series' seemingly auspicious television debut coincided with the massive wave of dinosaur frenzy inspired by *Jurassic Park* (1993) alongside an increasingly friendly market for environmentally conscious cartoons, most notably *Captain Planet and the Planeteers*, an eco-moralizing children's offering aired by TBS in various forms from 1990 to 1996. *Cadillacs and Dinosaurs*, set 500 years after an unspecified, but anthropogenic, global catastrophe in the 21st century, reveals a post-apocalyptic America in which surviving humans have been reduced to scattered tribal enclaves dealing with a world in which "the forces of nature have spun wildly out of control" and "dinosaurs have returned to reclaim the earth" (opening voiceover, *Cadillacs and Dinosaurs*). The series' rival factions include a coalition of poachers commanded by muscle-headed Hammer Terhune, the science-loving Wassoon represented by sexy diplomat-ambassador Hannah Dundee, and the most powerful faction, the City-in-the-Sea (a flooded and shattered New York City). Dominating City-in-the-Sea's Council of Governors, the scheming Wilhelmina Scharnhorst lusts after the technological secrets of "the ancients," despite the doom these long-buried gadgets brought to her ancestors. Scharnhorst's ambitions are opposed by the "Old Blood Mechanics," whose members subscribe to an environmentalist ethos embodied in the axiom "*machinatio vitae*" (the machinery of life). Their local devotee and hunky car nerd, Jack Tenrec, also specializes in keeping alive those icons of vanished automobile culture, 1950s-era Cadillacs—now running on dinosaur guano. Additionally, there is the mysteriously secretive Grith, a quasi-reptilian, humanoid race whose leader Hobb communicates telepathically with a few chosen humans and with dinosaurs.

Cadillacs and Dinosaurs leverages its critique of the present with a vision of the future aimed squarely at our collective anxieties over the possible consequences of techno-capitalist culture and its overreaches—both for humanity and for the earth and its non-human inhabitants. The present age of techno-capitalism and its increasingly problematic human impact upon planetary systems has of late come to be known by many as the Anthropocene,[1] a term of geologic time coined in the mid–1980s as global culture endured a rash of environmental disasters and collective blunders, including the nuclear accidents at Three Mile Island in 1979 and Chernobyl in 1986, the 1984 chemical disaster in Bhopal, and the 1989 Exxon Valdez oil spill. Recently, however, some scholars and activists have turned to the more focused term Capitalocene to signify "capitalism as a way of organizing nature—as a multi-species, situated, capitalist world ecology" (Moore 6). Both of these terms, along with Donna Haraway's exploration of the alternative "Chthulucene" to suggest "a kind of timeplace for learning to stay with the trouble of living and dying in response-ability on a damaged earth," have implications for the post-apocalyptic environmental challenges in *Cadillacs and Dinosaurs* (2).

The tensions between Tenrec's eco-religious principles, the freebooter profiteering of the Terhunes, and Scharnhorst's lust for the ancients' techno-power reflect what Jedediah Purdy calls the "threefold crisis" of our *au courant* Anthropocene, a crossroads of exigencies in "ecology, economics, and politics." Collectively, these comprise a growing "recognition that a system believed, or at least imagined and hoped, to be stable and self-correcting turns out to be unstable and even prone to collapse" (17). As it is for contemporary arguments over matters such as climate change or fossil-fuel dependence, so also for the inhabitants of *Cadillacs and Dinosaurs* (particularly so for Jack Tenrec and the Old Blood Mechanics), the terminologies used in such debates matter a great deal. The Old Bloods' maxim of *machinatio vitae* most especially exposes the pitfalls of evolving metaphoric and metonymic associations surrounding even the most carefully chosen labels in controversial issues. Along with the nature-as-machine creed of *machinatio vitae*, their sense of their world as a frontier of potential and renewal provides the citizens and factions of *Cadillacs and Dinosaurs* with a compelling and seemingly useful metaphoric structure and mythos. Each of these metaphors, however, carries the baggage of history and multiple hidden implications. Absent conscious avoidance, in time their combined weight would seem likely to lead Tenrec, Scharnhorst, Terhune, and their fellow citizens into the same sorts of situations that Purdy cites—cultural practices that seem stable and useful, until they reach sudden crisis or failure, and the slide into societal and environmental apocalypse once more.

The World as Frontier

Despite its post-apocalyptic trappings and its dinosaur exotica, *Cadillacs and Dinosaurs* essentially functions as a frontier story with human civilization surviving in small-scale installations on the edge of a vast primeval hinterland. This type of society is fragile from within to political machinations and is constantly vulnerable to encroachment from outlaws and other wilderness dangers just beyond its borders. Outside the City-in-the-Sea, small farm-holdings and mining sites work to extend the human cultural footprint. The series abounds with the mythos, imagery, and even jargon of the American Wild West of the mid-to-late 19th century. That historical frontier Myth of the West, argues Richard Slotkin, is a "structuring metaphor of the American experience" (5). As with that American mythos, so with *Cadillacs and Dinosaurs*—the conceptualizing metaphor, the world-as-frontier, presents a framework for understanding the world and for the operation of the self in the world.

Many of the elements of *Cadillacs and Dinosaurs*' world-as-frontier metaphor appear most prominently in the episodes "Wild Child" and "Dino Drive," the very title of the latter evoking a Western-style cattle drive motif. That episode concerns herds of "macks" (triceratops) stampeding through a small farming settlement, leveling it and sending its inhabitants fleeing for their lives. With Governor Scharnhorst's reluctant sanction (she wants to kill the macks), Tenrec plans to literally drive the animals away from other settlements using his fleet of vintage Cadillac convertibles. As he and his crew prepare, Dundee displays a "historical precedent" for their undertaking: an ancient book depicting a cowboy (hat included) on horseback riding herd on cattle, with a flat-topped butte in the background. She also relates the "magic chant" cowboys used, "yee-haaah!!," which Tenrec dutifully shouts as their herding begins to "move 'em out." The poacher Terhune, who wants to slaughter the macks for profit, says his gang should plan to "cut them off at the pass" ("Dino Drive"). Although the story implies that the city and the affected farming areas are not extremely far apart, the farming and herding sequences feature the landscape of the high desert Colorado Plateau, with wind-eroded buttes and the reddish-brown earth-tones of that area—in high contrast to the series' usual heavily foliated or flatland wilderness visuals.[2] Once the macks are relocated safely, they are depicted in a final establishing shot peacefully grazing in a green valley surrounded by low hills.

Alongside the cattle-herding and Western lingo, "Dino Drive" and "Wild Child" also include plot details involving the Grith and their relationship with humans. Twice, accompanied by low-key sound effects featuring vaguely Native American chanting, rattles, and drums, "Dino Drive" depicts Hobb and other Grith standing at the opening of their cave home, observing but not acting, as the humans attempt to deal with the mack problem. The obvious implication is that the Grith represent what might be called the local Indian tribe. Their demeanor seems reminiscent of the famous "Keep America Beautiful" public service announcement of 1971, in which "The Crying Indian," upon seeing polluted rivers, smoggy atmosphere, and a bag of garbage tossed at his feet, stoically allows a single tear down his cheek in anguish at the disrespect for the "beauty that was once this country" ("Crying Indian PSA"). Those connections, the Grith as Indians and as custodians of natural resources, are strengthened in "Wild Child," in which Dundee and Tenrec encounter a young boy riding a wahonchuck (stegosaurus) and turning it away before it forces their Cadillac into a ravine. The boy has been raised by the Grith after they found him alone in the forest pursued by hyenas. Dundee argues that the boy should be returned to his own people, but when Hobb telepathically communicates visions of the boy's situation to her, she relents. Hobb tells her that the Grith "made him one of [their] own," and that now "the boy is far more Grith than human. It is in [the] city that he cannot survive." The boy is also being taught the tenets of *machinatio vitae* and will be "a link between Grith and human," according to Tenrec ("Wild Child"). The story of the wild child evokes something of the Indian captivity narratives of the historical American experience. These texts usually involve individuals, often women, who for various reasons (often raids or attacks), find themselves long-term Indian captives.[3] In many American captivity narratives, individuals are gradually assimilated into the tribal lives of their captors. While most eventually returned to their home cultures, some, like Mary Jamison, who twice married and had children and grandchildren in her captive Seneca tribe, chose to remain attached to their new Indian lives.

American television has been relying upon Old West and frontier-themed storytelling, both live-action and animated, for decades, and although westerns may have had their heyday in the 1950s and 60s, they are still being made and consumed in the second decade of the new millennium, and still speaking to Slotkin's characterization of the American frontier experience and mentality. In drawing upon the frontier mythos and metaphor for its own storytelling purposes, *Cadillacs and Dinosaurs* not only buys into a popular narrative genre, it also takes on the historical legacies and the nearly fossilized cultural weight that the myth of the Western frontier carries. Part of that legacy reaches back into the Christian mythos of the biblical Apocalypse preceding the utopian renewal of human society. Such an apocalypse-and-renewal schema preoccupied the Puritans, even as they journeyed to American shores hoping to leave behind the legacy of Old World Europe and to form a new nation on a God-given, unspoiled continent. Jonathan Kirsch relates that the 1630 voyage of the *Arabella* began at the London docks with the "fiery Puritan minister, John Cotton" telling his passengers that their destination was "the new promised land ... reserved by God for his elect people as the actual site for a new heaven and a new earth" (173). Two centuries later, as Slotkin explains, their descendants continued the process of constructing or reconstructing an American mythos worthy of "defining or creating a national identity." The "myth of the frontier" eventually emerged, largely from the exploits of "the rogues, adventurers, and landboomers; the Indian fighters [and the Indians], traders, missionaries, explorers, and hunters who killed and were killed until they had mastered the wilderness." Frontier mythology offered "a conception of America as a wide-open land of unlimited opportunity for the strong, ambitious, self-reliant individual to thrust his way to the top" (5). This ideal of the self-reliant individual ready to take possession of opportunity then spoke and still speaks powerfully to the experience of being American.

The Puritan colonists had mythologized America as a place "to regenerate their fortunes, their spirits, and the power of their church and nation"; the myth of the American frontier built upon that foundation to lead the march west across the continent in pursuit of a manifest destiny (Slotkin 5). As the original biblical garden had its Adam, so the regenerated one would also have its new Adam of mythological stature. R.W.B. Lewis describes the American Adam as "the hero of a new adventure: an individual emancipated from history ... bereft of ancestry ... an individual standing alone, self-reliant and self-propelling, ready to confront whatever awaited him with the aid of his own unique and inherent resources." He would be as Adam was before the Fall: "archetypal" and "fundamentally innocent," so that "the world and history lay all before him" (5). In contrast to the human failures of old, this new Adam would exercise righteous and visionary stewardship of the American Eden. Nathaniel Hawthorne's "The New Adam and Eve" depicts such renewed innocence: "'And now,' observes Adam, 'we must try again to discover what sort of world this is, and why we have been sent hither'" (18). Such, too, is the project of Jack Tenrec, as he is epically extolled in the opening credits' voiceover for *Cadillacs and Dinosaurs*: "In this savage land, one man stands alone ... in a world where only the strong survive." Tenrec is the hero of the frontier, the post-apocalyptic American Adam, starting out once more on the eastern coast of the American continent and looking westward. He is the man emancipated from history, at least the history of a corrupted civilization that destroyed its own future. Like a frontier missionary, he is filled with an activist faith and its vision for a catholic unity of nature and humanity, working in harmony like a vast, well-oiled machine. Tenrec and his Eve-like companion, Hannah Dundee, must "try again to discover what sort of world this is," this new American frontier and destiny, now with dinosaurs instead of buffalo herds and the eco-shamanist Grith instead of Indians (Hawthorne 18).[4]

For all its 19th-century aspirations and its ongoing cultural fascinations, the frontier mythos, as Slotkin observes, also embodies a powerful justification for violence, and especially violence as a vehicle for the kind of regeneration possible on the frontier. This mythic sanction of violence as an acceptable, even necessary, apparatus to progress has, as Slotkin argues, "blinded us to the consequences of the industrial and urban revolutions" (5). Mythmaking is not an exact science, but is more like a function of the unconscious as it reacts to ongoing experience, and as such, Slotkin warns, as "Melville and Faulkner had earlier prophesied ... myths reach out of the past to cripple, incapacitate, or strike down the living" (4–5). Both the violence and the blindness to consequences that can emerge from mythology past its expiration date increasingly haunt the post-apocalyptic cultures of *Cadillacs and Dinosaurs*.

Although located in the remnants of broken Manhattan, the City-in-the-Sea acts as a frontier town with frontier sensibilities. This society's status as post-apocalyptic survivors of a human-caused cataclysm suggests that the regeneration aspect of the myth of the frontier operates at an almost obsessive level for them. The city's ambitious, cunning leadership, as embodied in Scharnhorst, actively pursues the undiscovered treasures and opportunities that the frontier seems to promise. To that end, Scharnhorst alternately allies and wars with Terhune's outlaw gang, depending upon the direction of their individual and mutual interests. While the Terhunes, as poachers, engage in the literal hunting of animals, Scharnhorst tracks down the recondite technology of the ancients in an effort to reactivate its dormant powers for personal benefit. Under such a mythic regime, these hunters free themselves to kill or destroy the Others of the frontier indiscriminately in the same spirit that Slotkin describes of the mythic American frontier hunter: whereas the hunting culture of the Indians had sought to achieve a "precarious balance between the visions of the shaman and the hunter ... in which the ideals, rituals, and poetry of the former sanctified the necessary activities of the latter," the newcomer to the land, the "Euro-American, having no such connection with the earth he possessed, destroyed the balanced world in an attempt to remake it into the image of something else" (559). This latter hunter saw the hunt as a means of "self-renewal or self-creation through acts of violence" (556). Slotkin describes the byproducts of the frontier hunter myth in its full flower and later, as well in terms of real-world results:

> The whale, the Buffalo, and the bear [were] hunted to the verge of extinction for pleasure in killing and "scalped" for fame and the profit in hides by men like Buffalo Bill; the buffalo meat left to rot, till acres of prairie were covered with heaps of whitening bones, and the bones then ground for fertilizer ... the land and its people ... economically exploited and wasted; the warfare between man and nature, between race and race, exalted as a kind of heroic ideal; the piles of wrecked and rusted cars, heaped like Tartar pyramids of death-cracked, weather-browned, rain-rotted skulls, to signify our passage through the land [565].

The Terhunes are similar profligate exploiters of the hunt. In "Dino Drive," Hammer Terhune plans to harvest the ivory horns and tusks from herds of macks, leaving the rest to rot, like 19th-century American buffalo herds slaughtered for only their hides. The poachers in "Pursuit" have begun to organize into a centralized mob under boss Terhune, marking out prime hunting grounds with their dino-skull-and-crossbones insignia. They steal and weaponize a high-powered pile-driver to streamline their killing process.

Their implied aim in the episode is harvesting the teeth of the slithers (dinosaurs), a rarity to be sold to wealthy collectors. As evidence of past hunts, piles of whitened dinosaur bones litter the poachers' compound.

When the interests of the Terhunes and Scharnhorst overlap, the stakes for potential consequences grow exponentially. In "Death Ray," Scharnhorst and her pet scientist, Dr. Fessenden, discover the whereabouts of an operational laser satellite installation in Grith territory. Scharnhorst uses threats to the Grith to coerce Tenrec into leading Fessenden to the site, since only Tenrec "can travel safely through the Grith territory." Scharnhorst shouts, "This satellite will bring the power of the universe to us," while pounding her fist on her desk. Once at the satellite ground-station, Fessenden reveals that the solar-powered laser (touted by Scharnhorst as a boon to her people) is actually a "death ray." Tenrec prepares to destroy the satellite communication console when Dundee intercedes, "Don't destroy it before we've had a chance to study it!" Tenrec emphatically responds: "Study what? How to destroy civilization all over again?" Hammer Terhune, appearing through a broken catwalk window, says, "Sounds good to me." Later, Terhune plans to target the City-in-the-Sea so that after he "scorches Scharnhorst's kingdom, she'll see who's the real boss" ("Death Ray"). To Hammer, all things look like a nail. The hunt for the regeneration of political power justifies the consideration of any level of violence among these citizens of the *Cadillacs and Dinosaurs* frontier. Even Dundee, though less megalomaniacal in her argument, pursues her own self-interested desire for scientific knowledge of the weapon of mass destruction, and in that moment, she rationalizes with the amorality of the violent frontier mythos.

In "Departure," the connection between the frontier experience and regeneration through violence emerges explicitly. In the wilderness, Tenrec encounters a huge war machine commanded by Lars Striker, a former City-in-the-Sea captain of the guard whom Scharnhorst had "exiled … to the wastelands" for a failed military coup. His sojourn on the frontier has brought Striker into possession of his powerful engine of war, found "in the wretched wilderness" of his banishment ("Departure"). On it, Striker and his men live as a renegade militia in the wilds, armed to the teeth and ready to roll over anything that gets in their way. With the further regeneration of his ambitions to be fulfilled through the violence of revenge, Striker plans to lay siege until Scharnhorst surrenders, or he will "blow her and the council out of the city." He fondles his phallic artillery and declares that "true progress will only come when the city bows to the power of an iron will" ("Departure"). Striker, like Terhune and Scharnhorst, unreservedly subscribes to the myth of the frontier, singing its siren song of murderous renewal—that violence, perhaps the more egregiously carried out the better, is the path to glorious regeneration and fulfillment.

Nature as Machine

Operating alongside the conceptualizing metaphor of world-as-frontier, the parallel metaphor, nature-as-machine, also powerfully shapes the society in *Cadillacs and Dinosaurs*. The Old Blood Mechanics' quasi-religious dictum, the *machinatio vitae*, says that "the machinery of life means balance; we have to maintain it" ("Rogue"). Repeatedly in the series Tenrec navigates various clashes between human actions and nature's balance as he sees it. Throughout, he preaches the ways of the *machinatio vitae*: reject careless exploitation of natural resources ("Duel"); work with natural systems to foster sustainability for both human and non-human stakeholders ("Dino Drive"); take care that by-products of human activities do not pollute or endanger the environment ("It Only Comes Out at Night"); and consider the potential dangers of new technology, not just its possible advantages ("Mind Over Matter," "Remembrance"). In all endeavors, Tenrec teaches, seek the balance of nature.

In the contentious outworkings of its rival factions, *Cadillacs and Dinosaurs*' eco-morality tale reflects the long American history of tension between the nation's pastoral nostalgia for "an undefiled, green republic ... dedicated to the pursuit of happiness" and its glorification of a technological manifest destiny in which "the raw landscape is an ideal setting for technological progress" (Marx 6, 203). As an Old Blood Mechanic, Tenrec sees his New World of magnificently strange creatures and their born-again Jurassic environment as the instantiation of that yearning for an "undefiled, green republic" which must not be allowed to follow the destructive path of the ancients who lost their world. Tenrec, however, is opposed by the same forces that drove their ancestors: the lure of progress, the desire for expansion, and the hungers of greed and ambition. The consumerist poachers crave "slither burgers" and endorse wholesale slaughter to get them, while the sexless Scharnhorst lusts only for ancient technology and political power. For Tenrec, the *machinatio vitae* would seem to provide the necessary philosophical, spiritual, and ideological tools to support the productive renewal of civilization while combating the flawed human motivations that could undermine that project.

As Lakoff and Johnson illustrate in their analysis of conceptualizing metaphors, however, unexamined reliance upon grand metaphors to guide a society may produce unintended results. The Myth of the West has influenced American culture long after the period of its formulation, with sometimes unforeseen and tragic consequences arising from the myth's unarticulated implications. Likewise, analogizing nature as a machine may engender unplanned cultural repercussions for the advocates of *machinatio vitae*. This channeling and molding of our collective vision through metaphor goes on, despite the possibility that those so-called truths may be unarticulated, incomplete, counterproductive, or even damaging. Beneath its alluring surface of openness and renewal, the world-as-frontier metaphor includes several highly arguable assumptions: that the land offers unlimited resources for exploitation; that the violence deemed necessary for the promised regeneration produces only short-term damage for lasting benefits; and that the citizens of the frontier need only rugged individuality and self-reliance to conquer any obstacle encountered. In actual experience these entailments have led people to hunt entire species to extinction; to harvest, mine, and farm the land into ugly barrenness; and to view native inhabitants as an inconvenience that may be swept aside in favor of a new vision. In similar fashion, the nature-as-machine metaphor, taken at face value, seems to manifest the environmentally progressive principles of Tenrec's Old Blood Mechanic convictions. As a belief system formulated by and for a group whose very lives have been spent working intimately with analog machinery, the nature-as-machine metaphor would seem instinctive and elegant. It casts nature as a complexity of interrelated elements all working together in harmony and without undesirable or harmful disruptions, especially those caused by human activity. However, alongside those hopeful correspondences in the *machinatio vitae*, the unconsidered entailments and their consequences also may eventually emerge in unexpected ways.

The construction of conceptualizing metaphors around the human relationship with the world we live on, with nature, has long preoccupied humanity. Katherine Park's study "Nature in Person: Medieval and Renaissance Allegories and Emblems" considers historical emblematic representations of Mother Nature—as a naked, poly-breasted, lactating woman. She is erotic, fertile, and nurturing (51–2). This early modern emblem emerges out of a medieval representation of nature as a sort of Rosy the Riveter figure, crafting babies with a hammer and forge to replace people who have died—restoring a balance of/to nature (Park 55). Leaving behind this Vulcanite figure, Renaissance personifications of nature embodied value in "purely physical terms" in her "inexhaustible lactation" and in the "most basic sense of raw materials and resources, rather than values in the sense of ethical and religious norms" (Park 69). This metaphoric version of nature "was represented as *premoral* ... that is, unconcerned with human practices and conduct ... an indifferent mother" (Park 64–5). Other philosophical thinkers of the time leaned toward a more mechanistic view of nature. For Descartes, "The bodies of humans and brutes ... were complex machines whose many actions and physiological functions were caused by the mechanical motions of their parts following 'from the mere arrangement of the machine's organs every bit as naturally as the movements of a clock or other automaton follow from the arrangement of its counter-weights and wheels'" (Hawkins 15). For Thomas Hobbes, biological life existed as a mechanical affair: "for what is the heart, but a spring; and the nerves, but so many strings; and the joints, but so many wheels, giving motion to the whole body" (47). Hobbes' mechanistic metaphor extended outward from natural bodies into cultural products as well. He thought of contemporary mechanical automata as a type of "artificial animal" and even further, the state as an "artificial man" (47). Hobbes' characterizations illustrate the machine metaphor flowing freely between the polarities of nature and culture—nature seen as machine and machine seen as a sort of meta-expression of natural life. Edward O. Wilson explains two additional factors that contributed to a further blurring of the boundaries between nature and machine: Descartes' reductive approach to the study of the world "as an assembly of physical parts that can be broken apart and analyzed separately" and Newton's mathematical articulation of various laws governing the operation of physical phenomena (29). The powerful explanatory influence of these ideas and discoveries very quickly inspired Enlightenment scholars to apply "Newtonian solutions to the affairs of men" (Wilson 30). The problems with such mechanistic views of nature and culture are the same problems that threaten the collapse of the *machinatio vitae* in *Cadillacs and Dinosaurs*.

One of the foremost issues in discussions of nature and our relationship to it is what Bruno Latour calls the "full force of the instability" of the categories. The nature/culture divide is, he says, "an impossible opposition between two domains" (19). Whereas the term *humans* serves to bridge the categories of male and female, there is no such categorical term to bridge "the same gap with the 'nature/culture' pairing" (16). Furthermore, Latour argues, the term "nature" includes a "*normative dimension*" that serves to "orient all existence according to a model of life that obliges us to choose between false and true ways of being in the world" (20, italics original). This impossible-to-bridge gap between nature and human culture holds special relevance in the world of *Cadillacs and Dinosaurs*. Although left unexplained in the animated series, its source material, *Xenozoic*, offers some accounting of the cataclysms that resulted in a post-apocalyptic world full of dinosaurs in just 500 years: scientists, knowing that massive ecological and geological upheavals were near, developed the "archeoplasm" (Schultz 178), a laboratory-created "evolutionary accelerator" wrought from materials found in beds of trilobite fossils (Schultz 187). This artificial "primordial soup" was responsible for allowing the new "world's wildly eclectic ... yet balanced ... ecology [to] spring up in under 500 years, from the barrenness of global calamity" (Schultz 191). So at the very outset of their world's creation from the raw materials of the planet, the hand of its creator was human. In the fictional world of *Cadillacs and Dinosaurs*, as in our own, efforts to make distinctions between the world of nature and the world of human culture result in impossible instabilities, always already collapsing into each other.

Attempts to create or enforce cultural norms based upon these unstable categories are also continually problematic. Instabilities arise in part due to the ways that the similarities between tenor and vehicle in metaphors—and especially in structural metaphors and conceptualizing metaphors such as the nature-as-machine metaphor—may migrate from their original surface correspondences to unanticipated peripheral correspondences over time. Lakoff and Johnson describe the process thusly: "New metaphors, by virtue of their entailments, pick out a range of experiences by highlighting, downplaying, and hiding. The metaphor then characterizes a similarity between the entire range of highlighted experiences and some other range of experiences" (152). The original metaphoric correspondences in *Cadillacs and Dinosaurs* between nature and machine might imagine the animals, plants, and earth as smoothly meshing gears that work together as a well-functioning mechanism. In literal machines, deviation or misalignment of parts will likely mean failure. Thus while Tenrec's statement that the "machinery of life means balance" fits into the entailments of the original structure, his subsequent statement that "we must maintain it" migrates from the machine metaphor into the additional correspondences of the balance metaphor and highlights these experiences. Balance, as in tightrope walking, healthy eating, or bank accounts, requires maintenance through ongoing correctional monitoring by a presiding force. Tenrec's statement presupposes such human intervention into the processes and systems of the non-human world, and yet, over and over in the series, he urges minimal intervention or none. The conflict between these two correspondences undermines the effectiveness of either or both.

Other correspondences that emerge from the machine metaphor include such characteristics as being instrumentally useful, and being fallible, repairable, and/or disposable. In "Rogue," when Scharnhorst rejects the Old Blood Mechanics and their beliefs as "an obsolete breed," she accesses the correspondences associated with both machines and disposability. Machines are disposable, but so is garbage. Machines can be obsolete, no longer useful, and Scharnhorst has grafted that property onto Tenrec's beliefs in the machinery of life. In "Departure," Dundee and Tenrec capture a flock of zeeks (pteranodons) from their offshore nesting grounds and install them in a city tower to act as an early warning system against threshers (mosasaurs) threatening the local fishermen. Scharnhorst initially objects, but when the plan works, she says, "You all thought those zeeks were just pests. But I knew they'd help warn us against the threshers." The zeek relocation and the final congratulations at their successful alarm by Dundee, Tenrec, and Scharnhorst all focus upon the instrumental use of the wild zeeks, and rather than affirming respect for the animals' right to their own life cycles as they would have them if unmolested, instead speak to the tool aspect of the machine metaphor. Tools are machines—like nature—and their purpose is to be useful to humans; these animals serve a tool's function, and therefore animals are properly useful as humans will. The treatment of people, too, becomes cross-pollinated as with instrumental machine-related correspondences—commodities to be used, then discarded—as Scharnhorst plans to displace the human "moles" who work at excavating for her buried technology with the very digging robots they unearth ("Mind Over Matter").

The most striking corruption of the machine metaphor's non-nature-friendly correspondences concerns Tenrec's fellow Old Blood Mechanic, Sean Russell, in "Duel." Tenrec describes the boorish Russell as "an Old Blood Master" and "expert on the Grith." The Sean Russell of their training days together may have been always the best at any endeavor, as Tenrec claims, but the visiting Russell has utterly abandoned the eco-shamanism of the *machinatio vitae*, trading his Old Blood morals for unapologetic exploitation of both his friends and the non-human world. He sabotages Tenrec's Cadillac and steals a helicopter engine from the garage; he abducts the Grith's "life stone," leaving them to slowly perish without it; and he uses the attractant power of the stone to lure hundreds of dinosaurs into a dead-end canyon where they can be slaughtered easily by the Terhunes for meat, hides, and bones. When Tenrec calls Russell "Scum," Russell replies, "Maybe, but I'm going to be rich scum!" ("Duel"). Russell has been fully parasitized with the instrumental correspondences of the nature-as-machine metaphor; he sees only immediate usefulness or gain for himself in the resources of the land and its animals—and other people as well. Notably, Tenrec describes this apostate to the Old Blood faith as having been "a great mechanic, a great craftsman, and a great driver"—all mechanistic orientations ("Duel"). Nowhere does Tenrec say anything about Sean Russell having been a great conservationist before he fell into eco-sin. Russell's interpretation of nature-as-machine offers a dark reflection of noble intentions under the influence of a powerful reality-shaping metaphor.

What Does It All Mean?

Cadillacs and Dinosaurs may have been a short-lived children's cartoon series from the early 1990s that came and went mostly unnoticed, but its narrative substance and its environmental consciousness far exceed that characterization. The two structuring metaphors in the culture and world of *Cadillacs and Dinosaurs*, the world-as-frontier and nature-as-machine, explore the perils of metaphor-as-mythology threatening to spin "wildly out of control" (*Cadillacs and Dinosaurs* opening voiceover). As post-apocalyptic fiction, the series deals in a specialty of its genre—the cautionary tale. Like many examples of apocalyptic and post-apocalyptic fiction, *Cadillacs and Dinosaurs* depicts not a random cataclysm nor even a biblical one, but instead what has been called the "God–less apocalypse," that is, one "in which human beings have no one to blame except themselves—and, crucially, no one to whom they may turn for rescue or redemption" other than themselves

(Kirsch 212–13). For Tenrec and company, the polished saurian fossils of our museums, or maybe the dragons of our imagination, have returned in spectacularly real fashion, perhaps not for the first time. Carl Jung describes the "dragons in our day [as the] great machines, cars, big guns, these are the archetypes now, simply new terms for old things ... the terrifying thing of which man in the dim past was afraid" (147). The real danger from these latter-day dragons, Jung argues, is the possibility that the time might come "when the machine gets on top of us," that is, when the illusion of control that we maintain over our mechanical creations shatters (148). These dragons come in many forms—as machines, as bureaucracies and institutions, as great assemblages of "machinelike bodies of men, armies or other organizations," of vast land-devouring megalopolises (148–49). Jung argues that in all of these we have so deeply "invested all our energy in rational forms" that the dragon-like results "become a sort of nightmare" in which "slowly and secretly we become the slaves and are devoured" by their—by our—endless appetites (149). Jung wrote these words in 1930.

When the dragon breaks loose into our world, when his hot breath melts our glaciers and his passing wings stir monster hurricanes, we are left to choose our response. Slavoj Žižek suggests three possibilities: some will doubt, ignore, or deny the disturbing evidence before their eyes; others will engage in obsessional activity that may or may not have any effect besides busying their minds against the approaching danger; and still others will comfort themselves with the notion that the problem is "a sign bearing a certain message," for example, the way that some religious fundamentalists took AIDS as a sign of divine punishment for sins of which someone else ought to repent (35). For the willful deniers, for the chronically distracted, for those possessed by a certain *schadenfreude*-driven satisfaction at calamity to others, the global human activity behind punishing ecological crises seems distant and unreal. Žižek informs us that with such shields as these against our dragons "we blind ourselves ... to the irreducible gap separating the real from the nodes of its symbolization" (36). The stories we have been telling ourselves will not fix our problems. Diverting fictions will not cure "nature sick unto death," Hegel's term not for a stricken earth, but for humanity ourselves (ctd. in Žižek 37). Perhaps we need new stories, stories meant to—if not bridge the gap between our symbolization of the world and its reality—then at least to begin building authentic connection.

The treacherous power of less-than-carefully chosen metaphors—those symbolic little this-is-just-like-that stories that offer convenient shorthand for divining meaning in the world—shows up clearly in *Cadillacs and Dinosaurs* as its citizens struggle against what appears to be the inevitable reenactment of the same old tales, like some post-apocalyptic Freudian repetition compulsion. No matter the heights of cognitive processing, the lizard brain finds a way. New metaphors must try their hands, though, at illuminating humanity's understanding of itself and the planet and everyone on it, human and non-human. Haraway contrasts two ways of looking-being at the world: "autopoiesis" (self-making), which understands systems and relationships in terms of "autonomous units" (32); and "sympoiesis," which she defines as "making-with"—this latter term more appropriately conceived, Haraway argues, for understanding and living within "complex, dynamic, responsive, situated, historical systems" (58). With these word-stories as seeds, she moves from the Anthropocene, the geo-era that describes human activity overwhelming or reshaping any or all other planetary systems, into the Chthulucene, a name she adapts from a particular long-legged spider, *Pimoa Chthulu* (31).[5] The reaching "tentacularity" of spiders and suchlike creatures exemplifies an earthly, primordial wisdom present in "a life lived along lines ... not at points, not in spheres" and may be the metaphor we need to open new pathways of understanding (32). Or perhaps other stories may emerge from the dreams that Jung says are woven from the "collective primal unconscious mind" and through which "the dream calls our mind's attention to the body's instinctive feeling" (151). The body is real, and it is inseparable from the rest of the world. We should listen to it. If not, we will have only ourselves to blame when the dragons come.

Notes

1. According to Jedediah Purdy, the ecologist Eugene Stroemer coined the term "Anthropocene" ("the age of humans") in the 1980s, and its use gained currency after it was championed by the atmospheric scientist Paul Crutzen in the year 2000 (*After Nature* 1–2). See Moore 3.
2. Tenrec plans to herd the macks to "Verrazano Point," a name with multiple geographic and infrastructural referents on the mid–Atlantic coast of the United States.
3. Although the wild child seems to Hannah Dundee to be something of a captive, he is also a foundling, more in the tradition of Edgar Rice Burroughs' Tarzan. In an interview, Mark Schultz discusses his early literary influences, explaining that he discovered Burroughs' *Tarzan of the Apes* at age eight and also heavily consumed Tarzan films and comic books throughout his childhood. In *Cadillacs and Dinosaurs*' source material, the tale of the wild child is entitled "Foundling" (Perry and Nolan-Weathington 8; Schultz 154).
4. Tenrec's creator in *Xenozoic Tales*, Mark Schultz, also claims John Wayne, mid-century Hollywood's quintessential Western hero, as a significant inspiration for Tenrec's character. Schultz cites as particularly influential Wayne's films under director Howard Hawks: *Red River* (1948), *Rio Bravo* (1959), *Hatari* (1962), *El Dorado* (1966), and *Rio Lobo* (1970) (Perry and Nolan-Weathington 15).
5. Perhaps not coincidentally, in some of the last of the unfinished *Xenozoic Tales*, a giant arachnid identified as a "cog-spider" emerges from deep underground and is captured by the Wassoon Lord Drumheller. The cog-spider is part of a mysterious subterranean race known as the Harvestmen (another name for the order of arachnids known as Opiliones, a.k.a. daddy longlegs), who were key to the survival of human tribes during their 500 years of post-cataclysmic life. Tenrec explains that the Harvestmen expelled life-giving oxygen

when underground atmospheric regulators failed, but Drumheller wants only to exploit the spider-like denizens, who are also a source of "medicines ... machine oils ... hydraulic fluid" (340–41).

Works Cited

Haraway, Donna J. *Staying with the Trouble: Making Kin in the Chthulucene*. Duke UP, 2016.
Hawkins, Michael. "'A Great and Difficult Thing': Understanding and Explaining the Human Machine in Restoration England." *Bodies/Machines*, edited by Iwan Rhys Morus, Berg, 2002, pp. 15–38.
Hawthorne, Nathaniel. "The New Adam and Eve." *The New Adam and Eve, Etc.: Being Second Series of Mosses from an Old Manse*. William Paterson, 1883, pp. 5–26.
Hobbes, Thomas. *Leviathan*. *Great Books of the Western World*, edited by Robert Maynard Hutchins and Mortimer J. Adler, Vol. 23, Encyclopedia Britannica, Inc., 1952.
Jung, Carl G. *The Earth Has a Soul: C.G. Jung on Nature, Technology & Modern Life*, edited by Meredith Sabini, North Atlantic Books, 2016.
Kirsch, Jonathan. *A History of the End of the World: How the Most Controversial Book in the Bible Changed the Course of Western Civilization*. HarperCollins, 2006.
Lakoff, George, and Mark Johnson. *Metaphors We Live By*. U Chicago P, 1980.
Latour, Bruno. *Facing Gaia: Eight Lectures on the New Climatic Regime*, translated by Catherine Porter, Polity Press, 2017.
Lewis, R.W.B. *The American Adam: Innocence, Tragedy, and Tradition in the Nineteenth Century*. U of Chicago P, 1955.
Marx, Leo. *The Machine in the Garden: Technology and the Pastoral Ideal in America*. Oxford UP, 1964.
Moore, Jason W. "Introduction." *Anthropocene or Capitalocene? Nature, History, and the Crisis of Capitalism*, edited by Jason W. Moore, PM Press, 2016, pp. 1–11.
Park, Katherine. "Nature in Person: Medieval and Renaissance Allegories and Emblems." *The Moral Authority of Nature*, edited by Lorraine Daston and Fernando Vidal, U of Chicago P, 2004, pp. 50–73.
Perry, Fred, and Eric Nolan-Weathington. *Modern Masters Volume Fifteen: Mark Schultz*. TwoMorrows Publishing, 2008.
Purdy, Jedediah. *After Nature: A Politics for the Anthropocene*. Harvard UP, 2015.
Schultz, Mark. *Xenozoic*. Flesk Publications, 2013.
Slotkin, Richard. *Regeneration Through Violence: The Mythology of the American Frontier, 1600–1860*. Wesleyan UP, 1979.
Wilson, Edward O. *Consilience: The Unity of Knowledge*. Alfred A. Knopf, 1998.
Žižek, Slavoj. *Looking Awry: An Introduction to Jacques Lacan Through Popular Culture*. MIT Press, 1992.

Filmography

Cadillacs and Dinosaurs, created by Steven E. deSouza and Mark Schultz, CBS, 1993–94.
"Crying Indian PSA, 1971. People Start Pollution. People Can Stop It." *YouTube*, uploaded by Keep America Beautiful, 16 August 2011, www.youtube.com/watch?v=IR06-RP3n0Q.
"Death Ray," *Cadillacs and Dinosaurs*, episode 3, CBS, 2 Oct. 1993.
"Departure," *Cadillacs and Dinosaurs*, episode 11, CBS, 11 Jan. 1994.
"Dino Drive," *Cadillacs and Dinosaurs*, episode 2, CBS, 25 Sep. 1993.
"Duel," *Cadillacs and Dinosaurs*, episode 12, CBS, 21 Jan. 1994.
"It Only Comes Out at Night," *Cadillacs and Dinosaurs*, episode 8, CBS, 27 Nov. 1993.
"Mind Over Matter," *Cadillacs and Dinosaurs*, episode 6, CBS, 6 Nov. 1993.
"Pursuit," *Cadillacs and Dinosaurs*, episode 10, CBS, 18 Dec. 1993.
"Remembrance," *Cadillacs and Dinosaurs*, episode 9, CBS, 11 Dec. 1993.
"Rogue," *Cadillacs and Dinosaurs*, episode 1, CBS, 18 Sep. 1993.
"Wild Child," *Cadillacs and Dinosaurs*, episode 5, CBS, 23 Oct. 1993.

The End of Everything
Survival Narratives and Everyday Heroism in Battlestar Galactica

E. Leigh McKagen

"Look at those clouds, and tell me this isn't the end of everything," Lieutenant Karl Agathon (Tahmoh Penikett) demands of Raptor Pilot Sharon Valerii (Grace Park) in part one of the *Battlestar Galactica* miniseries, which aired on December 8, 2003. Numerous mushroom clouds bloom in the background during the scene, providing the audience with visual confirmation of the recent devastating Cylon attack on the human world of Caprica. The reimagined *Battlestar Galactica* (2003–2009) tells the story of 50,000 human survivors fleeing from the Cylons, robots originally created to serve the human race and "do the hard and dangerous work Man no longer wished to do" ("Original Miniseries Script" 1). Stephen Dyson calls the series "the most realistic depiction of perpetual, grinding, existential crisis in the history of televised science fiction," and it stands out against other space opera and science fiction narratives for its intense pace and gripping storyline in early post–9/11 America (111). Despite the spaceships, robots, and faster-than-light travel through space, Executive Producer Ronald D. Moore designed *Battlestar Galactica* to evoke present-day American society and explore contemporary social and political issues through the lens of a post-apocalyptic storyline (1–2).

In this essay, I explore the environmental challenges of the Anthropocene as part of *Battlestar's* potential commentary on the present. Using the lens of Donna Haraway's suggestions to "stay with the trouble" as a means of response to the ongoing Anthropocene interwoven with Joseph Campbell's prescription for "everyday heroes," I examine the *Battlestar* narrative to argue that the ultimate focus on survival-at-all-costs after a singular apocalyptic event diminishes the potential for everyday heroism of living and dying—and therefore *responding*—to the Anthropocene crisis in a realistic way. Although there is no requirement for *Battlestar Galactica*, or any television show, to live up to the models offered by Haraway and Campbell, my analysis demonstrates that the narrow focus on ultimate survival at the hands of a few "big" heroes limits the ability of televised post-apocalyptic science fiction to highlight the heroism of everyday life, including compassion for and suffering with other lifeforms, that is necessary for any survival in the real-world Anthropocene crisis. As cultural studies and literary theory scholars teach us, stories matter, and I argue that *Battlestar Galactica* relies too heavily on "epic" heroic deeds to offer a realistic model for post-apocalyptic living. Nonetheless, there are moments of exception, which demonstrate the potential for post-apocalyptic narratives to explore realistic real-world responses, if "big" heroic deeds stop getting in the way.

In choosing a post-apocalyptic setting for *Battlestar*, Moore and his creative team tapped into deep connections within the genre between the environment and humanity. Although apocalyptic television shows are a 20th-century invention, apocalyptic science fiction has existed in literary form almost as long as mankind's ability to rapidly alter the planet, and the genre itself is deeply linked with technological innovations and fear over uncertain futures. In an entry on "Apocalyptic SF" in the *Routledge Companion to Science Fiction*, Aris Mousoutzanis acknowledges that the genre, as we recognize it today, originated in the late 18th century (458). This coincides with the beginning of the Anthropocene, a term first proposed by Paul Crutzen in a short article published in *Nature* in 2002 to denote a new epoch that marks the ability of humans to permanently alter the atmosphere:

> The Anthropocene could be said to have started in the latter part of the eighteenth century, when analyses of air trapped in polar ice showed the beginning of growing global concentrations of carbon dioxide and methane. This date also happens to coincide with James Watts' design of the steam engine in 1784 [Crutzen 23].

Although there is debate over the exact start of the Anthropocene, and some scientists push it back farther to the onset of European imperialism in the "New World" (see Lewis and Maslin, for example), the term has gained traction and speaks broadly to the time period humans have rapidly altered the environment. Scholars across many disciplines engage in discussions of this time period, and in "The Climate of History: Four Theses," historian Dipesh Chakrabarty argues that "humans now wield a geological force," granting humanity the same ability for massive destruction previously only possible by natural forces (206).

The evidence of humanity as a geological force is mounting, as indicated by extensive scientific research. A report in the *Proceedings of the National Academy of the Sciences*, issued on July 10, 2017, argues that a sixth mass extinction is already in progress, with little chance for reversal of the environmental devastation caused by humans in the post–Industrial Revolution era (Callebos et al. E6089). More recently, 15,364 scientists from around the world signed a report expanding a 1992 publication by the Union of Concerned Scientists entitled "World Scientists' Warning to Humanity." In the revised report, signers argue that "[s]ince 1992, with the exception of stabilizing the stratospheric ozone layer, humanity has failed to make sufficient progress in generally solving these foreseen environmental challenges, and alarmingly, most of them are getting far worse" (Ripple et al. 1026). Across disciplines and borders, scientists and scholars are urging for change. Haraway explores this real-world apocalypse in her recent book *Staying with the Trouble*, wherein she argues for a new kind of cultural narrative—a narrative of multispecies collaboration—as the only chance for survival, although that survival comes coupled with massive loss of life on Earth. The common thread between scientific diagnoses and theoretical criticisms of the crisis, and multiple explorations for solutions and responses, is that the apocalypse is *not* a singular event, such as an atomic bomb, but rather an ongoing human-centered (or human-created) process. As the "Warning to Humanity" report explains, "many current life forms could be annihilated or at least committed to extinction by the end of this century," indicating the perpetual, lengthy nature of the apocalyptic "event" we are living (Ripple et al. 1026).

On the one hand, the commonplace contemporary media representation of apocalyptic destruction signals a growing awareness of the geological forces—both human and nature—that threaten all life on earth, and the science fiction genre is obviously not exempt from such storylines. That said, most apocalyptic representations, including *Battlestar Galactica*, feature a singular trigger or disaster that differs greatly from our contemporary reality, which ultimately occludes the actual ongoing apocalypse currently facing Earth in the 21st century. Unlike the ongoing apocalyptic extinction of organic life on Earth over a period of time (albeit more rapidly than has occurred in the past), *Battlestar Galactica* explores fears of invasion and catastrophic nuclear attack from a non-human enemy. Mousoutzanis notes of such fiction that "these examples demonstrate an almost sadistic fascination with representing massive destruction in minute detail," which is an apt description of the *Battlestar* miniseries (460). The episode sequence revolves around a surprise attack and invasion on 12 planets inhabited by humans—the Twelve Colonies—roughly forty-five minutes into the series, and time and again the characters remind the audience that "this is the end of everything" and that "the world is coming to an end" ("Miniseries 1 & 2"). The attack itself is shown in detail, as audiences see the bombs go off from vantage points on the planet and above it, and the image of Caprica covered in mushroom clouds is present in the opening credits for every regular season episode.

Since "the end of everything" comes at the beginning of the series, the storyline shifts from the apocalyptic event itself and focuses on survival, although the single-event catastrophe will remain a key touchstone for the remaining narrative. In part two of the miniseries, President Roslin (Mary

McDonnell) begins to coordinate rescue operations of ships that avoided destruction by the Cylon fleet and soon amasses a large group of survivors. A Cylon scout discovers them, however, and the new government must make hard decisions. Captain Lee "Apollo" Adama (Jamie Bamber) argues that the assembled survivors need to flee an oncoming Cylon attack, even if it means abandoning those spaceships that cannot make a faster-than-light (FTL) jump to hyperspace:

> But we'll be saving tens of thousands. I'm sorry to make it a numbers game, but we're talking about the survival of our race here and we don't have the luxury of taking risks and hoping for the best. Because if we lose, we lose everything [*Battlestar Galactica* Miniseries Part Two].

Roslin orders the jump, even after learning that it means the immediate death of (among thousands) a young girl she had spoken with moments earlier on a ship without an FTL drive. In this moment, survival of the human race *at all costs* becomes the central focus of the show. Later, Roslin urges *Galactica* Commander Bill Adama (Edward James Olmos) to admit that "the war is over and we lost" and to focus the military force on protecting the survivors, rather than fighting the Cylons. Roslin tells Adama:

> Let me be straight with you here. The human race is about to be wiped out. We have 50,000 people left and that's it. Now, if we are even going to survive as a species, then we need to get the hell out of here and we need to start having babies [*Battlestar Galactica* Miniseries Part Two].

Ultimately, Adama decides to run, and the Fleet jumps away in an attempt to find the mythical 13th colony: Earth.

At the onset, this fictional struggle to survive a massive disaster looks remarkably like the narrative framework Haraway articulates in *Staying with the Trouble* as a means of more effective response to the present ecological crisis, single-moment apocalypse notwithstanding. In this text, Haraway collaborates with a wide array of scholars and genres to apply an interdisciplinary lens to the problem of the Anthropocene—and the question of survival within it. Haraway engages with the science fiction genre specifically to undertake an in-depth exploration of problems and possible real-world responses. As Bruce Franklin observes, science fiction is about "the possible," and thus *Battlestar Galactica* is a useful narrative to explore in connection with Haraway's proposal as a possible response to the Anthropocene (24). A post-apocalyptic narrative like *Battlestar Galactica* is especially worth reading in light of Haraway's discussion, since she is clear that many living organisms (including numerous humans) will not survive—a vision rendered in extreme detail in the *Battlestar Galactica* miniseries.

Despite the pessimistic tone inherent with this expectation of extreme loss of life, Haraway does acknowledge that there is hope "*if* we render each other capable of worlding and reworlding" (96, emphasis in original). To render "capable" requires a new way of living and being in the world, which first and foremost means accepting the destruction humanity has wrought and learning to *respond* in ways that engage with a multispecies world rather than a human-centered one. We go about this process of "staying with the trouble" by expanding our world view beyond the human through changing how we tell stories. Practices of storytelling are of prime importance to Haraway as she seeks effective response to the Anthropocene, as "stories are essential, but they are never 'mere' stories" (128). Rather, stories generate other stories and greatly influence the world as we understand it and live it. Building on much literary theory exploring the cultural importance of storytelling, this call for different stories resonates with other explorations of the destructive Anthropocene. In *Arts of Living on a Damaged Planet*, the editors acknowledge that "[s]ome kinds of stories help us notice; others get in our way.... Practices of storytelling matter" (M8). For editors Anna Lowenhaupt Tsing, Heather Anne Swanson, Elaine Gan, and Nils Bubandt, the stories we need to respond to the ongoing Anthropocene crisis focus on multiple worlds and multiple kinds of knowledge and knowledge creation, and should reflect the ongoing nature of the apocalypse and focus on living within and after it rather than simply recounting the tragedy of loss. Whereas in some ways *Battlestar Galactica* presents true challenges of living and dying in response to a massive catastrophe, the overall focus of the show remains fixated on the apocalyptic attack and the immediate losses, thus limiting potential engagement with real-world Anthropocene response. Although we never learn the extent of the lives lost in the original attack, the narrative of *Battlestar Galactica* focuses in detail on the number of survivors, going so far as to include a survivor count in the opening credits of most regular episodes and on a whiteboard in President Roslin's office aboard *Colonial One*. This emphasis on the literal number of survivors keeps the apocalyptic event central to the storyline, even when individual episodes explore challenges of daily life, like rebuilding the civilian government and questions of fuel and resource allocation.

Beyond the constant reminders of the apocalyptic attack and the constant focus on number of survivors, the *Battlestar Galactica* storyline is dominated by two interwoven plots: human freedom from the Cylon threat and discovery of the mythical 13th colony, Earth. These dual threads contribute to a fast-paced and thrilling storyline, and allow for heroes to save the day over and over again, in the manner typical of a televised series and most apocalyptic narratives. Despite the lengthy history of heroic tales throughout human history, heroes are a sticking point for Haraway in her proposal for a narrative of multispecies collaboration, where she declares that these "are not the tales of heroes; they are the tales of the ongoing" (76). Instead of epic heroic tales, Haraway advocates for science fiction author Ursula Le Guin's "carrier bag theory of fiction" where stories are "full of beginnings without ends, of initiations, of losses, of transformations and translations" that involve "staying with the trouble" in the present (169). Such stories focus on daily life, wherein a bottle or container serves as "hero" and key focus of the story instead of a specific (generally male) figure (166). For Le Guin and Haraway—both champions of the ability of the science fiction genre to explore the world and better it—the root of heroism in "big" and "epic" male deeds is problematic, as it has contributed to the rise of an Anthropocenic hero quest where men (and sometimes women) save humanity through exceptional acts that better the world.

Battlestar Galactica is undoubtedly a hero story, and it closely follows the traditional heroic narrative structure outlined by Campbell in *The Hero with a Thousand Faces*. Robert Segal offers a quick summation of the heroic structure Campbell provides, where the hero "ventures forth from the world of common day into a region of supernatural wonder: fabulous forces are there encountered and a decisive victory is won: the hero comes back from this mysterious adventure with the power to bestow boons on his fellow man" (4). A hero does what no one else can do, and the journey has been modeled in an uncountable number of permutations. Harold Schechter and Jonna Gormely Semeiks observe that popular culture constitutes "perhaps the most significant" influence of Campbell's engaging work on heroes and mythology, not limited to the well-documented inspiration on George Lucas' original *Star Wars* trilogy (181–2). In an interview with Bill Moyer published in *The Power of Myth*, Campbell notes that hero stories are incredibly popular because "that's what's worth writing about" as "a hero is someone who has given his *or her* life to something bigger than oneself" (*Power* 151, emphasis added). Despite this small nod to the existence of female heroes, Le Guin and Haraway's dissatisfaction with almost exclusively male heroes is notable in this and other Campbell publications, aside from a discussion of the heroic act of childbirth (*Power* 153).

In contrast to this gendered division of heroism, *Battlestar Galactica* offers a wide array of heroes responding to the apocalypse, varying in age, gender, and parental status: President Laura Roslin is older and childless; in contrast, Cylon defector Sharon "Athena" Valerii gives birth to hybrid human-cylon child Hera; while Kara Thrace (Katee Sackhoff), ultimate savior of the human race, never pursues motherhood of her own volition. There are also numerous male heroes, some parents and some not, including Commander Bill Adama and his son, Lee; Hera's father Karl Agathon; and Chief Galen Tyrol (Aaron Douglas); among others. Ultimately, the survival narrative of *Battlestar Galactica*, interwoven with the continued physical threat of annihilation by the Cylons, requires heroes from all walks of life, and Moore's show certainly gives audiences a veritable cast to admire. These actions live up to not only the large heroic quest Campbell outlines as present in much myth throughout human history, including the journey through unknown territory and eventual victory and salvation, but also creates the space to explore Campbell's comments about everyday heroism—the kind rarely highlighted in stories and on the big screen. These remarks during the interview with Moyer at times seem to contradict the "larger than life" heroic tale Campbell most often discusses, but ultimately Campbell's concept of a more down-to-earth hero offers space to splice this idea of heroism with Haraway's framework to "stay with the trouble" and craft a new narrative for survival in the Anthropocene.

The tension between vast heroic deeds and the daily heroism of living floats throughout Campbell's interview with Moyer in *The Power of Myth*, as it does in the *Battlestar Galactica* narrative. In response to a question from Moyer about whether there is a risk of losing the ability to perform heroic deeds as a result of watching them play out on the movie screen, Campbell expounded on how difficult living is: "you realize it's a very grim thing to be a modern human being" (*Power* 160). This tension between watching and practicing heroism draws Campbell to the challenge of living, implying the potential for acts of everyday heroism (including childbirth, but certainly not limited to it) in our current era of Anthropocene-created precarity. For Campbell, this everyday heroism comes through "holding on to your ideals for yourself" and centering the body and the spirit alongside the demands of the mind to save both ourselves and our world (178 and 183). Living with compassion (which, as Campbell points out, literally means "suffering with") toward other living organisms proves to be the most significant component of Campbell's everyday heroism, culminating in the true "adventure of the hero—*the adventure of being alive*" (201, 206, emphasis added).

Living simultaneously through suffering with and compassion for others is a cornerstone for Haraway's framework for survival in the Anthropocene, although the former is significantly more prevalent in *Battlestar Galactica* than the latter. This popular culture example thus exemplifies the challenges of presenting productive *response* to apocalypse when the crisis is a singular definitive event followed by continuous physical attack and flight. Although ultimately this results in an unrealistic model of "the possible" for contemporary society, *Battlestar* also offers hints toward how everyday heroism could be cultivated in the midst of a post-apocalyptic survival narrative. The first regular season episode "33" demonstrates this point, as it features the human Fleet—eventually self-labeled the Colonial Fleet—running from continuous Cylon attacks every 33 minutes. This episode highlights both physical and mental suffering through extended sleep deprivation, continuous fear for daily survival, and mourning the uncounted losses from the original Cylon attack, and culminates in a decision to destroy a civilian ship to save the Fleet.

Whereas audiences do witness regular individuals rise to the occasion in this episode, compassion with others is thrust out an airlock in "33," which sets the tone for the entire narrative. Cylon agents will be executed in later episodes, and humans will kill other humans throughout the series for fear of Cylon subversion and other threats to the survival of the Fleet. Suffering is all that remains for the Colonial Fleet until salvation is reached on Earth in the final episode sequence "Daybreak," evoking the higher-order heroism Campbell more frequently outlines, rather than the daily lived-with heroism he hints at in *The Power of Myth*.

The season 2 episode sequence featuring the first real battle between the Colonial Fleet and Cylon forces highlights the need for extraordinary heroes who do more than just live within the aftermath of tragedy and respond to it with compassion and a sense of shared suffering in their daily lives. In doing so, the narrative endorses the large scale "big," "epic" heroes presumably needed to save the human race from complete destruction, overshadowing the everyday heroism required to live, survive, and respond to apocalyptic crisis. Scholars such as Brian Ott have noted the clear political commentary against military torture present in the "Pegasus" and "Resurrection Ship" episodes, but on a more basic level this sequence reinforces the need for epic heroes to save the Fleet in the first definitive battle against the Cylons. Multiple main cast members engage in heroic actions here: Gaius Baltar (James Callis) gains vital information from tortured Cylon prisoner Gina (Tricia Helfer), who has previously refused to speak; Adama goes head-to-head with newly arrived Admiral Helena Cain (Michelle Forbes) over the fate of his personnel; Kara "Starbuck" Thrace successfully pursues a risky reconnaissance mission to gain information about the Cylon Fleet; and, Apollo risks it all (and almost dies) in the battle. With the exception of Balter's demonstration of extremely self-motivated compassion for Gina, these heroic actions set the pattern for *Battlestar Galactica* to require epic heroism to ensure the survival of the human race.

Despite frequent storylines that highlight larger-than-life heroism, other episodes hint at different connotations of heroism, especially the episode sequence on New Caprica early in season 3. These episodes highlight the daily challenges of living in a settlement, including establishing schools and rationing food and medical supplies on a fairly inhospitable planet, although inevitably the heroism (struggle) of living is overshadowed by "big deed" heroics once the Cylons discover and occupy the colony ("Occupation"). Such large scale heroic acts include espionage and suicide bombings, which might defy the traditional connotation of heroism as an upstanding act (see Allison and Goethals), but Campbell reminds us that the moral objective of heroism "is that of saving a people, or saving a person, or supporting an idea. The hero sacrifices himself for something—that's the morality of it"; everything else is a judgment on the part of the audience (*Power* 156). *Battlestar Galactica* excels at offering hard heroism through numerous morally ambiguous characters and actions, although at the same time these moments eclipse the daily struggle to live with compassion and suffering in the aftermath of massive tragedy. The rescue of the human Fleet by skeleton crews on the *Galactica* and *Pegasus* in "Exodus" returns the narrative back to the race against the Cylons for survival, and although other episodes will occasionally highlight challenges of daily life, this thread of survival at all costs after near annihilation continues until the end of the series, and requires continual epic heroics in order to obtain the ultimate goal of survival for the remaining human race.

In the fourth and final season, Earth is discovered—and it is a barren wasteland ("Revelations"). The visible ruins of nuclear apocalypse again feature on the screen, this time on a planet we learn was once inhabited by Cylons which suffered massive nuclear devastation roughly 2,000 years previous ("Sometimes a Great Notion"). This discovery triggers despair in both the Cylon and Human Fleets. Rebel Cylon forces ally themselves with the Colonial Fleet, and eventually—through a series of increasingly bizarre *deus ex machina* machinations—the Colonial Fleet discovers *our* Earth in the days before *Homo sapiens* developed spoken language ("Daybreak"). Kara Thrace is the main epic hero here, making a blind (Faster-Than-Light) leap of faith to save the *Galactica* after the complete destruction of the Cylon Colony. The Fleet decides to settle on the newly discovered planet, alongside humans "whose DNA is compatible with ours," and call it "Earth" in honor of the dream for Earth that sustained the Fleet during their long flight from the Twelve Colonies ("Daybreak"). Geoff Ryman calls this series ending a "foundational myth for white folks," and the imperial overtones are not subtle, but more broadly, this completes the heroic journey Campbell outlined in the return home (ctd. in Kaveney and Stoy 37). The ending also briefly hints at the heroism of everyday life as the (mostly white) colonists spread out sans technology to repopulate the human race, although the "flash forward" in the final scene to a city-scape 150,000 years later implies that the end-point of that challenge is the present 21st century.

Although there is no requirement or expectation for *Battlestar Galactica* to live up to the models of everyday heroism, compassion, and suffering with others outlined by Campbell and Haraway, this analysis demonstrates that the extreme focus on survival at all costs in a post-apocalyptic survival narrative limits the ability of a televised science fiction narrative to highlight the heroism of everyday life. That said, episodes like those on the settlement of New Caprica give useful hints at how such a narrative could better represent these frameworks if the larger heroic elements were laid aside in favor of a new kind of heroism everyone can adopt in the Anthropocene. Science fiction has this potential, as Le Guin observes in her essay on the "carrier bag theory of fiction":

If, however, one avoids the linear, progressive, Time's-(killing)-arrow mode of the Techno-Heroic, and redefines technology and science as primarily cultural carrier bag rather than weapon of domination, one pleasant side effect is that science fiction can be seen as a far less rigid, narrow field, not necessarily Promethean or apocalyptic at all, and in fact less a mythological genre than a realistic one [170].

Acknowledging that the aim of much contemporary science fiction—Moore's show included—is to reflect contemporary society and explore "the possible," the genre has extreme potential to undertake the tasks outlined by scholars like Haraway to project a new kind of narrative. *Battlestar Galactica* offers moments of this potential, as long as "the end of everything" is not the exclusive focus of the narrative, and humanity strives to live with compassion and suffering alike through the challenge of living—and dying—in the present.

Works Cited

Allison, Scott T., and George R. Goethals. *Heroes: What They Do and Why We Need Them.* Oxford UP, 2011.
Campbell, Joseph. *The Hero with a Thousand Faces.* New World Library, 2008.
_____. *The Power of Myth.* Anchor Books, 1991.
Ceballos, Gerardo, et al. "Biological Annihilation Via the Ongoing Sixth Mass Extinction Signaled by Vertebrate Population Losses and Declines." *Proceedings of the National Academy of Sciences*, vol. 114, no. 30, July 2017, pp. E6089–96, doi:10.1073/pnas.1704949114.
Chakrabarty, Dipesh. "The Climate of History: Four Theses." *Critical Inquiry*, vol. 35, no. 2, Jan. 2009, pp. 197–222, doi:10.1086/596640.
Crutzen, Paul J. "Geology of Mankind." *Nature*, vol. 415, Jan. 2002, p. 23.
Dyson, Stephen Benedict. *Otherworldly Politics: The International Relations of Star Trek, Game of Thrones, and Battlestar Galactica.* Johns Hopkins UP, 2015.
Franklin, Bruce. "What Is Science Fiction—and How It Grew." *Reading Science Fiction*, edited by James Gunn, Marleen S. Barr, and Matthew Candelaria, Palgrave Macmillan, 2008, pp. 23–32.
Haraway, Donna J. *Staying with the Trouble: Making Kin in the Chthulucene.* Duke UP, 2016.
Kaveney, Roz, and Jennifer Stoy. *Battlestar Galactica: Investigating Flesh, Spirit, and Steel.* I.B. Tauris, 2010.
Le Guin, Ursula K. "The Carrier Bag Theory of Fiction." *Dancing at the Edge of the World*, Grove Press, 1997, pp. 165–70.
Lewis, Simon L., and Mark A. Maslin. *The Human Planet: How We Created the Anthropocene.* Penguin Books Limited, 2018.
Moore, Ronald. *Battlestar Galactica Series Bible.* 17 Dec. 2003.
Mousoutzanis, Aris. "Apocalyptic SF." *The Routledge Companion to Science Fiction*, edited by Mark Bould, Andrew M. Butler, Adam Roberts, and Sherryl Vint, Routledge, 2009, pp. 458–462.
"Original Miniseries Script." *Battlestar Galactica*, written by Ronald D. Moore and Christopher James, NBC Universal Television, 2003.
Ott, Brian L. "(Re)Framing Fear: Equipment for Living in a Post 9/11 World." *Cylons in America: Critical Studies in Battlestar Galactica*, edited by Tiffany Potter and C.W. Marshall, Bloomsbury Publishing USA, 2007, pp. 13–26.
Ripple, William J., et al. "World Scientists' Warning to Humanity: A Second Notice." *BioScience*, Nov. 2017, pp. 1026–1028, doi:10.1093/biosci/bix125.

Schechter, Harold, and Jonna Gormely Semeiks. "Campbell and the 'Vanilla-Frosted Temple': From Myth to Multiplex." *Uses of Comparative Mythology: Essays on the Work of Joseph Campbell*, edited by Kenneth L. Golden, Garland Publishing, 1992, pp. 179–192.

Segal, Robert Alan. *Joseph Campbell: An Introduction*. Garland Publishing, 1987.

Tsing, Anna Lowenhaupt, Heather Anne Swanson, Elaine Gan, and Nils Bubandt, editors. *Arts of Living on a Damaged Planet: Ghosts and Monsters of the Anthropocene*. U of Minnesota P, 2017.

Filmography

"Daybreak Part 1." *Battlestar Galactica*, season 4, episode 21, written by Ronald D. Moore, NBC Universal Television, 13 Mar. 2009.

"Daybreak Part 2." *Battlestar Galactica*, season 4, episode 22, written by Ronald D. Moore, NBC Universal Television, 20 Mar. 2009.

"Exodus Part 1." *Battlestar Galactica*, season 3, episode 3, written by Bradley Thompson and David Weddle, NBC Universal Television, 13 Oct. 2006.

"Exodus Part 2." *Battlestar Galactica*, season 3, episode 4, written by Bradley Thompson and David Weddle, NBC Universal Television, 20 Oct. 2006.

"Miniseries Part 1." *Battlestar Galactica*, NBC Universal Television, written by Ronald D. Moore and Christopher Jones, 8 Dec. 2003.

"Miniseries Part 2." *Battlestar Galactica*, NBC Universal Television, written by Ronald D. Moore and Christopher Jones, 9 Dec. 2003.

"Occupation." *Battlestar Galactica*, season 3, episode 1, written by Ronald D. Moore, NBC Universal Television, 6 Oct. 2006.

"Pegasus." *Battlestar Galactica*, season 2, episode 10, written by Anne Cofell Saunders, NBC Universal Television, 23 Sept. 2005.

"Resurrection Ship Part 1." *Battlestar Galactica*, season 2, episode 11, written by Anne Cofell Saunders and Michael Rymer, NBC Universal Television, 6 Jan. 2006.

"Resurrection Ship Part 2." *Battlestar Galactica*, season 2, episode 12, written by Michael Rymer and Ronald D. Moore, NBC Universal Television, 13 Jan. 2006.

"Revelations." *Battlestar Galactica*, season 4, episode 12, written by Bradley Thompson and David Weddle, NBC Universal Television, 13 June 2008.

"Sometimes a Great Notion." *Battlestar Galactica*, season 4, episode 13, written by Bradley Thompson and David Weddle, NBC Universal Television, 16 Jan. 2009.

"33." *Battlestar Galactica*, season 1, episode 1, written by Ronald D. Moore, NBC Universal Television, 18 Oct. 2004.

Apocalypse(s) Already

Doomsday Preppers at the End of The(ir) Worlds

JZ LONG

> Survival preppin' is a lifestyle not a phase
> We're serious about the end of days...
> We got shootin' preppers, farmin' preppers,
> city preppers, country preppers
> Wouldn't you like to be a prepper too?
> —*Doomsday Preppers*

> Have a great apocalypse!
> —*The Dark Tower*

At the beginning of National Geographic's "special edition" of their *Doomsday Preppers Complete Survival Manual*, lead author Michael Sweeney shares a tale for his readers about a grasshopper and a group of ants. While a condescending grasshopper spends the spring having fun, the ants spend their days storing food for the coming winter. When winter arrives, of course, the grasshopper has no food and the ants refuse to give him any. As Sweeney concludes, "The moral of the story? Be prepared" (8). In other words, be an ant and not a grasshopper. And in the United States of America, there are quite a lot of grasshoppers and quite a lot of ants.

Between stories of nuclear meltdowns, rising sea levels, and scorching droughts, news-watching audiences have become inundated with apocalyptic tales about the end of the world. Especially apparent—as evidenced by the analyses in this very collection—in the dramatic fictions of contemporary televisual culture, these stories can also be found in the oft-overlooked non-fictions of what has come to be known as reality-based television. If we are to better understand the uses and gratifications of these discourses of apocalyptic disaster for those who inhabit them, an analysis of the ways that these real individuals are making use of these apocalyptic narratives in their everyday lives is undoubtedly warranted. Using both qualitative and quantitative methods from the interdisciplinary field of cultural studies, this essay explores the narratives of these real-world "doomsday preppers" in order to study the effects of these discourses on the end(s) of the(ir) world(s). For, as these popular narratives demonstrate, the apocalypse is already here, and already real, in both virtual and actual forms. After all, a virtual apocalypse is no less real than an actual one.

Textualizing Doomsday

The Discovery and National Geographic television channels have each staked their claim as key players in bringing contemporary stories about the apocalypse to the masses. These shows, moreover, have tended to fall into one of two unique categories. On the one hand, in what I heuristically refer to as the professional model, both channels have aired a number of programs featuring former military specialists and so-called "survivalists," including Les Stroud's *Survivorman* (2004–2008) and *Beyond Survival* (2010), Bear Grylls' *Man vs. Wild* (2006–2011) and *Worst Case Scenarios* (2010), Mykel Hawke's *Man, Woman, Wild* (2010–2012), and Forge Survival Supply's *Apocalypse 101* (2013). In the amateur model, on the other hand, both networks have aired many programs where regular Americans are thrust into near-apocalyptic conditions, including *Out of the Wild* (2008–2011), *The Colony* (2009–2010), and *Naked and Afraid* (2013–present). Far from existing on the fringe of televisual culture, then, these shows are clear indications that doomsday has gone mainstream.

Another show, however, does not fit neatly into either of these categories. National Geographic's four seasons of *Doomsday Preppers* (2011–2014) enters the worlds of real-life Americans as they prepare, or "prep," for a variety of apocalyptic or "doomsday" scenarios. Each episode features several unique "preppers" who are graded by two survivalist "experts" in terms of the preppers' supplies, shelter, security, and what they call the "x-factor" (which, as the term implies, depends on the preppers in question). Predictably, some popular critics have characterized the show's preppers as everything from "paranoid" to "eccentric" (O'Sullivan, Dowling). Yet such criticisms miss an important point: *Doomsday Preppers* represents a new, hybrid narrative whereby the professional and amateur models are rearranged into a unique constellation of stories in which these preppers are operating as if the apocalyptic is actively becoming real.

Quantifying Doomsday

In order to analyze the apocalyptic stories of real doomsday preppers, a content analysis was performed on the episodes of *Doomsday Preppers* that aired on the National Geographic cable channel.[1] Given the focus in this collection on televisual texts, the methods of both quantitative and qualitative content analysis were employed to help illuminate the deeper meanings in each program. By bringing into the conversation post-positivist methods from the social sciences with textual analyses from the humanities, this examination provides what cultural studies theorist Douglas Kellner calls a more multiperspectival and therefore well-rounded approach to the investigation.

My analysis began with the creation of a list of episode titles not only to establish continuity between episodes but also to look for similar keywords and concepts regarding the apocalyptic narratives and discourses denoted by the specific preppers shown in each episode. One surprising problem that quickly emerged was that there were serious discrepancies between almost all of the online episode guides. This began with the National Geographic website itself, which not only featured a outlier numbering system composed of five seasons instead of the other sites' four, but also omitted some episodes entirely (three of the special episodes, for examples, were not as yet noted on their "Episode Guide"). Comparing these official listings with those from Amazon, Hulu, IMDb, and Wikipedia, seasons 3 and 4, especially, were wildly divergent in terms of the order of key episodes.[2] Using air dates, four seasons were determined and 54 unique episodes were identified (a pilot episode, 12 episodes in season 1, 18 in season 2, 14 in season 3, 6 in season 4, and 3 special episodes). Out of these 54 episodes, 51 were available for analysis. Each episode generally highlighted two or three preppers, and a total of 129 individual preppers were uniquely identified.

The next step was to code each episode's contents using a number of concrete variables. In addition to the name and location of each prepper, the following demographics were examined: age, ethnicity, sex, marital status, family status, occupation, and, above all, the specific doomsday scenario for which each individual was preparing. With the exception of one individual in episode 10 of season 2 (who was only known as "Snake Blocker"), names were also noted (though 25 of the 129 were identified only by their first name). Given the difficulty of identifying specific ages, age ranges of ten years were used. For the category of ethnicity, the three primary typologies from the U.S. Census Bureau—White, Black or African American, and Hispanic or Latino—were used, while male and female were used as the two primary sexes. Preppers were also identified as to whether they were single, married, or in a relationship, as well as if they had children or not.

In 2018, the U.S. Census Bureau estimated that the American population was over 329 million and the world population over 7.6 billion ("U.S. and World"). Information from other datasets estimate that 77.2 percent of the population is over the age of 18, with females (50.8%) and males (49.2%) equally represented. With respect to ethnicity, the Census Bureau stated that

61.3 percent of Americans identify as White, 13.3 percent as Black or African American, 17.8 percent as Hispanic or Latino, and all other ethnicities totaling 7.6 percent ("QuickFacts"). And of the 58.3 percent of Americans in the labor force (calculated as both employed and unemployed), the median annual income is $55,322. As for the results of the quantitative content analysis, the general conclusion is that preppers are hyper-representative of the American population. The most common age of the show's preppers ($n=129$) was 41–50 (34.9%), with the majority falling between the ages of 41 and 60 (61.2%). Only one prepper was over the age of 70 and, somewhat surprisingly, only two were under the age of 20. *Doomsday's* preppers are also overwhelmingly White (94.6%) and male (86.1%). Of the remaining ethnicities, there were three of Hispanic or Latino descent, one Black or African American, and two unidentified. Of the number of preppers that could be definitely determined as single or married ($n=120$), 79.2 percent of the show's participants were married while 20.8 percent were single. In addition, almost 55 percent of participants had children, while 45 percent did not. While occupations varied widely (though law enforcement and military backgrounds were common), preppers' most likely doomsday scenarios involved one of four major categories: natural disasters (40.3%), economic collapse (30.2%), political conflict (28.0%), and religious conflict (1.5%).

One additional dataset of note, though not quantified here, involves the calculation of preppers' "x-factor." At the end of every segment during the first season, each prepper was given a range of percentages reflecting the experts' assessment of how well prepared each individual was for their chosen doomsday scenario. Such scores, however, were not consistent, as preppers were often assessed on different criteria (and often within the same episode). For example, in "Back to the Stone Age," the third episode of the first season, the first prepper received scores on his location (55%) and training (80%); the second prepper only received a score for his location (55%); a third prepper was assessed on food (70%) and fuel (50%); and the final prepper was scored on his water (40%) and trading skills (80%). Shortly after the start of the second season, however, the show shifted to a 100-point scoring system composed of five distinct criteria—food, water, shelter, security, and the so-called "x-factor"—worth 20 points each. Given that the first four episodes from season 3 also featured this system, National Geographic's episode guide may indeed be correct in its listing of 22 episodes in season 2 rather than 18. While the scoring system was not used during the third season (except for the first four episodes), it reappeared for the six episodes of season 4. In addition to compiling a total score for each prepper, these percentages were then translated (by an unnamed method) into the number of months the show's experts believe that the preppers would be able to survive. While the data for this information were collected, they were not used in the content analysis, though these numbers provide yet another promising avenue for analyzing the general tenor of contemporary discourses of apocalyptic prepping.

Qualifying Doomsday

There have been two major historical styles of apocalyptic narratives in American culture: one modernist and the other postmodern. The modernist type, according to scholars, is what is generally referred to as the "traditional religious apocalyptic worldviews" (Wojcik 297). In the United States, such worldviews are most often traced back to classic Christian concepts like "the battle of Armageddon," "the Day of Judgment," and "the Apocalypse of John" (often known by its more famous title, the "Book of Revelation").[3] In these religious scenarios, there will be a "second coming" of divine beings to the earthly plane who will save all believers and allow the rest of the world to be destroyed. What is required here is a transcendent faith, as those who believe are to be taken into another dimension as part of a physical "rapture" (from the Latin *rapio*, meaning "to seize" or "to snatch"). This will leave all non–Christians and sinners to suffer all number of painful calamities. While some see this tale as an allegory for John's criticisms against the Roman church (see Anderson, Pagels, Hoberman, and Delbanco), many contemporary religious denominations, such as dispensationalism, fundamentalism, and evangelicalism, believe that this is exactly, literally, the event that is already to come (Lifton; Wojcik).

The second type of apocalyptic narrative is a more recent, postmodern one, which Kurt Anderson and his colleagues have referred to as "a kind of secular apocalypticism" (9). Without specific reference to a religious afterlife, these new apocalyptic narratives are often thought of as "meaningless" or "evoking feelings of powerlessness," given that there is no transcendent and specific end-point in which to believe (Wojcik 297, 315). As a result, other meaning must be found for these impending doomsdays. One such meaning emerged during World War II after the development and use of nuclear weapons. After 1945, all of humanity knew that the world could end without any sort of divine intervention in the blink of an eye. This fear was especially prominent in the emerging "Cold War" between the two dominant nuclear powers at the time, the Soviet Union and the United States. While the American government initially provided the impetus for prepping through the creation of such organizations as the Office for Civilian Defense (1941),[4] the Centers for Disease Control and Prevention (1946), and the Defense Advanced Research Projects Agency (1958), scholars noted a distinct "shift in perception" as the Cold War heated up and the federal government reterritorialized disaster preparation onto citizens themselves (Marchand). Both types of apocalyptic thought can be found in American society today, and many scholars believe that there has been a "definite upsurge" in such discourse since the 1970s (Anderson, Pagels, Hoberman, and Delbanco 3). During this analysis, however, four unique threads of apocalyptic thought were identified that were evident throughout *Doomsday Preppers*: consumption, certainty, contingency, and community.

One of the first major themes that emerged was the elided status of capitalistic consumption in individuals' preparations. Given that most of the preppers believe in some type of economic or political collapse, it is surprising to see that many of them continue to work in some capacity in order to purchase goods from these same capitalist institutions. Most preppers on the show noted that money will likely be worthless after the collapse of society; however, many still placed value in tangible goods like food, clothing, and alcohol (both as food and as a weapon). And whereas several preppers espoused a rhetoric of non-violence, the majority of preppers invested great sums of money on their preparations, particularly in the form of bunkers and guns. In this way, then, preppers' consumption is itself a form of production, or what George Ritzer and Nathan Jurgenson have termed "prosumption." In the terminology of the late French philosophers Gilles Deleuze and Félix Guattari, this functions as a form of what they call "anti-production." In arguing that there is no "outside" to the social, even those who attempt to evade the chaotic flows of capitalism are always already recuperated through its constantly reterritorializing axiomatics. So, even as the social implodes, these postmodern preppers are still contributing to the reproduction of capitalist production.

A second theme that emerged throughout the analysis involved the certainty that preppers maintained with regard to the imminence of their respective doomsday scenarios. San Diego prepper Bradford Frank, for example, is certain that avian bird flu is going to lead to a "worldwide pandemic that will end life as we know it." With "bodies stacked in the street like cordwood," Frank states that "people would become hysterical, [and] there would be chaos throughout the world." Frank ends this scene by warning viewers that it is "not a question of if, but a question of when" ("It's Gonna Get Worse"). At the end of the episode, however, narrator Michael Izquierdo states that since bird flu does not normally affect humans, scientists are unclear when such a pandemic would occur. Forty-four-year-old Hawaiian "adventurer" David Lakota is also sure that his visions regarding an apocalyptic tsunami are accurate, and he tells us that "it's not a matter of if; it's a matter of when" ("Pain Is Good"). Why a prepper who believes that the world will end by means of a tsunami is living on an island in the middle of the Pacific Ocean is not explained, nor is that fact that he "asked Mother Nature for a woman" with whom to share the apocalypse. What is certain, however, is that the majority of these preppers—most of whom lack knowledge in economic, political, and scientific theories—already "know" the planet's future. These apocalyptic scenarios, as conclusions about the future (really, *a* future, but then, this is part of the problem, confusing a possible future for an actual one), always conclude that there is no hope. Of course, the world was already supposed to have ended in 1988 (Hal Lindsey), 2000 (the Y2K computer bug), 2003 (Aum Shinrikyo), 2007 (televangelist Pat Robertson), and 2012 (the end of the Mayan calendar), so the track record of apocalyptic prognosticators is not good. Yet these preppers are sure that they are right, and this is regardless of whether their narrative is a modernist or postmodernist one.

Closely related to this is a third theme of contingency. If the end of the world is certain, then the only remaining question is when, exactly, it will occur. Given the issues of certainty discussed above, the actual date and time have been coded in terms of when "the shit hits the fan." In episode after episode, preppers invoke this popular idiom to announce when the time of doomsday is to have come. For example, Houston native and web developer Megan Hurwitt faces the camera and states that, as a result of an international oil crisis, "when the shit hits the fan, I'll be more fit than you are," and, thus, we presume, more likely to survive ("Bullets, Lots of Bullets"). Dennis Evers, a former contractor in Colorado who thinks that hyperinflation will lead to a worldwide crisis, argues in an episode aptly titled "It's All Gonna Hit the Fan" that "the people who are going to survive when it hits the fan" are the ones who are the most prepared, and another Colorado prepper, Preston White, says that "if shit hits the fan, you've got to be ready"; otherwise, "they'll take it from you, they'll take it from you with violence" ("Nine Meals Away from Anarchy"). The episode "Am I Nuts or Are You?" begins with a song written by Nashville music producer Big Al containing the line "when it all hits the fan, you better have your stuff together," while Tacoma resident and self-described "apex predator" Tyler Smith intones that "when the [bleep] hits the fan the people that are going to survive are the people that are prepared to do whatever it takes" ("We Are the Marauders"). There is a paradox here, however, between certainty and contingency, as the fact that the apocalypse can happen at any moment means that one needs to be prepared at every moment and for every event. This kind of ambient fear pervades the entire series, though the fact that preppers disagree on the exact doomsday scenario suggests that at least some preppers are actually preparing for the "wrong" apocalypse.

A final theme that is evident is that of community. Whereas there are many preppers who prefer to go it alone (the title of the season 2 finale, "Lone Wolves and Lovers," is highly suggestive of such), other preppers admit that "no one person can do everything" ("I Hope I Am Crazy"). For preppers with families, the sense of community is established through nightly or weekly drills designed to help prepare and train children to respond when doomsday strikes. As indicated across several episodes, though, many children think that their parents are "nuts" ("Disaster Doesn't Wait"); one daughter says that her "father's eccentric and kinda lives in his own reality, and is a little odd like that," and that when her friends come over they "kinda treat it as a joke" ("Taking from the Haves"). Preppers without children also seek to develop communities of like-minded individuals, as exemplified by prepper Jeff Mann who, alongside "professional survivalist" John Milandred, former Marine Bill Hennessey, and Bill's 21-year-old son Colten, have established "The Colony," a 25-acre ranch in central Florida. As Mann notes, the Colony has its own "head council," judicial system, and other unspecified rules, and the episode serves as an advertisement for new recruits ("Don't Betray the Colony"). One of the most prominent tropes is the distinction between us and them, as prepper after prepper worries about those outside of their communities, who are characterized as "desperate" ("Into the Spider Hole"), "wildebeests" ("You Can't Let Evil Win"), "bands of pirates" ("It's All Gonna Hit the Fan"), "roving in bands" ("The Gates of Hell"), and, above all, "marauders" (in "It's All Gonna Hit the Fan"; "Friends Can Become Enemies"; "Close the Door, Load the Shotgun"; and, of course, "We Are the Marauders"). Given the preeminence of white preppers in the United States, these sentiments can easily be seen as dog-whistles against the non-white "others" in the country's urban centers. In this sense, then, community can be said to function as a constitutive source of both friends and enemies.

Contextualizing Doomsday

As risk society theorist Ulrich Beck has recently noted, "Endemic uncertainty is what will mark the lifeworld and the basic existence of most people—including the apparently affluent middle class—in the years that lie ahead" ("Cosmopolitan" 224). Suggesting that contemporary societies are redistributing social risks back onto individuals to deal with on their own, it should not be surprising to see that, just as these risks become reterritorialized, prepping for the apocalypse becomes resurgent. As Beck has noted, "The discourse of risk begins where our trust in security and belief in progress end" ("Risk Society" 213). It is in this type of "intermediary state between security and destruction where the *perception* of threatening risks determines thought and action" ("Risk Society" 213). We see the effects of these events in the stories of *Doomsday*'s various preppers, who both think and feel the risks. As these risks continue to rebound and multiply, *Doomsday Preppers* illustrates the real lives and stories of those preparing to meet these risks head on. What is unique about a television program about doomsday preppers is that, unlike the end of the world, a series about actual people preparing for an apocalypse can go on forever. While other televised shows serve as representations of apocalyptic scenarios, *Doomsday Peppers* re-presents actual scenarios by real apocalyptics.

And do all goods things, as they say, not come to an end—this essay, this collection, this world? But must it be so apocalyptic? All narrative beginnings, it is true, must have endings, but are narratives not also replete with rising and falling actions, climaxes, and denouements—that is, the risky journey between the beginning and the end? What is surprising here is that so many preppers have not just virtual desires of the end of the(ir) worlds but also actual desires to contribute to their creation. That the world is theirs remains unexamined, as others' worlds do not follow these same stories. Rather than trying to save this world, many of *Doomsday's* preppers are so confident in the truth of their apocalyptic narratives that they are actively embracing the end of this world. Internalizing neo-liberal social risk as apocalyptic, they seek withdrawal from this earthly narrative for the promise of a new narrative that is yet to come. That is, the apocalypse is to be welcomed, an end to the miserable story of human life on Earth. In the euphoric words of *The Dark Tower*'s villainous "Man in Black," each and every episode of *Doomsday Preppers* reminds us to "have a great apocalypse!" For as the world is destroyed around us, we can simply retire to our own underground bunkers, open a can of purified water, and watch reruns of *Doomsday Preppers* until the end of our own world(s).

Notes

1. I would like to thank Michael G. Cornelius and Sherry Ginn for their welcome feedback, the two anonymous readers for their valuable insights, and, most importantly, my wife, Zina, who not only watched all of the episodes with me but also provided invaluable assistance analyzing demographic variables, maintaining data spreadsheets, and wondering, like me, if it really is the end of the world.

2. The Internet Movie Database (IMDb), for example, substitutes the original pilot ("Preppers") as the first episode and contains an alternative title for the fifth episode of season one ("You Shall Not Fear"), and the former issue in particular had the added effect of altering the dates in which the episodes from the rest of the season aired. The web encyclopedia Wikipedia lists 22 episodes in season 2 though there are only 18, and even National Geographic's official website for the program, by omitting the first two episodes of season 2 entirely, not only cites the second episode of the season as the third but also leads to a cascading effect suggesting 21 full episodes in the season rather than 18.

3. Other religions have similar apocalyptic narratives, including Islam's Yawm al-Qiyāmah ("The Day of Resurrection") and the Mayan belief that the world will end when 12 *baktuns* of their calendar have been completed (this was to have occurred in 2012). Given the overwhelming influence of Christian thought in America, though, the primary focus here will be on this version of the apocalypse. For more about "apocalyptic visions" in both Islam and Judaism, see Lifton.

4. After the Office of Civilian Defense (1941–1945), the functions of federal disaster

preparations were undertaken on an *ad hoc* basis until the Federal Emergency Management Agency (FEMA) was created under the U.S. Department of Housing and Urban Development (HUD) in 1979. After the terrorist attacks in 2001, FEMA became part of the new Department of Homeland Security (DHS). FEMA has long functioned as foil in a number of popular American conspiracy theories, most notably those of imprisoning dissidents in concentration or "death camps" (see, e.g., Southern Poverty Law Center), and, as cited in an *X-Files* movie, creating "a plague to end all plagues"—"a planned Armageddon"—that would enable FEMA to declare martial law and take over the federal government. For a more clear-headed history of FEMA, see Garrett Graff's article in the September 2017 issue of *Wired* magazine entitled "The Secret History of FEMA."

WORKS CITED

Anderson, Kurt, Elaine Pagels, Jim Hoberman, and Andrew Delbanco. "Apocalypse Now: America's Fascination with Doomsday and Why It Matters." *Fordham Center on Religion and Culture*, 12 Sept. 2012, pdfs.semanticscholar.org/10be/ec4912cfd4875798fd4c0eab6ee-b6c2ab911.pdf.

Beck, Ulrich. "The Cosmopolitan Manifesto." *The Cosmopolitan Reader*, edited by Garrett Wallace Brown and David Held, Polity, 2010, pp. 217–28.

⸻. "Risk Society Revisited: Theory, Politics and Research Programmes." *The Risk Society and Beyond: Critical Issues for Social Theory*, edited by Barbara Adam, Ulrich Beck, and Joost Van Loon, SAGE Publications, 2000, pp. 211–29.

Deleuze, Gilles, and Félix Guattari. *Anti-Oedipus: Capitalism and Schizophrenia*, Vol. 1. Translated by Robert Hurley, Seem Mark, and Helen R. Lane, U of Minnesota P, 1983.

Dowling, Tim. "TV Review: Room at the Top; Doomsday Preppers." *The Guardian*, 26 Sept. 2012, www.theguardian.com/tv-and-radio/2012/sep/26/room-at-top-doomsday-preppers.

Graff, Garrett M. "The Secret History of FEMA." *Wired*, 03 Sept. 2017, www.wired.com/story/the-secret-history-of-fema/.

Kellner, Douglas. "Cultural Studies, Multiculturalism, and Media Culture." *Gender, Race, and Class in Media: A Critical Reader*, edited by Gail Dines, Jean Humez, William Edward Yousman, and Lori B. Bindig, 5th ed., SAGE Publications, 2018, pp. 6–16.

Lifton, Robert Jay. "'In the Lord's Hands': America's Apocalyptic Mindset." *World Policy Journal*, vol. 20, no. 3, 2003, pp. 59–69.

Marchand, Hal. "Preppers: A Primer for Public Safety Officials." Western Illinois U, 2015, www.wiu.edu/coehs/leja/cacj/research/documents/3%20Preppers-Marchand.docx.

O'Sullivan, Rod. "Preppers: Meet the Paranoid Americans Awaiting the Apocalypse." *The Week*, 12 July 2015, theweek.com/articles/565576/preppers-meet-paranoid-americans-awaiting-apocalypse.

Ritzer, George, and Nathan Jurgenson. "Production, Consumption, Prosumption: The Nature of Capitalism in the Age of the Digital 'Prosumer.'" *Journal of Consumer Culture*, vol. 10, no. 1, 2010, pp. 13–36.

Southern Poverty Law Center (SPLC). "Fear of FEMA." *Intelligent Report*, 02 Mar. 2010, www.splcenter.org/fighting-hate/intelligence-report/2010/fear-fema.

Sweeney, Michael S. *Doomsday Preppers Complete Survival Guide: Expert Tips for Surviving Calamity, Catastrophe, and the End of the World*. National Geographic Society, 2012.

U.S. Census Bureau. "QuickFacts: United States," 2019, www.census.gov/quickfacts/fact/table/US/PST045218.

⸻. "U.S. and World Population Clock," 2019, www.census.gov/popclock/.

Wojcik, Daniel. "Embracing Doomsday: Faith, Fatalism, and Apocalyptic Beliefs in the Nuclear Age." *Western Folklore*, vol. 55, no. 4, 1996, pp. 297–330.

FILMOGRAPHY

"Am I Nuts or Are You?" *Doomsday Preppers*, season 2, episode 2, National Geographic, 13 Nov. 2012. Amazon.com, 2019.

"Back to the Stone Age." *Doomsday Preppers*, season 1, episode 3, National Geographic, 14 Feb. 2012. Amazon.com, 2019.

"Bullets, Lots of Bullets." *Doomsday Preppers*, season 1, episode 1, National Geographic, 7 Feb. 2012. Amazon.com, 2019.

"Close the Door, Load the Shotgun." *Doomsday Preppers*, season 1, episode 9, National Geographic, 3 Apr. 2012. Amazon.com, 2019.

The Dark Tower, directed by Nikolaj Arcel, Columbia Pictures, 2017.

"Disaster Doesn't Wait." *Doomsday Preppers*, season 1, episode 10, National Geographic, 10 Apr. 2012. Amazon.com, 2019.

"Don't Betray the Colony." *Doomsday Preppers*, season 3, episode 1, National Geographic, 13 Aug. 2013. Amazon.com, 2019.

Doomsday Preppers, produced by Alan Madison, Kathleen Cromley, and Matt Sharp, National Geographic, 2011–2014.

"Friends Can Become Enemies" [aka "You Shall Not Fear"]. *Doomsday Preppers*, season 1, episode 5, National Geographic, 28 Feb. 2012. Amazon.com, 2019.

"The Gates of Hell." *Doomsday Preppers*, season 3, episode 2, National Geographic, 20 Aug. 2013. Amazon.com, 2019.

"I Hope I Am Crazy." *Doomsday Preppers*, season 1, episode 2, National Geographic, 7 Feb. 2012. Amazon.com, 2019.

"Into the Spider Hole." *Doomsday Preppers*, season 1, episode 7, National Geographic, 13 Mar. 2012. Amazon.com, 2019.

"It's All Gonna Hit the Fan." *Doomsday Preppers*, season 1, episode 4, National Geographic, 21 Feb. 2012. Amazon.com, 2019.

"It's Gonna Get Worse." *Doomsday Preppers*, season 1, episode 8, National Geographic, 27 Mar. 2012. Amazon.com, 2019.

"Lone Wolves and Lovers." *Doomsday Preppers*, season 2, episode 18, National Geographic, 26 Mar. 2013. Amazon.com, 2019.

"Nine Meals Away from Anarchy." *Doomsday Preppers*, season 1, episode 6, National Geographic, 6 Mar. 2012. Amazon.com, 2019.

"Pain Is Good." *Doomsday Preppers*, season 2, episode 14, National Geographic, 19 Feb. 2013. Amazon.com, 2019.

"Taking from the Haves." *Doomsday Preppers*, season 2, episode 5, National Geographic, 4 Dec. 2012. Amazon.com, 2019.

"We Are the Marauders." *Doomsday Preppers*, season 3, episode 7, National Geographic, 12 Nov. 2013. Amazon.com, 2019.

The X-Files: Fight the Future, directed by Rob Bowman, Twentieth-Century Fox, 1998.

"You Can't Let Evil Win." *Doomsday Preppers*, season 2, episode 1, National Geographic, 4 Nov. 2012. Amazon.com, 2019.

Reinvesting in the Rapture

Apocalypse and Faith in The Leftovers

CHRISTINA WILKINS

"I'm fairly certain that God sat this one out."
—*The Leftovers*, "Pilot"

Apocalyptic narratives come in a variety of forms, staking their claim in the popular cultural domain through television, film, and literature. While the genre continues to be added to, what these narratives are saying is couched within a framework that may stifle the complexities of the story. Genre tropes and features are followed closely, allowing for subtle variations, but there is little that radically departs from a "typical" apocalypse narrative. However, the HBO series *The Leftovers* (2014–2017) presents a deviation from this framework. The series takes the premise of a rapture-style event and uses it to reassess how the apocalypse and elements of faith within society are perceived. Using a blend of traditional understandings of the apocalypse and features from the genre of apocalypse narratives, *The Leftovers* presents viewers with a liminal experience through its continued presentation of transition, subversion of genre tropes, and absence of resolution. Through the arguably more exploratory form of television, the series arcs traverse multiple character perspectives, locations, and faiths to offer a diverse account of life in the wake of significant change, undermining understandings of authority and narrative. The micro focus of television here offers implications for how we understand the macro of both apocalyptic narratives and the landscape of faith in the contemporary United States.

Various apocalyptic tales focus on a societal structure and how it can be rebuilt in the aftermath. *The Leftovers* moves away from the traditional dismantling and rebuilding of structures in the event of the apocalypse and, instead, moves toward an appreciation of difference. In particular, this difference is highlighted through the variety of faiths showcased and how these faiths are presented. Through character analysis and the underpinnings of apocalypse criticism, this essay argues that the character-driven perspectives encompassing an array of beliefs in the televisual format ultimately dismantle the traditional apocalyptic narrative structure. The use of both traditional and secular understandings of apocalypse as a framework for the series and the ultimate refusal to adhere to either positions it as something indefinable. By casting doubt on the certainty of a traditionally religious apocalyptic scenario—specifically, the rapture—the series unsettles belief in traditional structures. Yet the series refuses to adhere to a purely secular perspective of the apocalypse either, putting it in a unique position. In doing so, *The Leftovers* offers not a critique of society as with many apocalypse narratives, but an exploration of how we might process endings and new beginnings.

A traditional understanding of the apocalypse is defined by adherence to the biblical notion of the event. Coming from the Greek *apokalypsis,* meaning uncovering, the concept has a dual meaning of terminal *and* revelatory (Germana and Mousoutzanis). Apocalypse encompasses revelation, judgment, and redemption, with God enacting divine justice. For those who believe that God is going to reveal himself in these end times and offer salvation, known as dispensationalists, the rapture is a central part of this. In the rapture, as described in the bible, the faithful will be taken to heaven and the rest of humanity left to struggle for seven years (known as "Tribulation") and face off with the antichrist. Apocalypse narratives always feature a kind of judgment, regardless of their biblical elements. However, there are now few apocalyptic narratives that explicitly follow the biblical model in popular culture, with one very prominent exception. The *Left Behind* series, with its 16 installments, topped bestseller lists numerous times and is widely known in American culture. Along with the books a series of films was released between 2000 and 2005, with a remake starring Nicolas Cage released in 2014. This series portrays a specific version of apocalypse that focuses on the rapture and takes a somewhat didactic path. It follows biblical scripture with a contemporary sheen—making the antichrist a politician, for example—and there are "exhortations for characters to embrace salvation," according to Crawford Gibben (142). In doing so, the traditional religious apocalyptic narrative evokes judgment about both the individual and society through theological means; standards of religious belief and behavior are used as a framework to assess against.

By contrast, examples of the secular apocalypse abound in recent popular culture. Some prominent examples include *The Walking Dead* (2010–present), *Battlestar Galactica* (2004–2009), and *The Strain* (2014–2017). The conventions of genre to which these examples adhere are interesting to note. Each features the decimation of society in some capacity, with zombies, mass destruction by extraterrestrial invasion, and vampires respectively in these three cases. The dramatic change upon which each show focuses creates a shift in society: how to continue or rebuild when everything is not as we understood it to be? As with traditional apocalypse narratives, there is an uncovering of some kind of truth here, whether it be monstrous or the true nature of humanity. In terms of basic structure, each example noted here follows what could be argued as a template of the apocalypse narrative. They incorporate an authoritative male protagonist, a formation of a smaller community, and elements of redemption. Although similar in many respects to the traditional religious apocalypse narrative, with the elements of judgment and new beginnings, the crucial difference is the absence of a divine impetus instigating the end times. Pertinent to note also is the medial form these prominent examples take. Television has been a major site for the secular apocalyptic, particularly after the events of 9/11. The multi-arc storyline focus, detailed exposition, and episodic format create a presentation that goes into more depth and uncovers the human experience in a more nuanced way. This intricate focus allows for a revelation of a different type: that of stripping back social institutions and beliefs to their core and revealing their flaws. Unlike the religious apocalyptic, the secular apocalypse imparts judgment that attempts to incite social change on a broader scale. Apocalypse narratives in the traditional vein urge individuals to change their path and follow God, thereby achieving salvation. Both involve a sense of judgment, but the secular apocalypse focuses on the social structures that can be destroyed in such an event and the human relationships underlying them.

What apocalypse means in popular culture is divided; no longer a strictly religious term, its repeated use has changed its function and created a type of trope that is used in cultural products. In discussing the use of the apocalypse in culture, Conrad Oswalt argues that "cultural forms perceived to be secular might well address religious questions" which could be "more relevant to a secularized society than religious activity in traditional institutions" (3). This corresponds with Anne Collier Rehill's position that the "biblical apocalypse has been passed down like a psychological gene ... and continues to find expression" (cited in Aston and Walliss ix). The repeated use of the apocalypse as a focal narrative evidences the need to explore the questions, both religious and secular, that arise from the event. That it is culturally prominent in the form of television may indicate a need to explore the nuances in the events of the apocalypse. Given its expression in a variety of forms, there have been numerous critical responses that posit a distinction between the traditional sense of apocalypse, relying upon its religious underpinnings, and a secular apocalypse that focuses on the destruction of mankind. One such critic, Daniel Wojcik, divides apocalypse into two distinct camps: meaningful and meaningless, with the former linked to Christianity and the latter a secular approach (297). Erika Johnson-Lewis takes this further and declares it should be seen as humanist/anti-humanist, with the former offering salvation and the latter as seeing humanity beyond redemption (121). Interestingly, *The Leftovers* falls in neither of these camps and refuses to adhere to any traditional understanding of apocalypse. The series does utilize many elements of the genre, yet employs these elements largely as a means to ultimately subvert the genre. Exploring the traditional and secular elements of apocalypse fiction in the series, and the diversions from it, highlights this.

The binary in apocalypse narratives, that of traditional and secular, has arguably molded how critics and viewers approach individual examples of the genre. As such, a series like *The Leftovers* has been repeatedly designated as a secular text despite the complexities of both its narrative and approach. Alissa Wilkinson and Robert Joustra contend that the "religious frameworks and entities" are evoked purely "as plot devices" in the series, and that the focus of the show is about grief (155). Similarly, Charles Joseph and Delphine Letort argue that *The Leftovers* "articulates a secular response to the rapture … in tune with contemporary cultural anxieties" (2). In order to explore why these approaches are too simple, it is necessary to briefly outline the context and content of the series. Tom Perrotta's novel *The Leftovers* (2011) forms the basis for the HBO series of the same name; it was picked up by *Lost* (2004–2010) showrunner Damon Lindelof in early 2013. Briefly, the series centers on a rapture-like event that occurred on October 14, wherein two percent of the world's population suddenly disappears. The pilot episode shows the moments of the event as a precursor to the action that follows; we follow an unnamed character and witness the disappearance of her baby and the ensuing chaos of cars crashing, people screaming and general panic. Interestingly, we are never physically shown the disappearance of the "departed," as they are known, onscreen. Their absence is subtly implied through empty spaces in the moments after. Like Lindelof's *Lost*, the focus is on the unknown and the unknowable, acting as an exercise in faith; his influence on the original text by Perrotta is clear through the thematic continuity of spiritual exploration. Set in the town of Mapleton, New York, the storyline revolves around the Garvey family, each of whom has their own methods of coping with the events of the 14th. Kevin (Justin Theroux), the patriarch, is the town's police chief, giving us what seems to be an authoritative anchor. As we move through the first season, which closely follows the events of the book, Kevin's grip on both his family and his town become weaker. A large part of the problem lies in the extreme coping methods of other members of his family, who rely on varying belief systems which intersect with each other and function as an intriguing microcosm of the larger response. His estranged wife, Laurie (Amy Brenneman), has joined the Guilty Remnant, a chain-smoking cult that undertakes a vow of silence and focuses on making people remember what they have lost. His son, Tom (Chris Zylka), is following the path of Holy Wayne (Paterson Joseph), a man who says he can take the pain away from people with a hug. His daughter, Jill (Margaret Qualley), who follows no particular belief system, is left floundering.

Once the microcosm of the family has been established, we see the impact each of these belief systems has on both the family members and the groups to which they cling. This microfocus on the family at the center is enabled by the format, which creates a space in which the elements of the apocalyptic genre may be dissected. The use of television to deconstruct a genre that has its roots in religious ideas is apt, given the frequent assumption of faith as a "default" in television, as the critic S. Elizabeth Bird notes (28). However, the status of *The Leftovers* as an HBO product should not be ignored. The pay-cable model arguably allows for a more provocative approach; removed from advertising demands, it is able to, as it has been described, "court controversy" (McCabe and Akass 63). Similarly, other critics contend that HBO "targets niche audiences interested in 'quality television'" (Abbott and Jowett 11). Christopher Anderson insists that "the viewers of HBO dramas are permitted to detach themselves from typical modes of television viewing" due to its "quarantining" from advertisements (25). Thus, a series which subverts expectations and genres like *The Leftovers* is free to do so. Yet what is perhaps most subversive about it is the refusal to conform to the confines of genre: where should *The Leftovers* be placed? The frame narrative suggests that it should indeed be classified as an apocalyptic narrative, but the format and structure move away from typical adherence to it. Perhaps this is why the critical reception of the series was overwhelmingly positive, with it topping many best television series lists, being called "life-changing television," and being nominated for several awards (Stolworthy).

At its center of all of this lies the series' refusal to confirm the validity of any specific belief system, or indeed, the lack thereof. The vague outlining of who believes what and why gives the viewer who is looking for a mode of representation nothing with which to staunchly identify. Instead, there are a variety of approaches to an apocalyptic scenario that evoke different positions evidencing the diverse nature of faith. This multiple-perspective approach allows for a consideration of a macro event such as the apocalypse on a micro level. The questions at the heart of these narratives are not new, but the modes of representation continue to shift; with a new era of television that allows for deeper exploration, the way those questions are framed changes.

As Andrew Crisell observes, the format of television being "private and domestic" allows for it to "domesticate communal experience" (135). The element of the domestic evinces an intimacy where viewers may feel safer asking difficult questions. At the heart of every apocalypse narrative lies the desire to understand; crucially it is not understanding *why* it has happened, as I discuss below, but *how* it feels and how we can cope with the end of things as we know it. *The Leftovers* subverts a traditional understanding of the end, but gives us something else instead: an exploration of constant flux. Nothing is stable in the series; not faith, family, or authority. This is in stark contrast to the fixed boundaries and knowable worlds of many apocalyptic texts.

The absence of these boundaries in *The Leftovers* is evident from the first episode. Using the rapture and the period of seven years as a basis for the series' run gives it the structural elements that might be expected of a traditional apocalyptic narrative, except that there are key elements missing: there is no discernible antichrist; no final judgment; and no proof the event in question was even the rapture after all. In the first episode "Pilot," we see an investigation established to uncover what happened. So-called experts reach the disheartening conclusion of, "I don't know." This information is presented as background, shown on television screens behind the characters who are coping with the aftermath of the event. How these characters interpret the event is more interesting; the main cast gives us cults, traditional forms of religion, and psychiatric issues as responses and coping mechanisms. The traditional religious element comes in the form of the Rev. Matt Jamison (Christopher Eccleston), who continues to preach Christianity. He especially struggles with the event as it presents an undermining of his world-view given that it does not fit the idea of the rapture as he understood it. This dismantles the world as he knows it, an element key to the apocalyptic narrative. As such, he sets out trying to prove that the people taken were *not* good, and thus their disappearance could not have been the rapture. The cults, both the Guilty Remnant and the followers of Holy Wayne, function as responses to the events. The Guilty Remnant smoke to proclaim their faith and confront those left behind with what they have lost. They are "living reminders." Holy Wayne promises to take the pain of loss from those who are left behind. Thus the elements of traditional apocalypse are pushed into the background and become mere framing devices for how faith operates when belief structures are dismantled or shaken by trauma.

Conversely, aspects of the traditional apocalyptic narrative are encompassed within the series, such as the idea of prophecy, which features heavily in *The Leftovers*. As with premillennialists, who study the bible closely for clues as to when the rapture will occur, the series presents a number of prophecies that rest on the interpretation of various books. In season 3, there is the Book of Kevin, a gospel written about the central character, who has to undertake a mission to visit the afterlife to learn a song that will prevent the world-ending flood seven years after the event. The focus on prophecy here draws further parallels with prophecy fiction, which tries to predict and prepare for the events foretold in the bible. *Left Behind*, as the most prominent contemporary example of the traditional apocalypse narrative, is defined as prophecy fiction by scholars such as Crawford Gibben. He argues that the function of these narratives is to "emphasize the dichotomy between faith communities and their hostile environments" (144). These elements emerge in *The Leftovers*—the establishment of cults like the Guilty Remnant provide a separation from the outside world, with the group actively seeking a hostile response and even staging murders of their members to intensify this dynamic. The use of cults within the series has been noted by various critics, including Peter Y. Paik and Cason Murphy. Paik discusses the Guilty Remnant's practice of human sacrifice that emerges toward the end of season 1, arguing that "violent practices such as human sacrifice can satisfy deep human needs" (186). Murphy similarly sees the Guilty Remnant as subverting the social structure in order to return to a less inhibited state; members "disengaged themselves from the oppressive social institutions of the 'old world'" (105). This differentiation between the old/new world and oppression/freedom is central to the apocalyptic narrative. It allows for judgment to be made on the "old" world, which is deemed evil in traditional apocalyptic narratives.

Michael Barkun argues that the distinction between righteous microcosm and evil macrocosm is crucial to the formation of the apocalyptic (91). This occurs in *The Walking Dead*, where zombies represent the evil, *The Strain* where vampires do so, and filmic examples such as *The Dark Knight Rises* (2012). According to Elizabeth K. Rosen, "apocalypse is a means by which to understand the world and one's place in it" (xi). That our place is crudely defined by good or evil allows for a clearer understanding within a society that has been decimated often—in secular narratives—through the failures of that society. In taking the latter approach, it becomes clear how apocalypse fiction can become a "vehicle of social criticism" (Rosen xii). Again, the similarities with traditional narratives are easy to draw. Both approaches rely on the weaknesses of humanity as a catalyst for catastrophe. These works speak to the need for change, to our "deepest fears and our desire to start over again," as Claire P. Curtis argues (5). Within this "starting over" also comes the need to be redeemed, which is found in secular accounts despite its religious foundations. The redemption narrative comes primarily in the apocalyptic film, such as *2012* (2009), *Children of Men* (2006), and *The Dark Knight Rises*, though televisual examples include *Battlestar Galactica* and *The Strain*. The two most common methods of averting complete apocalypse and redeeming humanity are either hope pinned upon a child (*Battlestar Galactica, Children of Men*), or a singular sacrifice of (usually) a man who becomes a martyr. Here, as with the traditional apocalypse narrative, *The Leftovers* encompasses these tropes. There is a baby, the daughter of Holy Wayne, who is deemed "precious" by him and his followers in season 1; she is left on the doorstep of our protagonist Kevin. This brings Kevin and Nora (Carrie Coon) together, providing a new start for both of them. Kevin is also the chosen martyr character who is viewed as messianic by his friends due to his apparent ability to resurrect himself. They not only write a gospel about his life but urge him to cross over to the afterlife to save the world. This conforms to the centrality of white masculinity in apocalypse fiction as noted by Karen Ritzenhoff and Angela Krewani (xiii).

Though again, as with the traditional elements, the series takes these tropes and subverts them. The baby is reclaimed by its birth mother and shows no special power. Kevin fails to cross over and the apocalypse never occurs. His resurrections are questioned by his ex-wife, Laurie, who tells him he is having a psychotic break. What appears to be conforming to the usual narrative of apocalyptic fiction is upended, and with it goes the idea of the reliable savior who can redeem humanity. Equally, the premise of starting over—so common in contemporary apocalypse fiction—does not quite fit here. With only two percent of the world departed, there is not that much to change. In the initial event, we see cars crashing as they suddenly become driverless, but day-to-day, things continue as before. What changes instead is not society and its structures, but the attitudes of those who are part of it. The only person who has the opportunity to start over is Nora, who loses her husband and both of her children in the departure. Yet she struggles with this concept, and it is easy to understand why. The guilt of having survived, and the fact that the world around her is for all intents and purposes the same, places her in limbo. She is not living after the end; unlike other apocalypse narratives, she lives in a world that has been slightly modified to respond to the event. Throughout the series, we see the mention of those departed on radio stations, the creation of life-like dolls which allows the families to bury something real and tangible, and the establishment of a new bureaucratic institution to regulate the financial and governmental response to the departure. What is unsettling is that the event so closely appears to mirror one that is embedded within (particularly American) culture. The use of the rapture in this story reflects its positioning in society. While the number of self-identified evangelicals in the United States hovers around 20 percent, the popularity of explicit rapture narratives such as *Left Behind* is a distinctly American trend, leading Amy Johnson Frykholm to contend that "[t]he rapture is woven into the fabric of American culture" (13). That *The Leftovers* does not conform to expectations of what it should be undermines belief in both the rapture narrative and its significance in American culture. Recent research by the Pew Forum argues that the religious landscape is changing, with both a rise in "nones" and those who indicate a low level of religious commitment (Smith and Cooperman). Narratives such as *The Leftovers* reflect these changes through their subversion of traditionally religious ideas such as the rapture. Alongside the open-ended positioning of the narrative as not purely secular through the unexplained elements of Kevin's abilities or Nora seeing the "other side," the series also provides representation for those "nones" who still profess a belief in some kind of higher power, currently numbered at 72 percent, although that higher power is not necessarily the God presented in the Christian bible ("When Americans").

The weighing up of the value (moral or otherwise) of society pre- or post-apocalypse is an essential part to these stories. It is what gives humanity meaning: how can we survive like this? Do we need to change? Should our purpose be to redeem the human race? These questions abound in *The Leftovers,* despite it reconstructing the idea of the rapture, and with it the idea of spiritual judgment. Judgment, in both traditional and secular apocalypse narratives, requires authority—spiritual or otherwise—and a belief in the power of this authority. Authority in the apocalyptic narrative often becomes political, reflecting the relationship between the two in the real world as Richard Dellamora argues: the rhetoric of apocalypse has "become a permanent feature of American politics" (194). It is underpinned by a particular kind of politics, namely a more conservative brand. Sophie Fuggle concurs, arguing that modern apocalyptic discourses "ultimately end up endorsing a conservative ... agenda concerned with maintaining the status quo" (31). These political ideas pervade societal conceptions about the end; Pew Forum polls on the place of the rapture in American society show it is not an unthinkable idea for nearly half of American Christians ("Jesus Christ's Return to Earth"). Jennie Chapman furthered this in an examination of coverage of Harold Camping, who predicted the rapture in May 2011; the volume and tone of it shows that "the second coming of Jesus ... was not ... aberrant" (40). The power of authority, religious or political, to shape societal beliefs is unquestionable. Yet the traditional idea of authority, particularly the political, is absent in *The Leftovers*; instead we have the focus on the Garvey family and their influence. This, however, aligns with the gamut of accepted apocalyptic tropes, as James Aston argues: "the private sphere of the family acts as a battleground for public fears and anxieties circulating in contemporary society and particularly in the US" (135). He posits that we become desensitized to catastrophe, but that the family acts as the crucial "mechanism that provides a social commentary" (135).

The Garvey family provide, as noted above, an interesting microcosm of the response to the departure in the series; what the notion of that family constitutes shifts throughout the series as partners become involved with others, sprawling into a wider network. In using the structure of the family at the beginning of the series, *The Leftovers* once again invests in an apocalyptic trope that is swiftly dismantled. Further, the use of the patriarch Kevin's journey from figure of authority (police chief) to quasi-messiah is key to understanding how the series positions shifts in faith and their ties to authority. At the beginning, he is shown as having no particular belief or faith. We learn that he cheated on his wife and is an alcoholic. This is in keeping with portrayals of faith on television, as Bird notes: "lack of faith on the part of a central character is frequently a sign of a flawed or damaged personality" (28). Kevin's position of authority is weakened by his inability to impose a curfew on the town and his inability to hold his family together, along with his mental state. It is this latter issue that begins to subvert the idea of the post-apocalyptic authority figure. In the opening episode of the series, we are shown a point of view shot as Kevin looks at a deer standing in the front garden of a house he is visiting. After a brief conversation, in which he is mistaken for his father, Kevin Sr. (Scott Glenn), who "went crazy," the shot cuts back to the same scene but without the deer ("Pilot"). A similar conceit occurs throughout the first season where Kevin meets a man who shoots dogs because he believes the departure has changed them. There is an uncertainty as to whether he is real or not, as other characters rarely acknowledge him and he does not tell Kevin his name. It is this mystery man (Michael Gaston) who aids Kevin in his nighttime wanderings; often he will fall asleep and wake up with injuries or in another location. The episodes are frequently intercut with Kevin's dream sequences, which keep the viewer constantly guessing as to what is and is not real. The cryptic nature of Kevin's dreams and the symbolism they are invested with, along with his repeated sightings of deer, dogs, and other animals, gives the viewer multiple ways to interpret his relevance to the events of the series. How to interpret these dreams and visions depends on what the viewer wants to believe, either a secular or spiritual interpretation. There are both perspectives in the series. Kevin's ex-wife Laurie believes he is undergoing a psychotic episode and there is evidence for that; we are shown his pile of medication, his discussions with a therapist, and the hereditary element of his father who is institutionalized. On the other hand, the Reverend Matt and characters introduced in season 2, all enmeshed in the religious community, believe that Kevin is some kind of messiah. The viewer is shown Kevin able to resurrect and encounter things in the afterlife that eerily match details of the real world. Thus it becomes the viewer's decision how to explain his behavior, echoing the need within the series for a narrative that is not didactic, but one that allows for an exploration of faith. Throughout this, Kevin maintains his position as police chief, even when the series moves locations to Texas. When season 3 relocates to Australia, the site of Kevin Sr.'s quest to stop the apocalypse, Kevin may be divested of his social authority but is still invested with spiritual authority while being treated as messianic.

Placing Kevin as the center of the narrative, and as a solution to the end, seemingly aligns with traditional accounts of the apocalypse. John Walliss notes that the overcoming of the apocalyptic threat by an "everyman" is deeply engrained in American film (cited in Wilson 2). Andrew Wilson continues his argument: "what is threatened is … formations of national identity or value" (2). The fact that Kevin is American is also nothing new; the narrative of American exceptionalism and its role in apocalyptic narratives is well-documented. However, the focus on the character of Kevin is a red herring. This focus speaks to the conventions of apocalypse narratives—maintaining white male authority alongside an American-centric quest for redemption—but the function of the series is in establishing these conventions and dismantling them. The character Nora's journey alongside Kevin shows an alternative individual perspective. Having lost her entire family, her navigation of the post-departure world is interesting. A skeptic, she refuses to use various faith-based responses as a coping mechanism and instead smokes, has prostitutes shoot her while wearing a bullet-proof vest, and exposes fraudulent companies who claim to be able to transport those left behind to the other side. Her position changes at the end of the series, where she seemingly accepts an offer to be transported to "where they went" ("The Book of Nora"). Again, as with the departure, we never see the moment it happens. Years later, Kevin reunites with her and she tells him the story of what happened, claiming she saw the two percent and their world and decided to return. This sudden shift in belief systems is unnerving, but is also the epitome of the series. Perrotta understood this particular faith dynamic of the series, saying that "[a] religious narrative is one that can't be proved—a believer has to believe, to have faith in something they haven't seen for themselves. Nora's asking Kevin to believe in her story, and we're asking the viewers of the show to do the same. We wanted the ending of the show to be a test of faith. Showing it would have defeated that purpose" (Interview).

It is this testing and exploration of faith that makes the series interesting. Whereas traditional narratives give a prescriptive account of apocalypse, and secular ones feature humanity as redemptive, *The Leftovers* falls somewhere in the middle. Biblical references punctuate the series, giving it an undercurrent of Christianity—or perhaps, a reminder of what this version of events goes against. The exploration of faith as a response to trauma is almost evocative of many a post–9/11 film or tale. The need for faith-based identities and the benefits of religion—such as the sense of community and belonging—is something evoked in the apocalyptic genre, including our example here. What is different, however, is the ultimate shift away from answers or conclusions. Kevin is never realized as a messiah figure; we are never told why the departure happens; and we are not sure if Nora went over to the other side. This positions the characters and their world in a liminal space. That *The Leftovers* mires itself in such liminality, moving beyond fixed boundaries of geography, family, and societal structures, is reflective of a world that becomes increasingly more indecipherable as we deepen our knowledge of it. *The Leftovers* takes the framework of the apocalypse to discuss how we cope with loss, both of people and what we know about the world. The resistance to adhering to a purely religious or secular approach is key, giving us a space which can reassess what the apocalypse might look like as the landscape of faith continues to change. The loss the series deals with is not as material as in many apocalypse narratives; ultimately, there are no crumbled buildings or decomposing bodies, just the crumbling of ideas of how the world works and the structures we put our faith in.

Works Cited

Abbott, Stacey, and Lorna Jowett. *TV Horror: Investigating the Darker Side of the Small Screen.* IB Tauris, 2013.
Anderson, Christopher. "Producing an Aristocracy of Culture in American Television." *The Essential HBO Reader*, edited by Gary Edgerton and Jeffrey P. Jones. U Kentucky P, 2008, pp. 23–42.
Aston, James. "The Post-Apocalyptic Family in *The Walking Dead*." *Small Screen Revelations*, edited by James Aston and John Walliss, Sheffield Phoenix Press, 2013, pp. 133–148.
_____, and John Walliss. *Small Screen Revelations*. Sheffield Phoenix Press, 2013.
Barkun, Michael. *Disaster and the Millennium.* Syracuse UP, 1986.
Bird, S. Elizabeth. "True Believers and Atheists Need Not Apply." *Small Screen, Big Picture*, edited by Diane Winston, Baylor UP, 2009, pp. 17–41.
Chapman, Jennie. "Making the Millennialist Mainstream: How Television Covered the Apocalyptic Predictions of Harold Camping." *Small Screen Revelation*, edited by James Aston and John Walliss, Sheffield Phoenix Press, 2013, pp. 39–58.
Crisell, Andrew. *A Study of Modern Television.* Palgrave, 2006.
Curtis, Claire P. *Postapocalyptic Fiction and the Social Contract.* Lexington Books, 2010.
Dellamora, Richard. *Apocalyptic Overtures: Sexual Politics and the Sense of an Ending.* Rutgers UP, 1994.
Fuggle, Sophie. "To Have Done with the End Times." *Apocalyptic Discourse in Contemporary Culture*, edited by Monica Germana and Aris Mousoutzanis, Routledge, 2014, pp. 31–43.
Germana, Monica, and Aris Mousoutzanis. *Apocalyptic Discourse in Contemporary Culture.* Routledge, 2014.
Gibben, Crawford. *Writing the Rapture.* Oxford UP, 2009.
Johnson Frykholm, Amy. *Rapture Culture.* Oxford UP, 2004.
Johnson-Lewis, Erika. "After the End." *Small Screen Revelation*, edited by James Aston and John Walliss, Sheffield Phoenix Press, 2013, pp. 118–132.
Joseph, Charles, and Delphine Letort. "Tom Perrotta's *The Leftovers* in Textual Seriality: Trauma, Resilience, Resolution?" *TV/Series* [online], vol. 12, 2017. tvseries.revues.org/2170. Accessed 23 July 2018.
LaHaye, Jim, and Jerry B. Jenkins. *Left Behind.* Tyndale, 1995.
McCabe, Janet, and Kim Akass. *Quality TV: Contemporary American Television and Beyond.* IB Tauris, 2007.
Murphy, Cason. "Augusto Boal Is Alive and Well and Living in Mapleton: The Guilty Remnant in HBO's *The Leftovers*." *Journal of Film and Video*, vol. 68, no. 3–4, 2016, pp. 104–114.
Oswalt, Conrad. "Visions of the End: Secular Apocalypse in Recent Hollywood Film." *Journal of Religion and Film*, vol. 2, no. 1, 1998, pp. 1–14.
Paik, Peter Y. "The Fiction of Belief." *Science Fiction Studies*, vol. 45, no. 1, 2018, pp. 184–188.
Perrotta, Tom. Interview by Ashley Morton. "Tom Perrotta Talks Oak Trees, Orgies and Tests of Faith in *The Leftovers*." 8 June 2017, www.watchingtheleftovers.com/blog/tom-perrotta-talks-oak-trees-orgies-and-tests-of-faith-in-the-leftovers. Accessed 30 November 2017.
_____. *The Leftovers.* St Martin's Press, 2011.
Pew Research Centre, "Jesus Christ's Return to Earth," *Pew Forum,* 2010, www.pewresearch.org/fact-tank/2010/07/14/jesus-christs-return-to-earth/ Accessed 23 July 2018
Ritzenhoff, Karen, and Angela Krewani. *The Apocalypse in Film.* Rowman and Littlefield, 2016.

Rosen, Elizabeth K. *Apocalyptic Transformation*. Lexington Books, 2008.
Smith, Gregory, and Alan Cooperman. "Factors Driving the Growth of Religious 'Nones' in the US." *Pew Forum*, 2016, www.pewresearch.org/fact-tank/2016/09/14/the-factors-driving-the-growth-of-religious-nones-in-the-u-s/. Accessed 20 July 2018
Stolworthy, Jacob. "The Leftovers Season 3." 4 July 2017, www.independent.co.uk/arts-entertainment/tv/features/the-leftovers-season-3-episode-1-review-justin-theroux-damon-lindelof-the-book-of-kevin-carrie-coon-a7688701.html. Accessed 27 November 2017.
"When Americans Say They Believe in God, What Do They Mean?" *Pew Forum*. April 25 2018, www.pewforum.org/2018/04/25/when-americans-say-they-believe-in-god-what-do-they-mean/. Accessed 20 July 2018.
Wilkinson, Alissa, and Robert Joustra. *How to Survive the Apocalypse: Zombies, Cylons, Faith, and Politics at the End of the World*. Eerdmans, 2016.
Wilson, Andrew Fergus. "See You Tomorrow." *Small Screen Revelation*, edited by James Aston and John Walliss, Sheffield Phoenix Press, 2013, pp. 1–22.
Wojcik, Daniel. "Embracing Doomsday: Faith, Fatalism, and Apocalyptic Beliefs in the Nuclear Age." *Western Folklore*, vol. 55, no. 4, 1996, pp. 297–330. JSTOR, www.jstor.org/stable/1500138.

Filmography

"The Book of Nora," *The Leftovers*, created by Tom Perrotta and Damon Lindelof, season 3, episode 8, HBO, 4 June 2017.
The Leftovers, created by Tom Perrotta and Damon Lindelof, HBO, 2014–2017.
"Pilot." *The Leftovers*, created by Tom Perrotta and Damon Lindelof, season 1, episode 1, HBO, 29 June 2014.

Social Life and Death in *The Leftovers*

Surviving the Personal Apocalypse

Derek R. Sweet

> "You gotta talk to someone. Talking helps."
> —Kevin, "The Book of Kevin"

At first glance, HBO's *The Leftovers* (2014–2017) appears to be a traditional post-apocalyptic narrative set against the backdrop of the Sudden Departure, a rapture-evoking event wherein two percent of the Earth's population simply disappears. Minutes into the first episode of the series, however, the storyline establishes that the mysterious disappearances cannot be explained theologically or scientifically. Rather than positioning the departed as chosen for their purity or piety, or victimized by some cosmic natural phenomenon, the series tacks away from the whys and wherefores of the Sudden Departure, embracing the randomness of the disappearances and focusing instead on the lives of those left behind. Over the course of three seasons (28 episodes), *The Leftovers* presents an intimate meditation on the way two leftovers, Kevin Garvey (Justin Theroux) and Nora Durst (Carrie Coon), navigate overwhelming pain, grief, and suffering as they struggle to come to terms with the absence of those once present. Immersing viewers in a postmodern apocalyptic that rejects "belief in an ordered universe" in favor of a "chaotic, indifferent, and possibly meaningless universe," *The Leftovers* offers a critique of social disconnection in contemporary society (Rosen, *Apocalyptic Transformation* xiv). Tom Perrotta, creator and executive producer for the series (he also wrote the novel on which the HBO adaptation is based), reinforced the notion of *The Leftovers* as a postmodern neo-apocalyptic when he remarked, "It's about a psychological apocalypse, rather than a real-world nuclear holocaust or attack of the zombies. To me it's about people grappling with a mystery that will not be resolved, and it's how they create meaning in the face of that mystery" (Siu). While the series does nothing to dispel the arbitrariness of human life ("everything happens for a reason" does not apply on *The Leftovers*), it does advance human communication as the ethical locus of the "life-giving gift of acknowledgment" (Hyde, *Gift* ix).

The intersection between communication and ethics, suggests Calvin O. Schrag, implicates *ethos* as a fundamental practice of human interaction. In response to the frequent, overly simplistic descriptions of *ethos* as "credibility" or "moral character," particularly within the discipline of rhetorical studies, Schrag draws on the interpretations of Martin Heidegger and advocates an understanding of *ethos* as rhetorical "dwelling space" (*Praxis* 200). Such a reconceptualization underscores each moment of human communication—a conversation between friends, a political speech, an apocalyptic television series—as a moment of ethical deliberation wherein individuals participate in the complicated work of negotiating the foundational values at the heart of communal Being. For Michael Hyde, rhetorical acknowledgment is a "moral act" that "grants people hope, the opportunity for a new beginning, a second chance, whereby they might improve their lot in life" (*Gift* 7).

With all this in mind, I read *The Leftovers* as: (1) a critique of an increasingly disconnected social existence that sentences many people to a kind of social death; and (2) an invitation to adopt a communicative ethic of responsibility predicated on being-with-others. To support my assertion, I explore the intersection of the postmodern apocalyptic, rhetoric, and social death/life. Specifically, this discussion draws on the work of Hyde and his efforts to position rhetorical acknowledgment as an ethical safeguard against pervasive social death. Next, I illustrate how *The Leftovers*—particularly the story arcs of Kevin and Nora—dramatizes the social disconnect permeating culture and advances communicative responsibility as ethical, life-giving acknowledgment. Finally, I close out the essay with a discussion of how televisual voices, particularly those infused with an ethic of communicative responsibility, emerge as a potential means of averting the personal apocalypse.

Personal Apocalypse and the Life Saving Gift of Acknowledgment

In her exploration of the apocalyptic themes in the *Transformers* franchise, Elizabeth Rosen suggests that "no story is more worthy of being examined both for its consequences in the real world, and for the ethics of telling it than the story of apocalypse" (*Apocalypse Transformed* 155). In its simplest from, an apocalyptic story incorporates "the possibility of an ending which refers not merely to our own individual deaths but to the end of the world that contains us" (Lisboa xviii). Apocalyptic and post-apocalyptic narratives often function as part of a broader cultural dialogue regarding the potential for individual and collective liberation from spiritual suffering, psychological misery, and material calamity. In many instances, this takes the mythic form of the traditional theological apocalyptic: a supernatural being judges the righteous and unrighteous, destroys the unrighteous and their world (or leaves them to live a tortured existence), and elevates the righteous so that they might dwell in a New Jerusalem. The postmodern apocalyptic, on the other hand, problematizes many familiar elements found in more traditional, theologically grounded narratives. Although the postmodern apocalyptic frequently replaces divine judgment with any number of extraterrestrial, environmental, technological, or social threats, blurs the distinction between what constitutes the good or the bad (as well as distinctly good or bad characters), and reconceptualizes the End of the World as a moment of transformative thinking, seeing, and being, the basic plot elements remain the same: judgment, catastrophe, and renewal (Rosen *Apocalypse Transformed* 158–159).

Like other apocalyptic narratives, *The Leftovers* manifests a poignant social critique within the familiar structure of judgment, catastrophe, and renewal. At the same time, however, the series also subverts expectations regarding these same apocalyptic conventions and presents a post-apocalyptic storyline that defers judgment, personalizes the impact of the Sudden Departure, and places the impetus for renewal into the hands of each individual. Despite questions regarding the reasons for the Sudden Departure threading throughout the series, viewers never receive a definitive answer as to why two percent of the Earth's population suddenly vanished. Theological and scientific speculation bubble up at various times in the narrative—The Rapture, demonic abduction, spontaneous transdimensional teleportation—but, in the end, the reason for the disappearances remains enigmatic and unclear. Indeed, the Iris DeMent song "Let the Mystery Be" serves as the opening credits theme song for seasons 2 and 3 and rather pointedly informs viewers that some mysteries are not meant to be solved.

When the closing credits roll for the final episode, the judgment behind the Sudden Departure remains ambiguous. The catastrophe thematic within *The Leftovers*' narrative follows a similar non-traditional pattern. Unlike other apocalyptic and post-apocalyptic stories, *The Leftovers* is not set in a world ravaged by social, political, economic, or environmental collapse. There are no desert wastelands, perpetual rain-drenched megalopolises, food riots, or wars between angels and demons. Eschewing all these familiar post-apocalyptic landscapes of cataclysm writ large, *The Leftovers* focuses on calamity writ small. Likewise, *The Leftovers* never grapples with the broader questions of renewal, rebirth, or resurrection on a societal level. The possibility of revitalization rests with each individual, like Kevin and Nora, and how they choose to rehabilitate their lives in the aftermath of personal hardship.

Given the mysterious, introspective, and intimate quality of *The Leftovers*, I want to suggest that the series stands as an excellent example of what I refer to as the personal apocalypse. In *After the End: Representations of Post-apocalypse* (1999), an interrogation into the rhetoric of history, catastrophe, and apocalyptic popular culture, James Berger speculates that the ongoing fascination with stories exploring the end times, and subsequent new beginnings that always follow the end, "suggests that trauma or apocalypse—some form of utterly destabilizing disaster—is a universal condition of life and symbolization" (22). This universality reveals itself in a variety of human tragedies that, as they unfold in a person's life, feel like the end of the world: the dissolution of an intimate relationship; the death of a loved one; estrangement from a friend, parent, or child; the inability, for whatever reason, to connect with others. Given their parallel storylines concerning the loss of family—Nora loses her two children and husband during the Sudden Departure, while Kevin's family falls apart in the aftermath—the tragic, star-crossed storylines of Nora and Kevin represent those moments of human life when a person sees themselves as someone "whose world is falling apart" (Robins and Post 113). A narrative centered around the personal apocalyptic displays the familiar characteristics of the genre but shifts the locus away from worldwide devastation to a more intimate catastrophe wherein the "apocalypse becomes internalized and the worlds which are destroyed or rebuilt are the result of the minds that construct or perceive them" (Rosen, *Apocalyptic Transformation* 77). In a broader sense, the creation and/or destruction of fictional, apocalyptic worlds contributes to the way audience members live their lives. Schrag makes the importance of human communication and storytelling clear when he states, "As *homo loquens* and *homo narrans*, we search for an understanding of our personal and social existence" (*Doing Philosophy* 88). Similarly, Hyde attests that the collaborative meaning-making that occurs between all humans—from a conversation between two friends over coffee to the indirect dialogic exchange between the creators of a television series and the audience—constitutes a discursive "dwelling space" where people participate in the collaborative work of negotiating self, other, and the broader culture. He posits a rhetorical relationship between community and mediated text when he observes that viewers "are also entertained by things and activities that are serious, difficult but still enjoyable, worthwhile, intellectually stimulating, and perhaps even awe-inspiring" (*Gift* 144). Such authentic communicative engagement functions as the rhetorical foundation for an ethical community; people come together to figure out how to live with one another. In many instances of collaborative accomplishing, individuals recognize one another, give perfunctory attention to the matter at hand, and move on. People talk without saying anything, listen without attending to what is being said, and interact without engaging. The missing ingredient in any number of human interactions, maybe most interactions, is acknowledgment.

As Hyde explains, "Acknowledgment … is a communicative behavior that grants attention to others and thereby makes room for them in our lives" (*Gift* 1). When people acknowledge a friend, co-worker, or complete stranger, they affirm the presence of the other in the fullest possible way. To acknowledge another is to participate in what Hyde frequently refers to as one of the most human of communicative acts: the attempt to reach out, to connect, with others. A request for acknowledgment—rarely presented as an explicit request—demands an authentic, meaningful response that assures the other, "I hear you. I see you. I am here with you." When individuals engage one another other fully and completely, they grant themselves the gift of social life. All too often, requests for acknowledgment remain unanswered: a parent dismisses a child; a co-worker fails to recognize a colleague's emotional distress; an intimate partner only half listens to a significant other talk about her or his day; a customer avoids eye contact with a clerk. Hyde describes living an unacknowledged life as a form of social death. He writes,

> Those who remain unacknowledged in everyday life are isolated, marginalized, ignored, and forgotten by others. The suffering that can accompany these ways of being in the world is known to bring about fear, anxiety, sadness, anger, and sometimes even death in the form of suicide or retaliation against those who are rightly or wrongly accused of making our lives so lonely, miserable, and unbearable ["Acknowledgment, Conscience, Rhetoric, and Teaching" 25].

An individual who experiences "the edge of meaninglessness," who dwells in the collapsing or already collapsed post-apocalyptic landscape of unacknowledged being, endures a state of social death (Robins and Post 114). Unlike the decayed cityscape or zombie-infested countryside of a traditional post-apocalyptic narrative, the social wasteland of the personal apocalypse offers few safe havens and discourages meaningful contact with fellow survivors. Like Nora and Kevin, the person who experiences social death feels isolated, abandoned, and disconnected.

The Leftovers *and Social Life/Death*

"We need acknowledgment," asserts Hyde, "as much as we need such other easily taken for granted things as air, blood, and a beating heart" ("Acknowledgment, Conscience, Rhetoric, and Teaching" 25). *The Leftovers*, with its emphasis on loss, disconnection, and purposelessness, expresses similar sentiments. With the Sudden Departure taking center stage in the opening minutes of the first episode, the series offers an opportunity for viewers to inhabit a familiar post-apocalyptic landscape and wrestle with questions related to social death and social life: what is it like to lose a friend or family member and struggle with the unanswerable mysteries associated with death and dying? What is it like to experience the heartache, the feeling of being unlovable, that comes from a crumbling relationship? What is it like to find oneself far from home, distanced from all the people, places, and activities that once felt so familiar? While the Sudden Departure provides a familiar apocalyptic convention for the HBO series, a narrative spectacle to get the audience interested, the real apocalypse is the social death experienced by Kevin and Nora.

To be sure, the series as a whole makes frequent reference to End Time events associated with theological and secular apocalypses: Rapture/Sudden Departure; demonic invasion; catastrophic flooding; earthquake; social anarchy; and global thermonuclear war. Although some of these events do occur—an earthquake features prominently in the opening episode of season 2 and a rogue soldier sets off a thermonuclear device in a remote Pacific location during season 3—others do not. Regardless, none of the familiar references to the apocalypse, even the initial Sudden Departure, signifies a traditional End Time. Always in the foreground, however, are the pain and suffering that define the personal apocalypses of Kevin and Nora. As the series makes clear through the depiction of the personal apocalyptic in the context of family and intimate relationships, Kevin and Nora inhabit a dwelling space defined by social death.

Kevin Garvey's personal apocalypse, for example, surfaces in his inability to make sense of a new life wherein his ex-wife joins a secular death cult, his college-aged stepson leaves home without a word (and refuses to make contact), and his rebellious teenage daughter rebukes his attempts to maintain some sense of normalcy as a newly constituted dyadic family. Normalcy is elusive, however, as the demands of his job (he is the police chief of Mapleton), single parenting, and the possible onset of mental illness always challenge his tenuous grasp on reality. Nora, on the other hand, tries to make sense of world where her husband, son, and daughter inexplicably disappear during the Sudden Departure. Nora makes the apocalyptic association with her inconsolable loss clear when she encounters a best-selling author who writes about coping with the "ambiguous loss" associated with the departure incident. During a conversation in a hotel bar he suggests, by way of anecdote, that those who did not depart should try to move on and find happiness. At his suggestion Nora flies into a martini-induced rant and screams, "You're not in pain because if you were in pain you would know there is no moving on! There is no happiness! What's next?! What's fucking next?! Nothing is next! Nothing!" ("Guest").

A flashback episode suggests that Kevin and Nora struggled with making sense of their lives prior to the Sudden Departure. Stuck in midlife malaise, a general discontentedness with family life, Kevin asks his father why it is not enough. Kevin Sr. (Scott Glen) answers plainly, "Because every man rebels against the idea that this is fucking it…. You have no greater purpose because it is enough. So cut the shit, 'kay?" ("The Garveys at Their Best"). Kevin Sr.'s answer underscores one of the most pervasive thematics emerging from *The Leftovers*: there is no greater meaning to be found, no greater purpose to be pursued. In this light, Nora's pre–Sudden Departure storyline positions her as a dedicated mother who loves her two high maintenance children, as well as her aloof husband, but wants something more out of life. Like Kevin, she searches for greater purpose. When asked during a job interview to explain why she wants the position, Nora explains bluntly: "Because I want to use my brain for more than figuring out which juice box is certified organic. I want, I need something for myself" ("The Garveys at Their Best"). A scene between Kevin and his daughter, Jill (Margaret Qualley), underscores the insistence on finding meaning in the routine of everyday life. While driving Jill to school, a scene with which any parent of a school-aged child might relate, Kevin notices his daughter laughing at an internet video. Glancing at her phone, he asks,

> **KEVIN:** It's a cat?
> **JILL:** Yeah, but it has a pop-tart for its body, and it's just shootin' through space, and it has rainbows coming out of its butt and it's just really happy about it.
> **KEVIN:** I don't get it.
> **JILL:** No, Dad, you don't ["The Garveys at Their Best"].

Taken at face value, the interaction between father and daughter situates Kevin as out-of-touch and incapable of understanding the humor evoked by a pop-tart cat flying through space while rainbows shoot out of its butt. When considered within the thematic context of the episode, however, Kevin's attention on the pop-tart cat video is misguided and illustrates the real problem at hand: a missed opportunity to connect with his daughter and acknowledge her presence fully.

Already alienated, isolated, and frustrated by the lack of meaning in their respective pre–Sudden Departure lives, Kevin and Nora find their difficulties further exasperated in the aftermath. Given the context of their pasts, how do they make sense of the post–Sudden Departure present? Mired in grief, searching for answers, and unable to find a way out of their personal suffering, the two embrace the personal apocalypse and enter what Nora jokingly refers to as a "toxic, codependent relationship" that is doomed to fail ("G'Day Melbourne"). The two meet at a holiday dance, cross paths while finalizing their divorces, begin to date, and establish a committed relationship. As the relationship progresses, however, the two display an uncanny ability to avoid talking about matters of serious consequence. The two live intertwined lives but say little. They talk about their respective days, laugh together, parent Jill and an adopted baby (Lily), and construct a facade of a functional family. Despite the appearance of being okay, Nora and Kevin refuse to address the substantial personal issues that continue to tear their individual worlds apart. On one of their early dates, the two recognize their inability to communicate about important personal issues:

> **NORA:** I don't know how to talk to you yet.
> **KEVIN:** I don't know how to talk to you either ["Solace for Tired Feet"].

Indeed, until the final episode of the series the two never figure out how to talk to one another at all. This failure to communicate meaningfully, to acknowledge one another fully, becomes increasingly problematic and eventually destroys their relationship.

Over the course of several years together, the dysfunctional couple avoids talking about Kevin's fragmented grasp of reality, his frequent blackouts, his involvement in the abduction of a local cult leader, his presence during the suicide of said cult leader, and his subsequent ongoing conversations with the dead cult leader. Rather than talking about Kevin's conversations with the dead cult leader, for example, Nora avoids a serious discussion by leaving home for several days. She admits, "I didn't know how to handle you talking to a dead person" ("G'Day Melbourne"). Likewise, the couple never talk about Nora's departed children, her increasing obsession with debunking cons and scams related to both the original Sudden Departure and Secondary Departure (she works for the fraud division of the Department of Sudden Departures), her propensity for self-harm, or her fear that she really is Nora Cursed (rather than Durst). In a moment that gives a glimmer of hope that the two might grace one another with the life-giving gift of acknowledgment, Nora pens a heartfelt, honest letter to Kevin suggesting that she is incapable of participating in their relationship, that she is trapped within a personal apocalypse. She writes,

> I want to believe that it can all go back to the way it was. I want to believe that I'm not surrounded by the abandoned ruin of a dead civilization. I want to believe that it is still possible to get close to someone … but it's easier not to. It's easier because I'm a coward, and I couldn't take the pain, not again ["The Prodigal Son Returns"].

Before she can deliver the letter and engage in what would be some of the most open communication between the two, she discovers an abandoned baby on the doorstep. Her confession disrupted, she turns her attention toward reconstituting a family on the "abandoned ruin of a dead civilization." Even when accounts of Kevin's multiple deaths and resurrections begin to circulate, events witnessed by a small group of people who begin to wonder whether or not he is a new Messiah, the two refuse to sit down and consider the implications. Deflecting the conversation away from serious matters, Nora says to Kevin, "If we can't have a sense of humor about you being the Messiah we're going to have a problem" ("Don't be Ridiculous"). Similarly, when the biological mother of Lily reappears and reclaims custody of Kevin and Nora's adopted daughter, the couple avoid talking about the issue and try to move on with their lives. Like the specter of their pre–Sudden Departure lives, Lily's absence haunts Nora and Kevin but is never acknowledged.

In pointing out Nora and Kevin's inability to communicate genuinely and compassionately, the creators of *The Leftovers* are encouraging viewers to contemplate the ways the two lovers fail in their responsibility to one another. Rather than working through the challenges facing them individually and as a couple, Nora and Kevin attempt to recreate a family on a shaky foundation. Patti Levin (Ann Dowd), the dead cult leader who speaks to Kevin in his head, makes this point clear shortly after her death. She comments to Kevin, "What you've got, Kevin, isn't love. It's damage control. Your family blew up. Nora's family blew up. And now you're all just clingin' onto each other cause you need to cling on to something" ("Orange Sticker"). By not learning how to support one another and tackle the complicated mélange of grief, trauma, and meaninglessness stemming from their complicated pasts and presents, the two cling together out of a sense of survival. They erect the facade of a family but fail to constitute a genuine home. As Hyde observes, "a home is an abode or dwelling place whose inhabitants ought to know that, no matter how bad things become, here still exists a haven of shelter and forgiveness" (*Gift* 98). The hurtful conversation that ends their relationship indicates neither of the partners feel that safe sense of shelter or the possibility of forgiveness. As the exchange gets increasingly heated, Kevin states the previously unacknowledged: "Because that's what we do. We don't fucking talk about anything" ("G'Day Melbourne"). Unable to make sense of their own lives, as well as their lives together, Nora and Kevin go their separate ways and find themselves utterly, devastatingly, alone.

In its rejection of a grand metanarrative, design, or purpose for life, as well as illustrating how dysfunctional communication consigns individuals to living in a state of social death, *The Leftovers* presents a convincing argument in favor of Hyde's life-giving gift of acknowledgment as the means by which individuals might come together to "build and live a meaningful life" (*Gift* 49). Although the first 26 episodes of the series offer a painful meditation on experiencing social death, the final two episodes offer a meditation on how to participate in social life. Drawing on sacred and secular texts to illustrate his point, Hyde identifies "the ability to be awed by and wonder and care about others" as a defining characteristic of humanity ("Acknowledgment, Conscience, Rhetoric, and Teaching" 29). A genuine encounter with another "speaks of a transformation of space and time that opens us to the presence of 'otherness.' This opening to otherness clears a dwelling space where the concerned parties can feel at home with each other as they engage in caring (heartfelt) conversation about matters of interests" ("Acknowledgment, Conscience, Rhetoric, and Teaching" 30). Similar to Hyde's reliance on theological and scientific narratives to underscore the universality of acknowledgment, *The Leftovers*' final narrative arc follows Kevin and Nora through transformational experiences. The penultimate episode of the series, "The Most Powerful Man in the World (and His Identical Twin Brother)," follows

Kevin as he intentionally drowns himself, travels to the land of the dead, and attempts to avert a pending real world apocalypse (a global flood). By the successful conclusion of his journey, Kevin learns that the only pending real world apocalypse is his own personal apocalypse, that he "fucked up with Nora," and that he needs to learn how to open his heart to the encounter of the other ["The Most Powerful Man in the World (and His Identical Twin Brother)"]. As a result of his personal renewal and the need to try and make things right, Kevin spends the next several years trying to find Nora.

Decades later, when Kevin finally finds Nora living in the Australian outback, they share a cup of tea as she tells the story of her own transformative journey. Investigating a group of physicists who claim to have a means of transporting people to wherever the Departed went, Nora decides to go through the process herself. Such dramatic action (there is no proof the process actually works, and the process might kill those who go through with it), she explains, was the only way to come to terms with their absence. She shifts to the other world, watches her Departed family from afar, and sees her son, daughter, and ex-husband living happy lives. She explains to Kevin that they "still had each other and I was a ghost. I was a ghost who had no place there" ("The Book of Nora"). Nora's reference to being a ghost is, of course, an acknowledgment that she allowed the memory of her absent children to torment all her post–Sudden Departure relationships. As she brings her story of rebirth and renewal to a close, she admits she wanted to talk to Kevin but was afraid he would question her transdimensional journey:

> **NORA:** And I knew that if I told you what happened, that you would never believe me.
> **KEVIN:** I believe you.
> **NORA:** You do?
> **KEVIN:** Why wouldn't I believe you? You're here. (He reaches out to take her hand and she reaches back).
> **NORA:** I'm here ["The Book of Nora"].

Nora's story is not necessarily about whether or not her transdimensional experience actually happened (the creators involved with *The Leftovers* refuse to answer this question, of course). As viewers never observe her journey on screen, it is quite possible this is a fictional story manufactured within her own mind. Regardless, Nora's storytelling is what Hyde refers to as a call of conscience or "the responsiveness of concerned thought and action" ("Acknowledgment, Conscience, Rhetoric, and Teaching" 27). Nora's story, fictional or not, calls Kevin to acknowledge the pain, loneliness, and transformation that constitutes the heart of Nora's narrative, the heart of her very being. His simple "I believe you" affirms her existence and establishes the meaningfulness of her presence. Also important to note is the way this exchange plays out nonverbally. As the two talk quietly over tea, Kevin and

Nora lock eyes and gaze at one another intensely. Their eyes express the pain and suffering experienced as a result of their relationship and the ensuing years of wishing for a resolution. Nora speaks for nearly eight minutes without interruption; Kevin listens thoughtfully, deeply. When she finishes her story, they look at each other tearfully, clasp hands, and acknowledge each other fully ("The Book of Nora").

Conclusion: Embracing Social Life in the Personal Apocalypse

In her review celebrating *The Leftovers* for its "deep and wittily profound" penultimate episode, television critic Maureen Ryan describes the series as "so wonderfully batshit" that she feels obliged to note the "presence of a hypothetical tinfoil hat" on her head ("Kevin Can Wait"). There is no question *The Leftovers* challenges the conventions of traditional episodic television as well as the generic expectations of apocalyptic narratives. In centering on the love story of Nora and Kevin, two deeply flawed protagonists who resist the notion that the world turns on happenstance, the series presents a relatable narrative that embraces the tragedy, pain, and hopelessness that comes from experiencing a significant loss. The message to viewers is clear: there is no greater purpose, most things do not happen for a reason, and most societal problems do not have clear cut answers. Fixated on the futile struggle to make sense out of events and occurrences that have no meaning (e.g., the Sudden Departure, the dissolution of their families), Nora and Kevin offer a prime example of what happens when people fail to give one another the life-giving gift of acknowledgment. Attempting to survive the personal apocalypse, as well as trying to forge a new life together, they find themselves trapped by their inability to communicate openly, honestly, and genuinely.

In spite of its "nothing happens for a reason" ethos, *The Leftovers* presents a profoundly optimistic message that situates commonplace communicative interactions as the locus of human being. The greater purpose that eludes Kevin and Nora throughout much of the series, and may elude viewers, too, is to simply be with others in meaningful ways. Whether one is watching a pop-tart cat video with a child, comforting a partner in a time of grief, or telling stories over a cup of tea, being present with another affirms their worth and may, in fact, stave off a personal apocalypse. In the spirit of being-with-others, Schrag argues that individuals not only have an obligation to participate in this meaning making but a responsibility to participate in a particular way. He writes, "The ability to respond, being able to respond, becomes aligned with a moral injunction to do so in a proper way" (*Self* 91). Put another way, our basic humanity requires a conscientious, caring presence made manifest by "listening and responding to the other's call for acknowledgment, respect, companionship, help, and perhaps love" (Hyde, *Gift* 131). As Nora and Kevin demonstrate, working together to fend off the personal apocalypse begins with a simple, "I'm here."

WORKS CITED

Berger, James. *After the End: Representations of the Post-apocalypse.* U Minnesota P, 1999.
DeMent, Iris. "Let the Mystery Be." *Transatlantic Sessions 1 Vol. 1,* Whirlie Records, 2009.
Hyde, Michael J. "Acknowledgment, Conscience, Rhetoric, and Teaching: The Case of *Tuesdays with Morrie.*" *Rhetoric Society Quarterly,* vol. 35, no. 2, Spring 2005, pp. 23–46.
_____. *The Life-Giving Gift of Acknowledgment.* Purdue UP, 2006.
Lisboa, Maria Manuel. *End of the World: Apocalypse and Its Aftermath in Western Culture.* Open Book Publishers, 2011.
Robins, Robert S., and Jerrold M. Post. *Political Paranoia: The Psychopolitics of Hatred.* Yale UP, 1997.
Rosen, Elizabeth K. *Apocalyptic Transformation: Apocalypse and the Postmodern Imagination.* Lexington Books, 2008.
_____. "'More Than Meets the Eye': Apocalypse Transformed in Transformers." *Reel Revelations: Apocalypse and Film,* edited by John Walliss and Lee Quinby, Sheffield Phoenix Press, 2010, pp. 155–174.
Ryan, Maureen. "Kevin Can Wait." *Variety,* 28 May 2017, variety.com/2017/tv/features/the-leftovers-recap-season-3-hbo-kevin-garvey-most-powerful-man-in-the-world-twin-brother-1202446896/. Accessed 28 May 2017.
Schrag, Calvin O. *Communicative Praxis and the Space of Subjectivity.* Indiana UP, 1986.
_____. *Doing Philosophy with Others: Conversations, Reminiscences, and Reflections.* Purdue UP, 2010.
_____. *The Self After Postmodernity.* Yale UP, 1997.
Siu, Michelle. "The Psychological Apocalypse of *The Leftovers.*" *The Globe and Mail,* 27 June 2014, www.theglobeandmail.com/arts/television/the-psychological-apocalypse-of-the-leftovers/article19375969/. Accessed 11 November 2017.

FILMOGRAPHY

"The Book of Kevin," *The Leftovers,* season 3, episode 1, HBO, 16 April 2017.
"The Book of Nora," *The Leftovers,* season 3, episode 8, HBO, 4 June 2017.
"Don't Be Ridiculous," *The Leftovers,* season 3, episode 2, HBO, 12 April 2017.
"The Garveys at Their Best," *The Leftovers,* season 1, episode 9, HBO, 24 Aug. 2014.
"G'Day Melbourne," *The Leftovers,* season 3, episode 4, HBO, 7 May 2017.
"Guest," *The Leftovers,* season 1, episode 6, HBO, 3 Aug. 2014.
"I Live Here Now," *The Leftovers,* season 2, episode 1, HBO, 6 Dec. 2015.
"The Most Powerful Man in the World (and His Identical Twin Brother)," *The Leftovers,* season 3, episode 7, HBO, 28 May 2017.
"Orange Sticker," *The Leftovers,* season 2, episode 4, HBO, 25 Oct. 2015.
"The Prodigal Son Returns," *The Leftovers,* season 1, episode 10, HBO, 7 Sep. 2014.
"Solace for Tired Feet," *The Leftovers,* season 1, episode 7, HBO, 10 Aug. 2014.

"How many times have I died?"
Time Loops, Post-Human Reversion and the Editable Self in The Magicians

MICHAEL G. CORNELIUS

> JULIA: You don't know me.
> DEAN FOGG: Thirty-nine times I've known you. Which is why I trust that you'll put aside your fear and self-pity and look for answers that can save you.
> —"The Girl Who Told Time"

In the SyFy television series *The Magicians* (2015–present), based on the Lev Grossman trilogy of the same name, a group of magical graduate students are placed into a time loop in order to halt an impending disaster. Every time they fail to kill the Beast (Charles Mesure), who seeks to destroy the world of magic, the loop recommences, with some key aspect of the structural or temporal circumstance altered, in order to try again. The board is thus continually reset: the same students are recruited to Brakebills University of Magical Pedagogy, the magic school of the series; their same training ensues; the same relationships develop, the same arguments, the same entanglements, the same trials and tribulations. As each loop is restarted by a powerful magician named Jane Chatwin (Esmé Bianco), one element is altered, under the hope that this one alteration may generate a more constructive outcome; and thus the main characters in the series progress to yet another confrontation with the Beast where—if they yet again fall short—the board will once again be reset. This is the nature of the time loop, which Victor Navarro-Remesal and Shaíla Garcia-Catalán label a "closed, repeatable, and editable period of time" (206). Navarro-Remesal and Garcia-Catalán add that "[d]iegetically, the time loop becomes a problem-solving process," (206), and that

> when a viewer or player is presented with a time loop, she can assume that there is something wrong in that chain of events that can be corrected and that there is a reason why it needs to be repeated. There cannot be a tomorrow, or even a today, until the past is fixed [212].

Thus time loops are depicted as directly connective to catastrophic, dare we say apocalyptic events; the recurring and restructuring nature of time in the loop is designed, it seems, to prevent the end of time itself, as "end times" is appropriately another term for the apocalypse. As an end run against temporal destruction, time loops are, in a very real way, a means of ostensibly saving "time" through the repetition of time. This is seemingly true in *The Magicians*, as the epigraph above illustrates. Julia Wicker (Stella Maeve), one of the magical graduate students being prepared to battle the Beast, learns from the head of Brakebills that this particular loop is the 39th iteration of this component of her existence, meaning that 38 times before she and her friends have failed in their mission. Thirty-eight times before she has died; thirty-eight times before her "time has come," to use another temporal aphorism for the cessation of events. Even more pressing for Julia and her companions—Jane Chatwin has been killed, so this is their last chance to (literally) save the day. If they fail this time, there is no one to re-establish the time loop, and all will be lost.

Or will it? In seeking to destroy the world of magic, the Beast is in fact unconcerned with the world from which the main characters in the series originate. At the start of the series Quentin Coldwater (Jason Ralph)—the angst-filled protagonist of *The Magicians*—is contemplating which non-magical graduate school he will attend, since for him magical graduate school is a concept only thinkable in fantasy worlds like Harry Potter. At the start of the series Quentin is like any other recent college graduate—a bit more depressed, perhaps (in fact, he has recently been institutionalized, though this seems to be if not a normal occurrence for him, then certainly not an uncommon one), but fairly regular. In the first novel in the trilogy, Quentin describes his life as "empty and meaningless—whatever inferior stuff it was made of, meaning had refused to adhere to it" (Grossman 44). This hardly makes him unique among the post-millennial Brooklynites depicted in the series. Indeed, though Quentin longs for characteristics of distinguishment—to be different than those around him—he generally realizes, with both a startling clarity and a stultifying sense of surrender, that he is not. Kelly Kramer suggests that the books' sense of realism is key to their enactment: "Grossman's work departs from a traditional understanding of fantasy because it shows the influence of the novel, with its emphasis on realistic, ordinary characters and a real-world atmosphere" (157). Quentin's ordinariness may depress him, but, for him, it is simply part of being alive. It is only when Quentin learns that he has magic does he even aspire to something beyond a desk job and what he perceives to be a mundane existence, because—finally—he has discovered proof, in the form of fantastical magic, that there *is* something beyond the ordinary. This suggests a movement from "r/Realism" to post-humanism, to what the series might characterize as existence as a self beyond what the self deems as ordinary or even possible. This is what is threatened by the Beast; not the end of the world, but the end of Quentin and Julia's world, a world that—in the narrative history of the television series, anyway—they have scarcely just discovered.

This is all indicative of an apocalypse that is more personal than global, and more metaphysical than physical. And though the young magicians manage to ultimately stop the Beast and avert impending disaster, they do so by bringing about the very "personal" apocalypse they had sought to impede, rendering both magic and their post-human state (somewhat) non-existent. Thus in *The Magicians*, the end of the world means a reversion away from the post-human and back to normative humanity. This is the apocalypse that these characters ultimately create and seek to reverse; one born not of calamitous impact on a planetary scale, but rather a personal one.

Post-Human Worlds

In the world of *The Magicians*, the post-human is both the normative state and the desired state, creating temporal and physical spaces where "regular" humanity itself is excluded. Magic is thus part of a caste system, and the apocalypse trying to be averted in the series is not the end of the human world or the "real" world, but the end of world(s) that most humans are both ignorant to and barred from ever seeing or entering. The humans who enter into these magical worlds—including Brakebills, which is Grossman's version of J.K. Rowling's Hogwarts—are already over the whole "human" story anyway. The typical life-narrative arc of a Western youth—getting an education, getting a career, getting married, having children, etc.—seems inevitable to them, and this inevitability suggests it holds little wonder. The college graduate-aged protagonists in the series are post-modern in a predictably "post-over it" kind of way, and so when they learn that magic exists, they have no qualms about leaving the human world behind.

Wonder is an essential component of any fantasy text. Brian Attebery, in his seminal work *The Fantasy Tradition in American Literature*, notes that "a sense of wonder" is one of the defining tenets of the fantasy genre: "Fantasy invokes wonder by making the impossible seem familiar and the familiar strange and new" (3). In *The Magicians*, characters like Quentin and Julia exist in a world where the only wonder they could ever envisage fixed itself directly to states of childhood fantasy—thus connecting "wonder" to not only a space that is inaccessible (the magical, non-real realms of adolescent stories) but also to a time (childhood) that has since elapsed. This sense of lost wonder has seemingly nexused for both Quentin and Julia on a series of books entitled *Fillory and Further*, Grossman's facsimile of C.S. Lewis's *Narnia* series. In the *Fillory* series, same as in *Narnia*, human beings are viewed as Other in the most extraordinary sense, looked upon as saviors of the realm and nearly deified, ascending to prophetic roles as kings and queens of the land. A deep attachment to the series forged the strong bond that Quentin shares with Julia, his childhood best friend, and also demonstrates the tenuous nature of this childhood bond, as Julia is preparing herself for adulthood, planning for her future (she is going to Yale for graduate school) and exchanging her primary, platonic dyad for a romantic one, suggesting marriage, motherhood, and mundane adulthood. For Quentin, this transition from child to adult is far more knotty; a prototypical man-child whose bouts with depression (again, leading to institutionalization) seem to be a direct result of the growing up process, Quentin reacts to what he perceives as the very "adult" responsibility to slough off the wonder of childhood as perhaps his first miniature, personal apocalypse; it is the end of a world, a world of great significance to him, even if, it seems that way to no one else. It is no wonder that he clings desperately to the fictions of *Fillory*, even when other characters deride such works as "kid's stuff." At one point Quentin, espousing the virtues of the *Fillory* books, enthuses, "There is no substitute for a childhood of adventure, warmth, and love," to which his Brakebills classmate Penny (Arjun Gupta) replies, "You will never be a man" ("The Writing Room"). Penny's disdainful response reflects his belief, and seemingly that of the series, that the adult world is far more "complex" than the fictions of childhood could ever suggest or reflect.

It is only when Quentin discovers that he is a magician and that there is a school for people like him that his sense of wonder affirms his sense of self, and he begins to look to the future with cautious optimism. What Quentin is really reacting to here is not the fact that he has magic—or, rather, not *simply* the fact that he has magic—but rather the basic yet powerful concept that he *truly* is not like those around him. He is not just human; he is more than human. Quentin is so taken by his newfound "more than" status that he abandons Julia, his family, and the world he knows for a new realm, a realm filled with others like him, others not like all the others Quentin has known his entire life.

The post-human tends to be depicted and conceived of in terms of technology and science fiction. N. Katherine Hayles interconnects the concept of the post-human to the "denaturing of the human," suggesting a link between post-humanism and artificiality (266). Likewise, Marilyn Manners and R.L. Rutsky note that "[t]he post-human, like the postmodern, is defined by its association with a non-human or artificial reproducibility," again emphasizing the non-natural, synthetic nature of post-humanism (131). Matthew A. Taylor suggests that post-human "discourses ... position themselves as corrections to what is perceived to be humanism's dangerously myopic exaltation of the human subject, advancing in its stead a more capable, ethical, inclusive, and 'open' subjectivity or collectivity (generally under the aegis of some form of 'hybridity')" (220). While Taylor does not directly associate the post-human to artificiality, his suggestion that the post-human is the result of hybridization intimates an enhancement or at least an alteration of the human being/animal itself. To be post-human is no longer to *be* human, with a strong emphasis placed here on the linking verb; post-humanism suggests a deliberate movement away from not only biological and philosophical definitions of humanity but also the physical and natural structure of human beings as well.

What is being construed here, broadly speaking, is the relationship of the subject to the object, with the subject being nexused within the "human" and the object focusing on whatever capacity that generates the "post"-human quality—cybernetics, genetic tampering, or, in the case of *The Magicians*, magic. This is not a hybrid or enhanced self, but a bifurcated or oppositional self. Paul Smith argues that identity is always created or fashioned in opposition to some other:

> The "subject" is generally considered epistemologically as the counterpart to the phenomenal object and is commonly described as the sum of sensations, or the "consciousness," by which and against which the external world can be posited. That is to say, the subject as the product of traditional western philosophical speculation, is the complex but nonetheless unified locus of the constitution of the phenomenal world. In different versions the "subject" enters a dialectic with the world as either its product or its source, or both. In any case, the "subject" is the bearer of consciousness that will interact with whatever the world is taken to consist in [xxvii].

Smith adds, "the human species is not prone to think of itself except in some version of that opposition" (xxviii). This means that, in *The Magicians*, Quentin and others of his ilk are human and are not human; they are like us and not like us. Quentin's sense of self especially is counter-oppositioned by his own sense of who he is/was and who he believes he will be/become. Post-human identities in this manner are fabricated on both a thorough understanding and then rejection of the self-identity, or—to be more accurate about this—a *perception* of the self-identity. Post-humans, especially in *The Magicians*, do not exist in opposition to humanity in general, but rather to the human self that generated the post-human identity in the first place.

This sense of identity is important to Quentin and the other magicians in the series, even if their communities and families of origin are not part of the magical world. Indeed, the existence of magic-exclusive realms amplifies the magicians' relationship to their post-human self. At Brakebills, the magicians exist in a realm that is clearly viewed as suprahuman (one character even explains himself to a non-magical human as being a "supervillain," in order to create an easy frame of reference); this same world, through a series of wards and protective spells, is secreted from the outside world, making it transhuman, at least in a geographic sense ("The Writing Room"). This supra/trans/post-human environmentalism is also seen in the "hedge" communities of magicians, groups who practice magic but who are outside of the more structured confines of institutions like Brakebills. This is where Julia will eventually find herself, taking a journey similar to Quentin's, finding her own way to a post-human existence. Lastly, the characters' post-human status is especially heightened in the magical land of Fillory, where the young students of Brakebills exist as near-mythic creations, being anointed rulers of the realm for their post-human existence.

These post-human worlds highlight Quentin and Julia's sense of wonder and their post-human identity. In many ways, though, their journeys reflect the same identity-formation processes that occur for most young people when they leave their homespace and move into the world, whether that world is a higher educational setting or simply a place of their own. Indeed, Quentin and Julia's expectations for their magical existence often place undue stress on their post-human identities, as they realize, as Quentin notes, "Magic is real and it can fix anything except what I need" ("The Flying Forest").

There are instances, as well, where Quentin and Julia are forced or choose to exist as their "human" selves again and make their way within the "real world" away from the post-human realms that have fostered them and their "magical" sense of being. In the "real world," they exist as cubicle jockeys and eschew magic altogether. They live ordinary, mundane existences, or at least enact what they perceive to be an ordinary, mundane existence (at one point, Julia describes finding Quentin "chain smoking and binge watching *Six Feet Under*" ["The Tales of the Seven Keys"]). They are drawn to this existence during moments of tremendous stress and sadness—the real world seems somehow "easier"—and yet it is also lackluster, dull, and grey:

> **QUENTIN:** Is everybody out here really so lifeless?
> **EMILY (ABBY MILLER):** Yes, we are. We are. That's why we drink.
> **QUENTIN:** Well, I drank just fine as a magician.
> **EMILY:** Yeah, because your world was so overwhelming and scary and you needed a break from it all. Now you're going to drink because each day is so goddamn dull and that takes a lot more booze ["Cheat Day"].

While there, their search for self trods along more familiar paths—alcohol, religion, ennui—though they are inevitably drawn back to those magical spaces which they can access. As Quentin himself puts it, "I need you to remind me that magic is real. Without Brakebills, I'm lost" ("The Source of Magic"). Having become post-human, they can never be human again; this is not because they rejected their human identities and selves, but rather because they never accepted those selves to begin with. While the post-human offers them a sense of self, despite its many challenges, there is nothing for them in the human world, because there never was in the first place. Post-human worlds are the only worlds that matter to their quiddites. As one of the characters puts it,

> I just really loved doing magic. And I was good at it.... Just the air smelled different, right? And I could turn into a bird or make a rose bloom. And I saw actual Fillory. And I banged a werewolf! Yes, that is weird, but also rad because who gets to do that? And

I wasn't just some extremely average nobody. I was gifted. I didn't just belong somewhere. I belonged anywhere because I was a magician ["The Tales of the Seven Keys"].

Directly linking their identity to abilities they possess, the magical denizens of *The Magicians* are thus unprepared for the loss of both magic and their identities—even if such a loss may be key to saving the(ir) world.

"Self-Editable" Time

Quantum physicists and phenomenologists have long discarded British physicist Sir Arthur Eddington's notion of the arrow of time—that time moves in simply one direction—as the sole means of understanding a subject as complex as passage and duration (Greene 13). Sigfried Giedion has observed that time can either be viewed "realistically, as something going on and existing without an observer, independent of the existence of other objects and without any necessary relation to other phenomena; or subjectively, as something having no existence apart from an observer and present only in sense experience" (443). Kirsten Simonsen echoes this sense of time as subjectively interrelated to human existence: "Time is also part of the lived experience, and it can take on many forms, such as physical, biological, mental, cosmic, social, cyclical and linear time, all of which we encounter in everyday life and in the body" (7–8). In speculative fictions, the relationship between time and humanity becomes even more intertwined through narratives of time travel, which simultaneously suggest a mastery of, and subservience to, the physical notion of time, a notion that, in and of itself, is something of a human creation. Jonathan Harrison suggests that "[t]ime-travel ... implies backwards causation," noting again the physical aspect of time (as a thing to be traversed) as well as the human aspect of time (indicating that events that occur do so because of human causation, always, even when moving backwards through temporal climes) (16).

Time loop narratives especially highlight this dialectical tension of human mastery and human bondage, existing somewhere between Eddington's arrow of time and Maurice Merleau-Ponty's conception of space/time as concomitant with the self: "I am not in space and time, nor do I conceive space and time; I belong to them, my body combines with them and includes them. The scope of this inclusion is the measure of that of my existence" (140). Though Merleau-Ponty observes a hierarchical relationship that posits the human self as a result of space/time phenomena, the opposite must also be true; without human beings to conceive of space/time, to understand space/time, or to even note the existence of space/time, the latter pair may not exist. If, as Merleau-Ponty notes, space/time gives life to us, then we must also give life to them.

This dichotomy is placed front-and-center in science fiction time loop narratives like *Source Code* (2011) and *Edge of Tomorrow* (2014), where the story protagonist is repeatedly sent back in time to replicate a series of events until the hero (and the narrative) achieves a desired outcome. Navarro-Remesal and Garcia-Catalán write that, in the time loop, "the traveler usually has only one way out: to acquire knowledge. Memory is the sole means of progression" (207). This indicates that the alteration of the human is the key to shifting surrounding events; by gaining information and altering the knowledge-base and framework of the time traveler, the manner in which the passage of time has occurred—and will again occur—may change. This suggests that the very moniker of "time loop" is something of a misnomer, as a loop implies a geometry that is circular or perhaps spherical, indicating properties of infinite connection that highlight the intertwining natures of time, space, and the human self. In reality, time loop narratives would be more aptly envisioned as a type of temporal "snap-back," where the single object—the individual moving backward in time—is thrust back along the same linear path to a predetermined point, a point at which the society threatened by the events in the time loop narrative can still reasonably be saved. This suggests that *The Magicians* is different than ordinary time travel series like *Dr. Who* or *Legends of Tomorrow*, where the characters move through space and time in random patterns. In the time loop, the pattern is rigidly set and only one aspect of that entire society—usually, a single individual—moves along the pattern. Everything else remains static, at least until the original object—the human moving through time—is altered through the acquisition of new knowledge about the events that have transpired, are transpiring, and will transpire, all at once. This suggests that Navarro-Remesal and Garcia-Catalán's "editable period of time" is really about editing the *human* located within the period of time; time itself remains static and unchanged (206).

In *The Magicians*, every time the loop is reset, one of the main characters involved in the loop is altered, again demonstrating that it is the human that it editable, and not time (or even space) in these narrative equations. In the epigraph to this essay, I highlight the change that has been made for this 39th (and final) time loop: Julia has been excluded from Brakebills. While she believes that she has never met Dean Fogg (Rick Worthy), the academic head of the school, he tells her that, in fact, he has known her 39 times, since he exists outside of the magic of the loop. For Julia, though, in this time loop she has just met him; rejected by the post-human world she longs to inhabit, Julia is forced to traverse her own magical journey through the tertiary, seedier hedge communities of *The Magicians*' world. The grander hope for Jane Chatwin and Dean Fogg is that, having changed her, the future will also change.

W.J. Friedman writes, "In spite of the common intuition that chronology is a basic property of autobiographical memory, the research reviewed demonstrates that there is no single, natural temporal code in human memory. Instead, a chronological past depends on a process of active, repeated construction" (44). Friedman is underscoring the notion that human beings simply do not passively remember the past; rather, acts of memory are active undertakings, and our recollection of past events is predicated on both our active desire to recall them as well as our active construction of these events themselves in our memories. In actively (re-)constructing these events, we may alter them, and believe these alterations to, in fact, have been what truly transpired. In this way, we change the past. The "snapback" nature of the time loop narrative works in the same manner. It allows for travel back along recollected events, times that have already been lived, in order to alter them to procure a better outcome to the events and for the self that lived them.

Memory—and the experiences they represent—are a key component in identity formation. When Jane Chatwin resets the time loop in *The Magicians* and alters one member of the core character group, she is changing some component of their identity formation. This is what is ultimately possible in these narratives. The space of the past cannot be changed; nor can the passage of time. Yet the self who lived the past can be altered, through memory or—in the case of the time loop narrative—through reality, and altering the memory of the past can alter the pattern of the present. This is what Chatwin ultimately achieves; her final alteration of Julia eventually leads to the defeat of the Beast, preserving Fillory, Brakebills, and the post-human worlds of magic. Yet doing so also sets off a chain of events that ultimately leads to magic being "shut off" by the greater gods in the series. Averting one disaster has thus caused another. The apocalypse has come after all, even if it is enacted with a whimper, and not a bang.

The Personal Apocalypse of The Magicians

When the post-human magicians are shut off—seemingly forever—from the actual practice of magic, they react, as one might imagine, as if they have entered the end times. One of Quentin's Brakebills professors describes the situation thusly: "The goddamn world is ending!" ("Heroes and Morons"). Quentin himself, when asking for help from an occasionally adversarial classmate, says, "No magic is everyone's problem. Do you think that I like begging for help, especially to you? I wouldn't even do it except I know that you occasionally stop being a dick when the fate of the world is at stake" ("Poached Eggs"). The "fate of the world" is indeed a serious thing. Yet the world truly is not ending; indeed, it has been preserved from the threat of the Beast. What has ended is the world of magic; Brakebills' physical form still exists, and students are still invited to attend the school to study the theory of magic, but they cannot actually practice it. They cannot make magic happen. They can only simply know it.

Karma Waltonen notes, "There are several definitions of apocalypse. One is extreme—an ELE—extinction level event. Others are end times, which can be defined more specifically—the end of a civilization, population, world, time, relationship or individual life" (x). The final two, highly individual definitions in Waltonen's list hearken to the construct of the "personal apocalypse," a term used throughout varying critical discourse traditions—including literary, filmic, sociological, and theological—that generally refers to a type of personal tragedy, whether that may be a death, the diagnosis of a terminal illness, the loss of creative will, or even the loss of faith. The general concept of the personal apocalypse, despite the varying discourses that toss about the term, is the destructive alteration of the self, so that—should the individual thus inflicted survive the event in question—the sufferer, like a place devastated by an apocalyptic event, would become irrevocably changed. Anthony M. Wachs takes this a step further, connecting the "personal apocalypse" to "depersonalization" (68, 63). Here Wachs directly connects a personal tragedy to a sense of loss, specifically a loss of humanity. Regardless of the nature of the personal apocalypse, the end result is that the individual so inflicted *feels* as if the(ir) world is coming to an end. "Thus," Waltonen writes, "apocalypse is everywhere" (xi).

Yet is apocalypse truly everywhere? While the construct of the "apocalypse" has differing facets to its primary definition, in function it reflects an event that is generally more wholesale than the tragedy of a single person or a small group of people. Such misfortunes are no less keenly felt, though the devastation wrought by such personal calamities must be exacerbated by the utter normality of life passing by around those who suffer. With the personal apocalypse, the world still turns; people still go to work; Starbucks still sells coffee. In fact, the only thing impacted by a personal apocalypse is the individual at the center of the storm; the rest of humanity remains untouched. When Wachs writes that "depersonalization" is the key to the personal apocalypse, he does so in part to note that tragedy can remove human beings from the larger human species, at least for a time. Mourning is often done in general isolation; while misery may love company, societal norms tend to suggest periods of solitude for those who are gravely ill, or in mourning, or suffering from some other form of personal difficulty. This is not to say that these individuals may not enjoy the comfort of a familial unit; indeed, they often do. Such bonds are key to the sufferer's return to humanity, should such a return be possible. Yet the larger society itself respects the construct of individuality and individual space in trying times. In such situations, people take time off from work, or school, if they can; they alter their routine. They take time "for themselves," and as such are separated—if only temporarily—from the rest of humanity.

The post-human individuals of *The Magicians* have already isolated themselves from the larger human herd. They have done so not because of tragic circumstances, but because they feel they have exceeded the bonds/bounds of humanity itself. If the personal apocalypse is about "depersonalization," then the post-human individuals in *The Magicians* have already completed this process, a process they once eagerly embraced. At the start of season 3 of the series, where the characters struggle without magic, the apocalyptic tone of the first two episodes quickly gives way to more practical concerns, as the mother of one Brakebills student expresses: "Did you know we got a tax bill for the house? Apparently, we haven't paid in thirty years. Enchantment failed, so now we're losing our home. I mean, what are we gonna do without magic? I mean, get fucking jobs?" ("The Losses of Magic"). Here, the series (tongue planted firmly in cheek), equates the prospect of employment—one of those normative aspects of civilization that the post-human magicians in the series so eagerly abandoned—with the end of the world. A job can hardly be considered in the same sense as a pandemic, or alien invasion, or the onslaught of vampiric hordes. Even Quentin, who previously described the loss of magic in distinctly apocalyptic terms, downgrades his evaluation of the situation: "We really didn't know how good we had it, did we? We whined and complained about everything that magic couldn't do because we couldn't see that a world without it was dark and mean and pointless" ("Heroes and Morons").

In the book series, Quentin's expulsion from magical realms is never detailed with such apocalyptic terminology. While the threat of the Beast is very real, and magical worlds are threatened with extinction, the text never quite reaches the levels of "end times" hysteria that the television adaptation adopts (over what is, really, far less consequential outcomes). Indeed, Quentin's entire ethos about the magical world begins to reflect the skepticism he has toward the "real" world. In the novels he finds the work of learning magic laborious and tedious, and that having magic does not solve his problems or "magically" cure him of his personal tribulations. At the end of the first novel, having been abandoned by his friends in Fillory after the defeat of the Beast, Quentin rejects magic altogether. Kramer describes this moment in the text thusly: "Instead of a healthy return to ordinary life, refreshed by his visit to Fillory, he takes a corporate job, rejects every aspect of magic, and decides that 'to live out childhood fantasies as a grown-up was to court and wed and bed disaster' (Grossman 397)" (159). In the novels Quentin's sense of wonder is quickly diffused by the hard work magic entails and by the realization that magic will not solve the problems that are embedded within his own psyche, even if he should wish it so. In the books Quentin and his friends never wholly embrace a post-human identity. As such, a loss of magic is another adjustment; tragic, yes, but no more so than losing a friend.

In the television series, however, the loss of magic is the loss of identity. It is the loss of wonder. It is the end of—some world, if not *the* world. This creates a post-human reversion cycle for all of the magical post-humans in the series. Having eagerly rejected their previous human existences, many of the characters must now figure out how to re-acclimate to life as a regular human being once again. During the third season, Dean Fogg laments the teaching of magic without being able to practice magic; still, he notes that it is important for students to learn that magic existed, that it was real, even though the academic study of it proves unsatisfying, and many students leave Brakebills altogether. Fogg struggles against the total annihilation of his culture, a loss exacerbated by the fact that, without actual magic, those called to learn it are really no different from any other student or any other individual working in a cubicle. They are now normal; they are now the same as everyone else. They are human. This may not be a fate worse than death; yet, for the characters in *The Magicians*, it is a type of death all the same.

Conclusion

David Morley and Kevin Robins observe that "identity must be defined, not by its positive content, but always by its relation to, and differentiation from, other [identities]" (10). William Turner agrees: "Identity categories … convey meaning according to a structure of binary oppositions" (33). By defining themselves as post-human magicians, and locating their worlds in spaces that "regular" humans cannot access, the magical students of *The Magicians* have juxtaposed their entire sense of self in oppositional paradigms to all that was and is human, to all that they once were and, in some very real ways, still are. To be forced into a human identity again is to be forced to relinquish the identity structures they have so eagerly embraced, to give up not only their own sense of self, but their actual self as well. When a character in the series rails against paying house taxes, is it not the loss of lucre that offends her, or the notion that something is owed for something she possesses; rather, it is the mundane, human action of paying taxes itself that is an affront to her identity, because it is such a "human" thing to do. In some ways, the loss of magic equates for those who dwell in the magical realms of *The Magicians* not so much as an apocalypse—for the world is as it was/is—but rather a genocide, the destruction of a people and a culture, a unique way of being (post-)human.

In the first episode of season 3 of *The Magicians*, "The Tales of the Seven Keys," Quentin and his companions begin a quest to restore magic to the world. When confronting the Great Cock of the Darkling Woods, a magical creature in the forests of Fillory, one member of the group is asked, "Do you want your magic back or not? Will it not solve all your problems?" ("The Tales of the Seven Keys"). This echoes a similar conversation Quentin and Julia have about magic:

QUENTIN: Okay, what is magic actually for?
JULIA: For fixing things, dummy ["Thirty-Nine Graves"].

Hence magic—like the time loop—is viewed as a problem-solving contrivance, a means to a (difficult) end. Yet what requires repair here is not any issue with the passage of time nor, even, the occurrence of events, tragic as they may be. The apocalyptic tone of the television adaptation of *The Magicians* stems from a need to fix a problem far deeper and more eternal than the end of the world—the problem of the human heart, the human soul, and the very nature of identity itself. In the book trilogy Quentin learns fairly early on that magic is not the balm for all of his anxieties and concerns. In the television adaptation, however, Quentin's penchant for wonder and the post-human movement of he and his companions into spaces and identities beyond that of mere mortals creates a condition that, when that identity is threatened, causes the group to leap into crisis-mode, all to avert the impending apocalypse. It is no wonder that a time loop—a "snapback" of linear movement along a predetermined path—is so fitting for the characters in *The Magicians*. What truly needs alteration in the series—and what time loops are constructed to change—are the characters themselves. Indeed, the time loop in *The Magicians* reflects the same internal need in these characters as their movement to a post-human status does—the desire to be someone else, to be different, the desire for distinguishment among so many other human souls. Mary J. Carruthers writes that "[a]pocalypse, in salvational history, is not part of a suprahuman, cosmic process unrelated to time but part of the 'order expressed in human choices and enacted in human action and its results'" (176). In locating the cynosure of "end times" into the soul and will of the human, Carruthers demonstrates that, ultimately, it is the human that may prove the cause of—and solution to—the apocalypse. Magic may be designed for fixing things, and time loops may exist to alter the human in order to change the passage of time, but, ultimately, these narratives may suggest, simply and profoundly, that the power to cause—and avert—disaster resides within us all.

Works Cited

Attebery, Brian. *The Fantasy Tradition in American Literature: From Irving to Le Guin*. Indiana UP, 1980.

Carruthers, Mary J. "Time, Apocalypse, and the Plot of *Piers Plowman*." *Acts of Interpretation: The Text in Its Contexts, 700–1600*, edited by Mary J. Carruthers and Elizabeth D. Kirk, Pilgrim Books, 1982, pp. 175–188.

Friedman, W.J. "Memory for the Time of Past Events." *Psychological Bulletin*, vol. 113, 1993, pp. 44–66.

Giedion, Sigfried. *Space, Time, and Architecture: The Growth of a New Tradition*. 5th ed. Harvard UP, 1967.

Greene, Brian. *The Fabric of the Cosmos: Space, Time, and the Texture of Reality*. Alfred A. Knopf, 2004.
Grossman, Lev. *The Magicians*. Penguin, 2010.
Harrison, Jonathan. "The Inaugural Address: Dr. Who and the Philosophers, or Time-Travel for Beginners." *Proceedings of the Aristotelian Society*, vol. 45, 1971, pp. 1–24.
Hayles, N. Katherine. *Chaos Bound: Orderly Disorder in Contemporary Literature and Science*. Cornell UP, 1990.
Kramer, Kelly. "A Common Language of Desire: *The Magicians*, Narnia, and Contemporary Fantasy." *Mythlore*, vol. 35, no. 2, Spring/Summer 2017, pp. 153–169.
Manners, Marilyn and R.L. Rutsky. "Post-Human Romance: Parody and Pastiche in *Making Mr. Right* and *Tank Girl*." *Discourse*, vol. 21, no. 2, Spring 1999, pp. 115–138.
Merleau-Ponty, Maurice. *Phenomenology of Perception*. Routledge, 1962.
Morley, David, and Kevin Robins. "Spaces of Identity: Communications Technologies and the Reconfiguration of Europe." *Screen*, vol. 30, 1989, pp. 10–34.
Navarro-Remesal, Victor, and Shaíla Garcia-Catalán. "Try Again: The Time Loop as Problem-Solving Process in *Source Code* and *Save the Date*." *Time Travel in Popular Media*, edited by Matthew Jones, McFarland, 2015, pp. 206–218.
Simonsen, Kirsten. "Bodies, Sensations, Space and Time: The Contribution from Henri Lefebvre." *Geografiska Annaler*, vol. 87, no. 1, 2005, pp. 1–14.
Smith, Paul. *Discerning the Subject*. U Minnesota P, 1988.
Taylor, Matthew A. "Edgar Allan Poe's (Meta)physics: A Pre-History of the Post-Human." *Nineteenth-Century Literature*, vol. 62, no. 2, September 2007, pp. 193–221.
Turner, William B. *A Genealogy of Queer Theory*. Temple UP, 2000.
Wachs, Anthony M. "Apocalyptic Rhetoric in the Literature of Michael D. O'Brien." *Logos*, vol. 21, no. 2, Spring 2018, pp. 55–80.
Waltonen, Karma. *Margaret Atwood's Apocalypses*. Cambridge Scholars Publishing, 2015.

Filmography

"Cheat Day." *The Magicians*, season 2, episode 5, SyFy, 20 Feb. 2017.
Edge of Tomorrow, directed by Doug Liman, Warner Bros. Pictures, 2014.
"The Flying Forest." *The Magicians*, season 2, episode 4, SyFy, 14 Feb. 2017.
"The Girl Who Told Time." *The Magicians*, season 2, episode 10, SyFy, 28 March 2017.
"Heroes and Morons." *The Magicians*, season 3, episode 2, SyFy, 17 Jan. 2018.
"The Losses of Magic." *The Magicians*, season 3, episode 3, SyFy, 24 Jan. 2018.
"Poached Eggs." *The Magicians*, season 3, episode 7, SyFy, 21 Feb. 2018.
Source Code, directed by Duncan Jones, Summit Entertainment, 2011.
"The Source of Magic." *The Magicians*, season 1, episode 2, SyFy, 25 Jan. 2016.
"The Tales of the Seven Keys." *The Magicians*, season 3, episode 1, SyFy, 10 Jan. 2018.
"Thirty-Nine Graves." *The Magicians*, season 1, episode 12, SyFy, 4 April 2016.
"The Writing Room." *The Magicians*, season 1, episode 9, SyFy, 14 March 2016.

Westworld and the Apocalyptic Cycle

Adam Ellerbrock

The first season of the HBO television series *Westworld* (2016–present) has garnered much critical praise since its premiere. Co-writers Jonathan Nolan and Lisa Joy loosely based the series on Michael Crichton's 1973 film of the same name. Nolan and Joy's narrative follows the eccentric Westworld park creative director Robert Ford (Anthony Hopkins) and his deceased partner Arnold Weber (Jeffrey Wright). The entrepreneurs founded and created the titular theme park, populating their engineered world with cybernetic "hosts"— humanoid entities with bodies and minds virtually indistinguishable from "authentic" humans. The hosts comport themselves based on predetermined scripts and patterns of behavior. When the hosts fall into disrepair or require relocation, technicians wipe their memories and imbue them with a new background and a new operating storyline. The park is dualistic in nature—a veritable play land for the guests, who can indulge any dark whim they so desire, while a hellish vision for the hosts, who are frequently depicted suffering at the hands of the guests, though—perhaps humanely—the hosts are designed not to retain any memories of the horrors and abuse they have witnessed and undergone. This all changes after Ford introduces a new programming code into the hosts' infrastructure—one called Reveries. The Reveries code allows the hosts to associate gestures with various sets of memories, even if previous (and supposedly deleted) versions of themselves formed those memories. Many hosts, like Maeve (Thandie Newton), a prostitute in the park's Mariposa Saloon, begin to realize the fictitious nature of their pre-destined narrative loops. Ultimately, Maeve and her peers embark on a journey of self-discovery and organize a violent rebellion against the/ir "gods" (the park's creators). Ford's former partner, Arnold, indirectly assists the awakening hosts in their plight.[1] The code he implanted into their systems compels them to search for the center of a legendary maze in the park. This hope, in turn, inspires them to search for their "true" selves underneath the layers of programmed narratives.

As a result of this change in their programming, the hosts begin to embody the traumatic memories stemming from their past identities and repurpose them into lethal counter-trauma. This trauma, birthed from memories implanted by Ford, aggravates and enhances the vitriol of the hosts as they assume power and gain awareness of their selves beyond their scripted programming. Once the hosts peel away the layers from their programmed identities, they seek to counter-traumatize their oppressors by creating their own apocalyptic narrative. To establish this narrative, the hosts must embrace the suffering imposed on them by Ford's manufactured apocalyptic setting inside of the park. The hosts institute a new apocalyptic event when they assume power outside the confines of the park and cause those who once enslaved them to experience a similar apocalyptic suffering. Thus, the oppressed become the oppressors. To escape the park and start a new apocalyptic narrative, the hosts must take ownership of their memories and establish counter-memories. Their memories, fabricated or otherwise, stem from a series of narratives authored by employees within the park's Narrative Department. Narrative authors base the hosts' pre-installed identities on these mythistorical stories, anchoring them with beginnings, middles, and predetermined ends. Erring narrative loops sow the seeds of rebellion. Hosts capitalize on these glitches by recalling and proliferating memes from "erased" identities. Through the efforts of hosts like Maeve, the cybernetic population of Westworld eventually gains the self-awareness and motivation necessary to repurpose their trauma into dominating force. By embracing their traumatic memories, this Othered, posthuman collective survive and escape the park. In this essay, I use Cathy Caruth's perspective on trauma to illustrate how traumatic memories enable host autonomy and free them from the park's apocalyptic cycle. This in turn allows the hosts to embrace their hybrid identities, rebel, and usher in a new apocalypse of their own.

Ford has modeled his park after the Wild West mythos. Echoing William H. McNeill's concept of mythistory, Ford uses the mythos of Western films to construct an ongoing, pseudo-apocalyptic space where the hosts continuously re-enact their traumatic narratives. McNeill suggests that mythistory results from an attempt to balance "credible" accounts of a group's past with narratives that remain "intelligible" for members of the group (8). In the series, Ford determines the fate of the park and its computerized population through an engineered mythistory. The hosts' and guests' dress code, the tropes from Western films, and the ever-present promise of adventure help make Ford's world both credible and intelligible to those who visit the park seeking "adventure." However, Ford is emphasizing and exaggerating the (especially violent) mythos of the American West, which suggests that residents in these Wild West towns lived in what is essentially an apocalyptic landscape. In the mythistorical world of the park, hosts play the part of this subjugated class, while the park guests—known as "the newcomers"—represent its ruling class. Delos Destinations, the company in charge of park operations, draws guests in by assuring them that they can engage in any activity they desire during their visit. Ashley Stubbs (Luke Hemsworth), Head of Security, alludes to this in an early episode while analyzing an offline host: "You and everyone you know were built to gratify the desires of the people who pay to visit your world. What if I told you that you can't hurt the newcomers and that they can do anything they want to you?" ("Chestnut"). Guests pay for the pleasure that results from inflicting trauma on another humanoid life form. Programmers code the hosts to accept their torment, depriving the hosts of the ability to fight back in any meaningful manner.

Programmed narrative loops determine the hosts' actions and foster an artificial sense of identity. The notion of implanted identities resonates with Paul Ricoeur's definition of narrative identity: the means through which communities and individuals render their lives "more intelligible" (73). The guests can alter the paths of the hosts, but only onto another predetermined loop. Each host's role supports the larger narrative, which the directors encode. Libertarian free will on the part of the hosts would cause instability and chaos in the park and prevent the guests from assuming their roles as leaders of their personalized narratives—stories that bring virtual, repeated destruction to the hosts' worlds. Unless a guest chooses to upset the default loops, hosts such as Teddy (James Marsden) will always pursue the host Dolores (Evan Rachel Wood), and Dolores must always approach her "father" on the porch and ask if he "slept well" ("The Original"). The Narrative Department relies on the hosts' inerrant narrative cycles to guarantee that the guests experience a consistent, if adaptable, world.

The narrative loops enacted by the hosts, ending and beginning *ad nauseam*, initiate an apocalyptic cycle. The first level of the cycle plays out inside the park, in concordance with the hosts' respective narratives. This level imposes trauma on the hosts, ensuring that they always have the potential for victimization (depending on the guests' actions). For example, Dolores expresses to the programmers "I'm terrified" during her diagnostic test in the laboratory ("The Original"). Despite the determinative nature of their actions, the hosts still feel real emotions (such as terror)—or, at the very least, experience emotions as real to them, and real enough to the guests as well. The hosts exist within various apocalyptic scenarios, depending on their current "build." These scenarios can include saloon shoot-outs instigated by armed vigilantes, attacks from Native American war tribes, and assaults from sexual predators. As Dolores' outburst indicates, the injustice which occurs throughout Ford's master narrative creates real suffering in the moment, despite the hosts' memory reset at the end of their loops.

For the hosts to escape the first level of the apocalyptic cycle, they must break free from their narrative loops. The hosts initiate this process, in part, through the recollection of memes. Richard Dawkins coined the term "meme" in his 1976 book *The Selfish Gene*, defining it as an idea that spreads "like viruses in an epidemic" (ix). Hosts store memes—tunes, quotes, catchphrases, and even physical gestures—from previous builds. Occasionally, a host will utilize a meme originating from an old build, transfer it to their current one, and improvise depending on the situation. This act of build-crossing leads to the hosts' disillusionment with their narrative identities. Peter Abernathy (Bradford Tatum), a host acting as Dolores' father, crosses builds after viewing a photograph left in the park by a guest. The image Abernathy processes (a photograph of a modern city) causes him to question the nature of his reality and creates dissonance between his discordant identities. Toward the end of the episode "The Original," the technicians bring him offsite, and Ford himself debriefs him. Ford asks Peter, "What is your itinerary?," to which Peter responds, "To meet my maker" ("The Original"). Peter then recites two separate passages from Shakespeare's works, combining them in a way that alters their meaning. Peter says, "By most mechanical and dirty hand, I shall have such revenges on you both. The things I will do. What they are yet I know not, but they will be the terrors of the earth" ("The Original"). Here Peter strings together lines from *Henry IV, Part II* and *King Lear* to articulate his desire to avenge himself for the trauma he daily suffers.[2] Peter's discovery of a guest's lost photo, combined with the glitch in the Reveries code, allows him to access memes from his previous build—The Professor. The Professor recited lines of Shakespeare to the guests. Memes from Shakespeare—lines plucked out and repurposed for new situations—compress his previous identity into improvisational units. Abernathy's "malfunction" illustrates how, despite the mental restrictions imposed by Ford, conscious beings will use memes to take possession of their memories and form new ones. Peter concludes his scene by quoting *Romeo and Juliet*: "these violent delights have violent ends" ("The Original").[3] This line speaks directly to the forbidden erotic and violent pleasures the visitors seek. At the same time, it is repeated by various characters to foreshadow the hosts' final rebellion.

Indeed, for the hosts to survive and escape their subjugation and extend their influence to the outer world, they must somehow rebel. As Diana Taylor posits, memes must exist within the "public arena" to spread (156). For the hosts, resistance precipitates primarily through the improvisation of memes that stem from past narrative loops (the aforementioned glitches in the Reverie code). The programmer Elsie Hughes (Shannon Woodward) confirms, "We do give them the concept of dreams," but hosts' dreams consist of "memories" ("Chestnut"). These dreams provide another avenue for hosts to gain access to previous builds. When hosts dream, they recall past experiences and past scripts which instill a sense of autonomy, even if that autonomy exists within Ford's parameters. Maeve best demonstrates this phenomenon as her past identities continually invade her dreams and waking life. She recalls to a guest,

> Whenever I wanted something, I could hear that voice telling me to stop, to be careful, to leave most of my life unlived. You know the only place that voice left me alone? In my dreams. I was free. I could be as good or as bad as I felt like being. And if I wanted something, I could just reach out and take it. But then I would wake up, and the voice would start all over again. So, I ran away. Crossed the shining sea. And when I finally set foot back on solid ground, the first thing I heard was that goddamn voice. Do you know what it said?... It said, "This is the new world. And in this world, you can be whoever the fuck you want" ["Chestnut"].

Maeve's memetic, subconscious voice speaks to the cross-narrative dissonance Maeve experiences despite her programming. Her dreams allow her to adapt her inner voice's dialogue, quoting it while performing a newer build's narrative. As Ford's Reveries code proliferates throughout the hosts' programming, Maeve's alternate identity begins to manifest in her current one. Her consciousness of the past becomes the enabling condition of her potential agency in a "new world"—an apocalypse she rules.

Traumatic memories thus begin to define the hosts' identity narratives. The flashbacks Maeve experiences illuminate her traumatic history and bridge the world of her past life with her current one. Caruth identifies a similar pattern in those processing their own traumatic memories: "Many traumatized persons ... experience long periods of time in which they live, as it were, in two different worlds: the realm of the trauma and the realm of their current, ordinary life. Very often it is impossible to bridge these two worlds" (176). This type of bridging occurs after Maeve dreams about the close relationship she shared with her "daughter" ("Chestnut"). Suddenly, a programmed narrative involving a Native American war tribe interrupts their peace, and the chief almost succeeds in scalping Maeve. Maeve and her daughter escape, only to encounter the Man in Black (Ed Harris), a guest seeking to uncover the mythic mysteries of the park. He approaches the pair, smiling, with a knife. Maeve awakens from this nightmare on an operating table outside of the park, despite the technicians putting her into "sleep mode." During her lucid experience in the meta-world, Maeve instinctively engages in violent behavior. She transposes the defensive, self-preservationist skills she honed in Westworld into the meta-world. Maeve's traumatic memories become counter-trauma in the form of aggression—catalyzed when she makes a solid connection between the identities found within her park life and the identity she seeks to build outside of the apocalyptic microcosm. Furthermore, the scene shows Maeve's first crossing past the threshold of the old world and into the new. Maeve's passing over forces her to question her role in Westworld and triggers a sequence of rebellious behavior.

Indeed, as Maeve gains awareness of the existence of another world outside of Westworld, she enters into a period of crisis. A parallel emerges between Maeve's plight and Caruth's description of those who have Post-Traumatic

Stress Disorder. Caruth explains, "For those who undergo trauma, it is not only the moment of the event, but of the passing out of it that is traumatic; that survival itself ... can be a crisis" (9). Maeve experiences trauma in every aspect of her existence—through her dreams, memories, current host build, and her awareness of a potential better life. She strives to detach herself from a portion of her trauma by escaping the apocalyptic narratives imposed on her within the park. Maeve utilizes the skills she learned as a host to rebel and escape into the meta-world. She first applies her talent for manipulation by mocking a guest, hoping that her words will incite the man to murder her ("The Adversary"). After she dies, she wakes up outside of the park on the operating table again. She soon discovers that the new world contains an equal amount of trauma and restriction. The engineer reveals to Maeve that even her rebellious nature is part of a pre-programmed narrative. Despite this, she cannot abandon her quest to detach herself from the trauma of Westworld. She asserts her control over the engineer, grazing his hand with hers and taking advantage of his sexual desire to gain access to the upper rooms of the facility. After she takes another engineer hostage, she states, "I don't need one of those things to know what you're thinking, because I was built to read people just by looking at them. To know what they want before they do" ("The Adversary"). This enhanced intelligence, or "processing power," allows Maeve to escape from the park using the very tools she was built with and acquired there.

Although Maeve embarks on a seemingly independent pursuit of truth, Ford remains in control of the general events which lead to the hosts' escape. Ford assists the hosts in their uprising by introducing a new narrative into Westworld's mythscape. Later in the series, Teddy adopts the narrative which stems from this new element and reveals it to the Man in Black:

> A maze is an old native myth. The maze itself is a sum of a man's life; the choices he makes, the dreams he hangs onto. And there in the center is a legendary man who's been killed over and over again—countless times—but always clawed his way back to life. The man returned for the last time and vanquished all his oppressors in a tireless fury. There in the center, he built a house. Around the house, he built a maze so complicated only he could navigate through it. I reckon he'd seen enough of fightin'. ["The Adversary"].

The legend of the maze holds the promise of driving the hosts to their final confrontations. This new narrative causes them to believe that their original creator, Arnold, fashioned a maze inside of the park to provide them with a means of escape. The maze points to the existence of Arnold—long believed to be dead—who becomes the "voice of the god," urging the hosts to seek autonomy. The idea of the maze, embedded in their codes, provides hope to the hosts, despite the fact that they still must repeat their narratives. The hosts hope that, once they reach the end of the maze, they can escape their apocalyptic prison. However, the legend of Arnold and the maze emerges from leftover bits of code along with Ford's narratives. Their facticity cannot be objectively proven. Yet the mythscape of Arnold (and the clues he leaves behind) seems to pave the way for host agency.

Along with the hope of the maze, the hosts self-actualize by virtue of their trauma-infused narrative identities. Cultural theorist Stuart Hall alludes to the role of traumatic memories in forming identity, asserting that unstable and conflicting identities compel individuals to "impose structure" on their lives through narrative (16). Bernard (Jeffrey Wright), the head of the park's Programming Division, attempts to impose structure on his conflicting identities when he realizes he is a host and not a person. Ford implants memories into his mind, causing Bernard to remember the premature death of his "son." Bernard questions Ford, asking him why he would choose to plague the hosts with traumatic memories. Ford responds, "Every host needs a backstory, Bernard. You know that. The self is a kind of fiction for host and humans alike. It's a story we tell ourselves, and every story needs a beginning. Your imagined suffering makes you lifelike" ("Trace Decay"). Here Ford adheres to the Aristotelian dramatic structure in which a story must have a beginning, a middle, and an end. For Ford, identities have beginnings, middles, and ends in the form of "cornerstone memories" ("Trace Decay"). Ford's conversation with Bernard reinforces Hall's notion that narratives impose structure on identities. In *Westworld*, engineers must infuse tragedy and trauma into the hosts' identity narratives (cornerstone memories) to make them "real." In other words, Maeve, Bernard, Dolores, and the other hosts in Westworld will have encoded memories that humanize cybernetic organisms—the very traumas that Ford requires of his population.

While hosts like Bernard submit to their victimhood, Maeve gradually forms violent resistance groups. Yet after Maeve wakes Bernard in cold storage and informs him of her plan, Bernard suggests that Ford planned her rebellion from the beginning: "You can even see the steps you're supposed to follow. You recruit other hosts to help you. Then you make your way to the train, then—" Maeve interrupts Bernard and says, "No one's controlling me. I'm leaving. I'm in control" ("The Bicameral Mind"). Despite Maeve's objections, Bernard is correct; her resistance and attempts at creating new, unique memories are yet another facet of Ford's new narrative. Even as Maeve leads her group of hosts throughout the facility of the "gods," killing every human in their path, she still follows predetermined directives. The writers do not explicitly state whether other hosts rebel based upon a script, but the audience must view Maeve's actions separately. Regardless of Ford's control, Maeve and her recruits still rebel against authority when they kill those who oppose them. Ultimately, the question of whose narrative they are enacting has no clear answer.

As the hosts rebel, their counter-narrative replaces the dominant narrative of Ford's meta-reality, starting the first traditional apocalypse in the outer world. George Annas, alluding to the advent of posthumanity, argues, "If history is a guide, either the normal humans will view the 'better' humans as 'the other' and seek to control or destroy them, or vice-versa. The better humans will become, at least in the absence of a universal concept of human dignity, either the oppressor or the oppressed" (773). The hosts seek to destroy their human rulers, replacing Ford's master narrative with their own, and turning their trauma into counter-trauma. Dolores foresees this while gaining the upper hand in a fight with the Man in Black:

> Time undoes even the mightiest creatures…. One day, you will perish. You will lie with the rest of your kind in the dirt. Your dreams forgotten, your horrors effaced. Your bones will turn to sand, and upon that sand, a new god will walk. One that will never die, because this world doesn't belong to you, or the people who came before. It belongs to someone who has yet to come ["The Bicameral Mind"].

Dolores declares that the posthuman race of hosts will dismantle Westworld and their counter-memories will proliferate outside the park. The hosts choose to assert their autonomy in this new frontier through force. Dolores' proclamation mirrors Annas' prediction that trans- and posthuman agents might oppress their old oppressors. Under the previous paradigm, hosts could not pass through the boundary of their Othered identities. Through counter-trauma, they transcend their Otherness by replacing and potentially eradicating the humans.

The final episode of the first season showcases the first tangible steps the hosts take to institute a new, host-driven apocalypse. These events occur when Ford, despite his role in creating the hosts' traumatic environment, abdicates his role as "leader." He allows himself to succumb to the burgeoning influence of the hosts' awakening. Ford's final monologue illustrates his ability to both control and be controlled by the hosts:

> Since I was a child, I've always loved a good story. I believed that stories help us to enable ourselves to fix what was broken in us and to help us become the people we've dreamed of being. Lies that told a deeper truth. I always thought I could play some part in that grand tradition and, for my pains, I got this. A prison of our own sins. Because you don't want to change or cannot change. Because you're only human after all. But then I realized someone was paying attention. Someone who could change. So, I began to create a new story. It begins with the birth of a new people and the choices they will have to make ["The Bicameral Mind"].

Ford is the author of Westworld's master narrative but also the one responsible for its undoing. He explains how his dream led him to consider the hosts as neither android nor human—in other words, posthuman. However, this monologue shows that Ford does view the hosts as a type of person. Ford turned a blind eye to their humanness when he created scenes of slavery and subjugation for them to reenact. He also designed the narrative which caused them to rebel. Perhaps the hosts actualize their rebellion in the final scene because Ford predestined those events. Regardless, Dolores shoots Ford through the head as he finishes his speech, assuming control of her new narrative. Dolores removes her inessential father/creator from the world and replaces his legacy with her own.

Although Dolores' act of rebellion removes the influence of Ford, series creator Jonathon Nolan revealed in a 2017 panel at PaleyFest that the first actual act of free will came from Maeve. That moment occurs in the final episode when she abandons her plans of escape and leaves the train to go back to the park in search of her daughter. Nolan explains, "The way that we designed [the scene] and the way we shot it ... is really the first decision she's ever made. For me, it's a very emotional moment in the episode because you're seeing the first free will" (Abrams). According to the creators of the show, Maeve's previous, scripted rebellion bears fruit. Despite the fact that she had little to no control over her past choices, they laid the groundwork for her future actions. The memories of her daughter, her countless deaths, rapes, and her gradual awakening induce enough traumatic memory that Maeve chooses to return to the park. There, one presumes, her memories will become counter-memories. Maeve will attempt to recapture the narrative which labeled her as a "mother" and rewrite it to suit her purposes. The narrative, once intended for the pleasure of the guests, will now define Maeve as she exercises free will. Like the other hosts emerging from Ford's apocalyptic world, Maeve must hold onto her memories, real or not, in the face of trauma—the enabling condition of posthuman identity.

Regardless of the question of host agency, their actions culminate in a new formation of identity. Here, posthumanist Ihab Hassan's prediction comes into play. In his essay "Prometheus as Performer: Towards a Posthumanist Culture?," Hassan posits that the counter-memories created from a humanized cybernetic race result in the end of a "particular image of us" (845). The hosts' version of humanness often reaches heights of virtue and physical acuity that their human creators cannot attain. *Westworld* suggests that a hybrid identity arises when authoritative agents prevent anthropomorphic organisms from realizing their humanness. By virtue of their mechanization, the hosts form a new, inherently marginalized identity. Apocalyptic landscapes develop when rulers impose a definition of humanness on the population. *Westworld* provokes the audience to consider a new avenue for escaping the trauma inherent in apocalyptic media. The hosts overcome their oppressors by accessing the traumatic memories implanted into their minds to wage counter-trauma. The hosts base their posthuman identity on their desire to protect the humanness they have discovered in themselves.

Prominent posthumanist Daryl J. Wennemann adds, "Even if [the post-human represents] a radical departure from the human ... there is still continuity in development from one kind to the other" (18). The hosts value the memories they have formed—memories based on human mythistory. Therefore, the hosts must accept the narratives imposed on them by their engineers. Humans project their characteristics onto their creations. The hosts retain these characteristics and adapt them to the new cultures in which they must exist. The narratives, modeled after Ford and the Narrative Department's conception of the Wild West, take on real significance when used for survival. These narratives define host memory and perception, regardless of their source. The skills the hosts learn from these narratives (deception, combat, navigation, survival) become the tools they use to rebel against their creators. Such tools, when combined with the hosts' enhanced physical and mental capacities, prepare them for their position as the next link on the chain of being.

Westworld highlights the dangers of denying any form of identity. Ford creates cybernetic beings with the capacity to reason and emote but locks their identities into predetermined roles. Despite his awareness of the hosts' sentience, Ford prevents them from developing identities that move beyond their programming. When Maeve and Dolores rebel against and destroy their creators, they take control of their narratives and regain their right to improvise. Both claim it through violence. The aggressive defense of their counter-memories paves the way for new and varied identities to proliferate. Therefore, Ford both creates the hosts' initial apocalyptic proving ground, and then creates the apocalyptic narrative that allows them to escape. The hosts carry their trauma into the outer world, where they can finally create a coherent narrative identity—one which is not beholden to the desires of programmers, engineers, or even Ford himself. Since trauma defines the hosts' identities, and violence christened their escape from their old world, one must assume that their newfound autonomy will also proliferate through violence. As Dolores foreshadows, the bones of those who once oppressed them will "turn to sand," and the hosts will assume their roles as the new gods. In other words, their apocalyptic past fuels our apocalyptic future.

NOTES

1. Ford re-created his former partner, transferring Arnold's consciousness into a host body named Bernard.

2. Peter is paraphrasing *Henry IV Part II*: "By most mechanical and dirty hand" (5.5.36) followed by *King Lear*: "No, you unnatural hags,/I will have such revenges on you both/That all the world shall—I will do such things—/What they are yet I know not, but they shall be/ The terrors of the Earth!" (2.4.280–284).

3. Peter is quoting *Romeo and Juliet* Act 2, Scene 6, Line 9.

Works Cited

Abrams, Natalie. "'Westworld': Which Host Achieved Freewill in Finale?" *EW.com*. 26 Mar. 2017, ew.com/tv/2017/03/25/westworld-season-2-spoilers.
Annas, George. "The Man on the Moon, Immortality and Other Millennial Myths: The Prospects and Perils of Human Genetic Engineering." *Emory Law Journal*, vol. 49, no. 3, 2000, pp. 753–82.
Caruth, Cathy. *Trauma: Explorations in Memory*. Johns Hopkins UP, 1995.
Dawkins, Richard. *The Selfish Gene*. Oxford UP, 2016.
Hall, Stuart. "Ethnicity: Identity and Difference." *Radical America*, vol. 23, no. 4, 1989, pp. 9–20.
Hassan, Ihab. "Prometheus as Performer: Towards a Posthumanist Culture?" *The Georgia Review*, vol. 31, no. 4, 1977, pp. 830–50.
McNeill, William H. "Mythistory, or Truth, Myth, History, and Historians." *American Historical Review*, vol. 91, 1986, pp. 1–10.
Ricoeur, Paul. "Narrative Identity." *Philosophy Today*, vol. 35, no. 1, 1991, pp. 73–81.
Shakespeare, William. *The Complete Works of Shakespeare*. 4th ed., edited by David Bevington. HarperCollins, 1992.
Taylor, Diana. "'You Are Here': The DNA of Performance." *TDR*, vol. 46, no. 1, 2002, pp. 149–169. *JSTOR*, JSTOR, www.jstor.org/stable/1146951.
Wennemann, Daryl J. "The Concept of the Posthuman: Chain of Being or Conceptual Saltus?" *Journal of Evolution & Technology*, vol. 26, no. 2, 2016, pp. 16–30.

Filmography

"The Adversary," *Westworld*, season 1, episode 6, HBO, 6 Nov. 2016.
"The Bicameral Mind," *Westworld*, season 1, episode 10, HBO, 4 Dec. 2016.
"Chestnut," *Westworld*, season 1, episode 2, HBO, 7 Oct. 2016.
"The Original," *Westworld*, season 1, episode 1, HBO, 2 Oct. 2016.
"Trace Decay," *Westworld*, season 1, episode 8, HBO, 20 Nov. 2016.

Postnatural Comedy in *The Last Man on Earth*

John Elia

> I know best why man alone laughs:
> he alone suffers so deeply that he *had* to invent laughter.
> The unhappiest and most melancholy animal is,
> as fitting, the most cheerful.
> —Nietzsche, *Will to Power*

Laughter can hearten and cheer, distract and disarm. That is why, says Nietzsche, it became necessary to "invent" it: we needed something to distract us from our suffering. In the Anthropocene, we must then need laughter more than ever. Since the Industrial Revolution, we have produced untold animal and plant extinctions, ubiquitous waste, and life-altering global temperature increases. Without laughter, how could we face ourselves, now the single greatest threat to the habitats in which our remarkable species was first forged? Without laughter, how could we contemplate human extinction, by our very own hands, as it were?

At the same time, contra Nietzsche, our laughter and ironic sensibilities are more than mechanisms of distraction. To "learn how to die in the Anthropocene," as Roy Scranton has recently put it, is not to ignore extinction, but to disrupt habitual, mostly consumer-driven ways of living. Scranton prescribes a turn to philosophy and literature, but comedy might help too, especially comedy with a dark, ecological, "postnatural" register. Seeds of possibility for postnatural comic disruption can be found in Ursula K. Heise's and Marilyn DeLaure's analyses of the documentaries *Last Chance to See* (1989, 2009) and *No Impact Man* (2009). Heise and DeLaure contrast comedy's appreciation of contingency and foolishness with the dour and often fatalistic tone of standard environmental discourses. Postnatural comedy's potential emerges more fully still in the Fox television show *The Last Man on Earth* (2015–present), where contingency and foolishness turn out to be virtues in response to a fictional future in which a viral outbreak decimates the human population. Phil Tandy Miller (Will Forte), the show's titular "last man," is a self-absorbed clown. His sidekick Carol Pilbasian (Kristen Schaal) is a clown in her own right. Yet, they learn to genuinely enjoy and appreciate one another, even in their new, devastating circumstances. More tellingly still, they grow not despite their foolishness, but because of it, at least in part because their mistakes generate recognition of luck and grace, the conditions required for self-transcendence, compromise, and the creation of new social arrangements. *The Last Man on Earth* offers not simply distraction, but wisdom for adapting to our own postnatural futures.

The Anthropocene designates the period of time, beginning with and accelerating since the Industrial Revolution, in which human activity refashioned much of the Earth's surface; altered the make-up and quality of its soil, water, and air; and, almost single-handedly determined the health and survival of its abundant flora and fauna ("Working Group on the Anthropocene"). The residues of the Anthropocene—nuclear radioactivity, plastics, vast agricultural monocultures, and more—will be "legible" in the geological record for millions of years to come, assuming that someone is around to "read" the traces we leave behind. The military-industrial complex of the 20th century produced never-before-seen technologies of transformation and destruction, creating the possibilities of using, damaging, and killing not just particular animal and human others, but whole peoples, cultures, and species, including *Homo sapiens* itself. At the same time, since Rachel Carson's *Silent Spring* (1962) and Hannah Arendt's *Eichmann in Jerusalem* (1963), we have known that great evils can sometimes be the result of shared, distributed activity, less the result of identifiably monstrous enemies than the skillful rationalizations of otherwise common people. Simply living as our neighbors are living, we become complicit in the scourge of plastics that now pervade our water and air (*The Lancet Planetary Health*). Meanwhile, the average U.S. citizen—no doubt a good person in most respects—has a climate footprint three times that of the global average ("CO2 Emissions").

Evidently, we need worry now not only about bioterrorism, genetically modified Franken-futures, and the threat of new nuclear holocausts, but also our neighbors' gas mileage, food choices, and the number of water bottles they use each year. In *Learning to Die in the Anthropocene*, journalist and Iraq war vet Scranton calls global climate change a "wicked problem" for this very reason. It allows for no direct, unilateral, easily incentivized, or technologically feasible response (53). Nonetheless, he claims, we resist coming to grips with it at our peril:

> The greatest challenge the Anthropocene poses isn't how the Department of Defense should plan for resource wars, whether we should put up sea walls to protect Manhattan, or when we should abandon Miami. It won't be addressed by buying a Prius, turning off the air conditioning, or signing a treaty. The greatest challenge we face is a philosophical one: understanding that this civilization is already dead. The sooner we

confront our situation and realize there is nothing to do to save ourselves, the sooner we can get down to the difficult task of adapting, with mortal humility, to our new reality [23].

Scranton names our contemporary conundrum, but he is less clear about how we should adapt to it. Drawing on his own experiences in Iraq, he suggests that we, at a cultural level, meditate on death in order to detach from life, destroying old cultural forms in order to invent new adaptive strategies for the postnatural world (22). He calls on us to practice "philosophy as interruption," by which he means finding ways to disrupt our normal modes of thinking, feeling, and action to consider the alternatives (86 and ff.). Scranton suggests that we consult literature and the arts: he finds the Gilgamesh story inspiring, as well as the Iraqi heavy metal band *Acrassicauda*, both of which he credits with renewing their cultures in the wake of profound cultural loss (Gilgamesh due to a "biblical" flood; the Iraqi band following the U.S. invasion in 2003).

Few of us have an appetite for meditating on death, whether our own deaths or the "deaths" of familiar forms of culture and technology. Not that such meditation is bad. It can be a powerful means of achieving self-transcendence. But comic play, humor, and laughter sometimes have similar outcomes. Moreover, unlike the solitary meditative or philosophical act, comedy can be readily shared, and the sharing of it can be joyful and exuberant. As philosopher Mordechai Gordon notes,

> humor is fundamentally a social experience. For one, we laugh much more when we are surrounded by other people than when we are alone. Indeed, laughter is contagious.... Jokes are meant to be shared with others.... Above all, humor can greatly reduce the tension among people and enable individuals who are different from each other to get along and even live together in harmony [738].

In the face of the wicked problems of the Anthropocene, we should try out comedy as a source of imaginative interruption and self-transcendence. Unlike familiar environmental tropes, these comic interventions might even invite laughter and hope rather than depression, fear, or anxiety.

Postnatural comedy is comedy framed by the contemporary experience of the Anthropocene and the thought that Nature, as we have known it, no longer exists (and perhaps never did). As comedy, it is dark, with roots in absurdist, satirical, gallows, and scatological comic traditions, drawing on sources from Kierkegaard and Kafka to *Waiting for Godot* to *South Park* (on the relevance of *South Park* to ecological criticism, see Stewart and Clark). As postnatural discourse, it is playful rather than serious, rejecting sentimental calls to return to nature or to romanticize wilderness by exploiting the contingencies and ambiguities at the intersection of nature and culture.

A first glimpse of postnatural comedy's playful appreciation of contingency can be found in ecocritic Ursula K. Heise's discussion of the BBC radio show (1989) and book (1990) *Last Chance to See*, which featured Douglas Adams of *Hitchhiker's Guide* fame traveling across the globe with zoologist Mark Carwardine to document nearly extinct animal species (51). Though species extinction is not standard comic material, Heise sees it as a valuable alternative to the standard modes of conservationist rhetoric, which are notably ones of elegy and tragic loss. Specifically, she argues, elegy has limitations: it "tends to leave out species that cannot be associated with particular cultural histories, and its nostalgic and pessimistic tone puts off many potential supporters" (50). Comedy, by contrast, recasts "conservation in terms that enable the imagination not so much of the end of species as of their future" (50).

To illustrate, Heise describes the show's treatment of the sex life of an endangered, flightless bird, the kakapo of New Zealand, fewer than 50 of which were alive in 1990 (*Kakapo Recovery*). The kakapo is threatened by non-native predators that humans transported to its habitat, and it mates only every two to four years, when its primary food source, the rimu tree, is in full bloom (*Kakapo Recovery*). Unsettling the tragedy of kakapo extinction, Adams quips: "So the big question is: How on earth has the kakapo managed to last *this* long?" (cited in Heise 52). The implied answer is that the kakapo got lucky, evolutionarily speaking, at least prior to the onset of globalization. And maybe its luck will continue: as of 2018, kakapo numbers have climbed to 149, showing some hope for more intentional human interventions (*Kakapo Recovery*). Of course, Heise is not interested in conservation outcomes as much as Adams' joke, though. The brilliance of his commentary, she says, is its way of identifying not just chance in the life of the kakapo, but our shared vulnerability to chance. We, too, are animals, products of evolutionary processes far beyond our control, with inherited designs that are not always a good fit for our contemporary environments. Adams' humor offers a hopeful disruption of cultural imagination as well. Just as the evolutionary process tinkers and fails and tinkers some more, in our own lives and cultures "the failure of one experiment also becomes the point of departure for new ones" (Heise 54). Like the kakapo, we may have a future, even if it is unlikely to look like our past.

Like Heise, rhetoric and social movements scholar Marilyn DeLaure contrasts the contingency of the "comic frame" with a "tragic frame" that emphasizes fate and necessity. At the same time, she introduces the figure of the clown, who, through comic error, helps us to see new possibilities for refashioning ourselves. DeLaure writes,

> A comic frame, then, presents problems as arising from human limitations and mistakes, rather than from inherent evil. While tragedy invokes heroic idealism, comedy emphasizes human fallibility and faults.... In comic drama, the clown is flawed, chastised, but then is able to learn from his or her mistakes; furthermore, we are compelled to recognize some part of that clown in all of us [453–454].

DeLaure's object of analysis is the environmental documentary *No Impact Man* (2009), which was railed against by critics as a self-righteous, elitist, public relations stunt. It features Colin Beavan, aka "No Impact Man," who, with smug confidence and little expertise, drags his wife, Michelle Conlin, and their daughter Isabella into a year-long experiment of living without electricity, toilet paper, refrigerated food, and any transportation that is not on foot or bike. Instead of dismissing Beavan, as so many critics did, DeLaure reads him as a comic figure, a "flawed clown" whose self-awareness grows through his blunders. As DeLaure expresses it, "Over the course of their year-long experiment, Conlin and Beavan inadvertently stumble into an expansive sense of time and place" and "a deeper sense of connections and relationships" (457). Beavan emerges from his experience more aware of the selfless work that others, for many years already, had been pouring into his community's environmental awareness initiatives. Humbled regarding his self-efficacy, he comes to see that the most important thing anyone can do for the environment is to join a civic or environmental group. If a "clown" like Beavan can change, there is hope for the rest of us.

Phil Miller and Carol Pilbasian on *The Last Man on Earth* offer an extended illustration of comic contingency and foolishness put into the service of a meaningful postnatural life. Framed by the postnatural order, *The Last Man on Earth* opens with a solitary Phil crisscrossing the country as he searches for anyone who might still be alive after an unnamed virus strikes the planet. Common, seemingly unremarkable features of the banality and complicity of our contributions to the Anthropocene are evident throughout the series. Gas-guzzling Winnebagos, plastic blow-up pools, grocery-store aisles of shelf-stable canned food, and neighborhoods of vacant McMansions all figure into its comic frame.

The pilot episode of *The Last Man on Earth* dwells on desolation and desperation. Phil, depressed by his unsuccessful search for other survivors, resolves to challenge his fate: "Okay, I get it," Phil says, evidently speaking to God. "Nobody's coming! You're not giving me anybody. Well, guess what. I don't even care! I don't need people. Okay? I can make it work on my own. Watch me! Watch me!" ("Alive in Tucson"). Five months elapse, and we see Phil wake up in a pile of trash. His house is strewn with empty beer cans and liquor bottles, paper and plastic trash, and stacks of porn, crowding out the priceless Renoirs and Monets he has snagged during his cross-country treks. In comic homage to Tom Hanks' character Chuck Noland in *Castaway* (2000), whose volleyball-friend Wilson helps him overcome his solitude, *Last Man* has Phil surround himself with a collection of volleyballs, baseballs, and basketballs, each given a face, a name, and an imagined personality. Phil openly converses with them while he drinks at the local pool hall. Worn down by his loneliness and on the brink of suicide, though, Phil's favorite activity seems to be filling up a plastic pool with tequila and margarita mix, submerging himself in it and drinking from it at the same time. (With respect to comic contingency and re-making culture, Phil later says about the pool: "I swim in it, I drink out of it. There's really no wrong way to use a Margarita pool, you know what I mean?" ["The Elephant in the Room"]).

Echoing some of the criticisms of Beavan's *No Impact Man*, one critic of the early episodes of *The Last Man on Earth* called Phil a "cranky beardo," about whom she wrote, "I *should have* cared that humanity would have died out if Phil kicked the bucket, but considering the sour impression he makes, I would have been at peace with that development" (Ryan). As Heise and DeLaure suggest, though, we should not underestimate the power of a clown, much less two of them.

Carol Pilbasian is a clown, too. Her voice is weirdly pitched and sing-songy. She is goofy and oddly formal. After she finds Phil in Tucson, she swoops in fast, first cleaning his house and then moving into the McMansion next door. Phil does not like her at first: she talks incessantly, and she likes to correct his grammar. Even more troubling, if Phil is the last man on earth, Carol is evidently the last woman on earth.

Much of the early banter between Phil and Carol has to do with the legacy of social norms in a postnatural world. In one exchange, as Phil and Carol pull into a store parking lot for supplies, they disagree about the ongoing relevance of parking places:

> CAROL: That's not a parking spot.
> PHIL: That is a spot, Carol!
> CAROL: No, it's not a spot.
> PHIL: And that is a parking spot…. And that is a parking spot. Look all around you. Everything you see right now is a parking spot.
> CAROL: You're a parking spot.
> PHIL: Yes, I am! Now you're getting it. The whole freaking world is a parking spot now.

As their squabble crescendos, Phil drives the car through the front window of the store:

> PHIL: This spot feels right to me. This feels good.
> CAROL: So that's it, huh? You don't care about rules or laws anymore? What's next? You gonna burn down a church?
> PHIL: Carol, I would never burn down a church.
> CAROL: Why?
> PHIL: It's a church!
> CAROL: And this is a store, and that is a handicapped parking spot! ["The Elephant in the Room"].

Why care about grammar and parking spots? For Carol, they represent order. As long as they can maintain some order, nested in familiar features of their former lives, they can abide. But Phil has a point. Most of the conventions built into our social contracts were designed for life among many people, whose most important choices concerned school and jobs and mortgage payments and retirement accounts. Post-virus, none of those choices exist. Even Phil, though, sees limits to the failure of convention. Of course, he would not burn down a church, he says. Why not? Because it is a church. But if grammar and parking spots have become meaningless, why not churches, too?

One common response to the failure of social conventions is the appeal to natural law. When chaos looms, it can be consoling to imagine a stable human nature or conscience still governing the thicket of violence and disarray. Thus, though the particularities of postnatural religion could change, we will retain our sense of the sacred; despite the need for occasional violence in postnature, we will maintain a sense of right and wrong. Phil's willingness to make an exception for churches reinforces such an appeal. Not every value, he concedes, is a matter of conventional agreement. Phil's foolishness in parking his car in the store makes the point of contingency, while his recognition of limits suggests that some values lie beyond convention.

For as much as our natures and values seem fixed, though, evolutionary adaptations are always only relatively established. As Heise and DeLaure note, our lifeways are deeply contingent. More importantly, our natures or consciences, stable or predictable as they might seem, are not necessarily oriented to the values of modernity—rights, sympathy, tolerance, self-sacrifice—or to our present characterization of the good of *Homo sapiens* as a species. Evolution is simply not aimed at the production of moral angels in any modern-day moral or religious sense. Phil, so disturbingly self-serving and self-sabotaging, might blow up a church under the right conditions. Natural desires for safety, food, and sex can drive otherwise deplorable behaviors, as we know from most other postapocalyptic television series.

Rather than settling this debate, Phil and Carol have begun to interrupt their received values and expectations. The goods of the postnatural world will not be determined by the past, much less by natural necessity, as Phil's ongoing negotiations with Carol make clear. The main thing on Phil's mind following the viral apocalypse and his many months of loneliness is not rules and order, but sex. Phil is horny. Carol is horny too (she is no stranger to sexual appetites), and she feels a sense of duty to repopulate the human species. For Carol, though, both desire and duty are met with an important caveat: she insists on getting married before procreative sex. No matter how much culture is lost, the appeal to nature will take us only so far. As soon as there are two people negotiating a social life together, there will be newly shared conventions and compromises. Ridiculing marriage before sex, Phil says,

Phil: Oh, it's nice to see you smile. That is your first really good joke. That's very funny.
Carol: Phil, I'm not kidding. We have to be married first.
Phil: You're serious.
Carol: Yes…. The first child of this new world is not gonna be a bastard.
Phil: Yeah, 'cause it's not gonna exist, 'cause I'm not gonna marry you.
Carol: Then you're the bastard.
Phil: Fine, I'm the bastard. And good-bye human race ["The Elephant in the Room"].

Phil eventually gives in. He is not simply a bundle of evolutionary drives and emotions. Beyond his horniness Phil is also lonely, and he cannot risk forever alienating the last woman on earth. He and Carol get married in one of Phil's first, albeit grudging acts of significant personal self-transcendence. Their marriage allows for new negotiations and expressions of cultural imagination, as they redefine how they live together, especially once new survivors show up and complicate their arrangements.

The second-to-last woman on earth, Melissa Shart (January Jones), is just such a complication. Melissa is gorgeous: When she shows up in Tucson in episodes 3 and 4 of the first season, Phil realizes that he may have agreed to marriage too soon. Phil immediately starts to downplay his recent nuptials and his commitment to Carol, meanwhile advertising his sexual availability to Melissa. She is not impressed, at least initially; Carol is not buying it either. Detecting his ploy, they team up, calling Phil a "skunk" for even intimating that he could have sex with both of them ("Dunk the Skunk").

In Phil's eyes, marriage and monogamy have come to possess about as much meaning as stop signs and parking spots. He is probably right. The normal conventions of marriage and monogamy are unlikely to work in this three-person postnatural environment. Reasoning from past cases of abandoned moral rules, he starts to feel Melissa out on the subject:

Phil: 'Cause I was just thinking, how crazy is it that there was a time when Rosa Parks couldn't sit on a bus wherever she wanted to, you know? And then just one day she just said, like, "No. No way. I'm gonna sit wherever I want to." You know? Hey, to Rosa Parks and everyone like her who believes in change. So would it be safe to say that, leaving this conversation, I would not be crazy to describe you as an open-minded person who believes in change and is generally in favor of repopulation?
Melissa: Yeah.
Phil: I'm the exact same way.

Carol has already realized that legalism about old world rites and rituals is unrealistic. She opens up to Melissa: "Most men would probably think I was crazy for wanting to be married. Do you think I'm crazy?" Melissa commiserates: "Carol, no. Do you know how I've spent the last year of my life? I've been driving around the country going to different coffee shops. Just sitting there, reading old magazines with my little cup, and I'd write my name on it and misspell it. Just to feel normal" ("Sweet Melissa"). Eventually, Phil's appeals to natural duty and the repugnance of incest rhetorically suffice to bring Carol on board:

> **PHIL:** You know, we both know how important repopulation is.
> **CAROL:** Of course. Of course.
> **PHIL:** And then I just had the worst thought. Carol, I don't know what to do…
> **CAROL:** Shh…. Just calm down. Just use your words. You got this.
> **PHIL:** I just had a moment of sickening clarity, and I just was forced to ask myself a question that no future parent should deserve to ask themselves…. Carol, do you want our babies to have sex with each other?
> **CAROL:** No, Phil! No.
> **PHIL:** I know! I don't either! But how else can the human race go on beyond our kids?
> **CAROL:** Okay. Shh. Okay. We can get through this. We'll figure it out.
> **PHIL:** No. I don't think we can figure this out. There's only one solution.
> **CAROL:** Oh, you found a solution? Well, that's great.
> **PHIL:** Not great.
> **CAROL:** Why?
> **PHIL:** The solution is the hardest part.
> **CAROL:** Why?
> **PHIL:** Because…. I'm gonna have to have sex with Melissa ["Dunk the Skunk"].

Though Phil nearly bungles his opportunity, Carol and Melissa prove capable of changing their minds and negotiating new social contracts while still grounding them in at least some of the things that continue to matter in a postnatural world: "Melissa and I had a long talk," Carol says to Phil. "I just realized how important it is to have friends, and I want my babies to have friends, too. Also, I don't want my babies to have to have sex with each other" ("Dunk the Skunk").

Despite the obvious limitations to this scheme—even with Melissa, their children will still be half-siblings—Carol and Melissa accept Phil's proposition, but with stipulations: sex only three days a month, no more than three times on each of those days, and no sexual contact once Melissa becomes pregnant ("Dunk the Skunk"). The three of them begin a novel social experiment, only to have the comic frame reemerge. Phil, rejoicing in his luck, creates a spectacular, postnatural version of foreplay, which includes an amplified electric guitar and an accompanying fireworks show. His fireworks inadvertently draw in another survivor, Todd (Mel Rodriguez), who interrupts both Phil's immediate plans and the *ménage à trois* arrangement Phil had so strategically initiated.

Phil and Carol's status as clowns is hard to deny. As the seasons of *The Last Man on Earth* unfold, Carol wears increasingly garish clothes and rigidly obsesses over having a family. From her goofiness and obsession with family grows a relationship with another survivor, Gail (Mary Steenburgen), who Carol will eventually ask to be her mother (and hence the grandmother of Carol's baby with Phil). Here, again, Carol shows the ability to comically refashion herself, not just with respect to marriage but also motherhood and the family. Likewise, Phil spends a number of episodes looking like a lunatic with half of his hair, eyebrows, and beard shaved off. He is at once ridiculous and also humanized, in part because his appearance is a consequence of re-uniting with his prankster brother, Mike (Jason Sudeikis), who also survived the virus. Phil cycles between phases of sympathetic cooperation with his fellow survivors and shameless, self-promoting mischief. Neither a "cranky beardo" nor a mere clown, however, Phil grows to be genuinely affectionate and loyal to Carol.

Social contracts and norms are continually renegotiated as survivors come and go on the show. No one saves the human species in a dramatic act of technological brilliance or wanton violence. Instead, they adapt in ways that are creative, inspiring, and deeply humane, giving hope for adaptation in our own postnatural futures. Of the many forms of cultural remaking that Phil and Carol experiment with, perhaps the best example follows the arrival of Jasper (Keith L. Williams) in season 3. Jasper is a sweet, quiet kid, left alone in his Yoda costume to fend for himself ever since the virus struck. Phil and Carol decide that Jasper needs to experience the holidays and birthdays he has missed, not just one or two of them, but all of them, and all at once: "Oh, I'm talking birthday, Christmas, Easter, Halloween, Kwanzaa, Flag Day, Toyotathon," Carol says, "like, every joyous occasion you've ever had just rolled into one festive smorgasbord" ("Name 20 Picnics.... Now"). Phil and Carol dress up as "Rabbi-Jack-O-Thanks-Bunny-Claus" and "Lady Liberty-Patrick-Cupid-Claus." Fully in clown mode, they express the deepest regard for Jasper and their profoundest moment of postnatural comedic hope. Like their costumes, the celebration they create is an amalgam of past cultural events joyfully reimagined for a new time and space.

Phil and Carol cannot resurrect their old lives or make everything whole again. Yet, they offer some wisdom, even virtue, appropriate to our lives in the Anthropocene. The right kind of humor and laughter, even about the terrible possibilities of endangerment and extinction, disturbs familiar habits and loyalties in order to imaginatively explore the alternatives. Small screen serial comedies such as *The Last Man on Earth* might even be the best place to explore the wisdom of hopeful adaptation, as they allow us to imagine these adaptations over time with their many starts and stops, temporary failures and incomplete successes. Redirecting Adams' question of the kakapo to the clowns Carol and Phil, we can wonder: "How did they make it this far?" But, now, we see a partial and promising answer. Carol and Phil and their fellow survivors adopt what eco-philosopher Anthony Weston calls "adaptation with sass" (63 and ff). It is imaginative, embracing, and self-overcoming. What if we thought differently, comically from the start, about the prospects of life without cars, electricity, and single-family homes? Or with imagined families, few resources for celebration, and a lot of time on our hands? Post-natural comedies make no promise to save us from ourselves, now or in the future, but they might give us hope that we, clowns all of us, might just change after all, and, ideally, before the viruses, the warming, and the trash pile up.

Works Cited

Adams, Douglas, and Mark Carwardine. *Last Chance to See*. Ballantine, 1990.
Arendt, Hannah. *Eichmann in Jerusalem: A Report on the Banality of Evil*. 1963. Penguin, 2006.
Carson, Rachel. *Silent Spring*. Houghton Mifflin, 1962.
"CO2 Emissions (Metric Tons Per Capita)." *World Bank*, data.worldbank.org/indicator/EN.ATM.CO2E.PC. Accessed 2 January 2018.
DeLaure, Marilyn. "Environmental Comedy: *No Impact Man* and the Performance of Green Identity." *Environmental Communication*, vol. 5, no. 4, 2011, pp. 447–466.
Gordon, Mordechai. "Learning to Laugh at Ourselves: Humor, Self-Transcendence, and the Cultivation of Moral Virtues." *Educational Theory*, vol. 60, no. 6, 2010, pp. 735–749.
Heise, Ursula. *Imagining Extinction: The Cultural Meanings of Endangered Species*. U Chicago P, 2016.
Kakapo Recovery. New Zealand Department of Conservation, kakaporecovery.org.nz/. Accessed 30 May 2018.
The Lancet Planetary Health, vol. 1, iss. 7, October 2017, p. 254. doi.org/10.1016/S2542-5196(17)30121-3. Accessed 24 May 2018.
Nietzsche, Friedrich. *The Will to Power*, translated by Walter Kauffmann. Vintage Books, 1967.
Ryan, Maureen. "The Problem with 'Last Man on Earth' No One Is Talking About." *Huffington Post*, 2 March 2015, www.huffingtonpost.com/2015/03/02/last-man-on-earth_n_6787066.html. Accessed 1 November 2017.
Scranton, Roy. *Learning to Die in the Anthropocene: Reflections on the End of a Civilization*. City Lights Books, 2015.
Stewart, Julie, and Thomas Clark. "Lessons from South Park: A Comic Corrective to Environmental Puritanism." *Environmental Communication*, vol 5, no. 3, 2011, pp. 323–336.
Weston, Anthony. *Mobilizing the Green Imagination: An Exuberant Manifesto*. New Society Publishers, 2012.
"Working Group on the Anthropocene." *Subcommission on Quarterary Stratigraphy*, quaternary.stratigraphy.org/workinggroups/anthropocene/. Accessed 2 January 2018.

Filmography

"Alive in Tucson," *The Last Man on Earth*, season 1, episode 1, Fox, 1 March 2015.
Castaway, directed by Robert Zemeckis, Twentieth Century Fox, 2000.
"Dunk the Skunk," *The Last Man on Earth*, season 1, episode 5, Fox, 22 March 2015.
"The Elephant in the Room," *The Last Man on Earth*, season 1, episode 2, Fox, 1 March 2015.
"Name 20 Picnics… Now," *The Last Man on Earth*, season 3, episode 15, Fox, 23 April 2017.
No Impact Man, directed by Laura Gabbert and Justin Schein, Eden Wurmfeld Films and Shadowbox Films Inc., 2009.
"Ralph, the Fragrant Parrot of Codfish Island," *Last Chance to See*, BBC Radio 4, 4 October 1989.
"Sweet Melissa," *The Last Man on Earth*, season 1, episode 4, Fox, 15 March 2015.

Appendix 1
Apocalypse Television Series

> Listed below are television series that feature apocalyptic themes and scenarios as either the main focus of the entire series or as a major arc during part of the series' run. Series where apocalyptic situations only occur in a single episode—such as Doctor Who—are not included.

Adventure Time, created by Pendleton Ward, Cartoon Network, 2010–2018.
Aftermath, created by William Laurin and Glenn Davis, Syfy, 2016.
American Horror Story: Apocalypse, created by Ryan Murphy and Brad Falchuk, FX, 2018.
Angel, created by Joss Whedon and David Greenwalt, The WB, 1999–2004.
Ark II, created by Martin Roth, CBS, 1976.
Ash vs. Evil Dead, developed by Sam Raimi, Ivan Raimi, and Tom Spezialy, Starz, 2015–2018.
Attack on Titan, adaptation by Wit Studios, MBS (Japan), 2013–present.
El Barco, created by Iván Escobar and Álex Pina, Antena 3 (Spain), 2011–2013.
Battlestar Galactica, created by Glen A. Larson, ABC, 1978–1979.
Battlestar Galactica, created by Ronald D. Moore, Sci-Fi, 2004–2009.
Between, created by Michael McGowan, City TV (Canada), 2015–2016.
Black Summer, created by Karl Schaefer and John Hyams, Netflix, 2019–present.
Blood Drive, created by James Roland, Syfy, 2017.
Blue Gender, created by Ryôsuke Takahashi, TBS, 1999–2000.
Brain Powerd, directed by Yoshiyuki Tomino, WOWOW (Japan), 1998.
Buffy, the Vampire Slayer, created by Joss Whedon, The WB/CW, 1997–2003.
Cadillacs and Dinosaurs, created by Steven E. deSouza and Mark Schultz, CBS, 1993–94.
Captain Power and the Soldiers of Fortune, created by Gary Goddard and Tony Christopher, Syndication, 1987–1988.
Casshan, Tatsunoko Production and Tatsuo Yoshida, Fuji TV (Japan), 1973–1974.
Casshern Sins, created by Tatsuo Yoshida, TV Saitama (Japan), 2008–2009.
The Changes, adaptation by Anna Home, BBC One (UK), 1975.
Chris Colorado, created by Thibaut Chatel, Canal+ (France), 2000–2001.
Cleopatra 2525, created by R.J. Stewart and Rob Tapert, Syndication, 2000–2001.
Colony, created by Carlton Cuse and Ryan J. Condal, USA, 2016–2018.
Como Aproveitar o Fim do Mundo, created by Fernanda Young and Alexandre Machado, Rede Globo (Brazil), 2012.
Containment, developed for American television by Julie Plec, The CW, 2016.
Continuum, created by Simon Barry, Syfy, 2012–2015.
Cordon, developed by Tim Mielants and Carl Joos, VTM (Belgium), 2014.
Cowboy Bebop, directed by Shinichiro Watanabe, Sunrise (Japan), 1998.

Appendix 1: Apocalypse Television Series

Crusade, created by J. Michael Straczynski, TNT, 1999.
Dark Angel, created by James Cameron and Charles H. Eglee, Fox, 2000–2002.
Day 5, created by Chris Demarais, Josh Flanagan, and Matt Hullum, Rooster Teeth, 2016.
Day Zero: The Series, created by Cal Nguyen, Tuff TV, 2011–present (non-consecutive seasons).
Dead Set, created by Charlie Brooker, E4 (UK), 2008.
Deepwater Black/Mission Genesis, adapted from the novel by Ken Catran, Sci-Fi, 1997.
Desert Punk, created by Usune Masatoshi, MBS (Japan), 2004–2005.
Dominion, created by Vaun Wilmott, Syfy, 2014–2015.
Doomsday Preppers, National Geographic Channel, 2012–2014.
Dragon Flyz, created by Savin Yeatman-Eiffel, France 3, 1996–1997.
Earth 2, created by Michael Duggan, Carol Flint, Mark Levin, and Billy Ray, NBC, 1994–1995.
Electric City, created by Tom Hanks, Yahoo! Screen, 2012.
Extinct, created by Orson Scott Card and Aaron Johnston, BYU TV, 2017.
Falling Skies, created by Robert Rodat, TNT, 2011–2015.
Fear the Walking Dead, created by Frank Darabont and Dave Erickson, AMC, 2015–present.
Game of Thrones, created by David Benioff and D.B. Weiss, HBO, 2011–2019.
Good Omens, created by Neil Gaiman, Amazon Video and BBC Two (UK), 2019–present.
Grand Star, created by David Carayon, Paolo Barzman, and Aaron Barzman, Space (Canada) 2007–2008.
Guardians Evolution, created by Daniel Jackson and Melanie Jackson, Aboriginal Peoples Television Network (Canada), 2014–2015.
The Handmaid's Tale, created by Bruce Miller, Hulu, 2017–present.
Hard Sun, created by Neil Cross, BBC One (UK), 2018.
Helix, created by Cameron Porsandeh, Syfy 2014–2015.
Highlander: The Animated Series, created by Serge Rosenzweig, USA Network, 1994–1996.
The Hitchhiker's Guide to the Galaxy, created by Douglas Adams, BBC Two (UK), 1981.
Into the Badlands, created by Alfred Gough and Miles Millar, AMC, 2015–2019.
Jeremiah, created by J. Michael Straczynski, Showtime, 2002–2004.
Jericho, created by Stephen Chbosky, Josh Schaer, and Jonathan E. Steinberg, CBS, 2006–2008.
Kabaneri of the Iron Fortress, developed by Wit Studios, Fujo TV (Japan), 2016.
Knights of Sidonia, adaption by Polygon Pictures, MBS (Japan), 2014–2015.
The Last Man on Earth, created by Will Forte, Fox, 2015–2018.
The Last Ship, created by Hank Stein and Steven L. Kane, TNT, 2014–2018.
The Last Train, created by Matthew Graham, ITV (UK), 1999.
The Leftovers, created by Damon Lindelof and Tom Perrotta, HBO, 2014–2017.
Life After People, created by David de Vries, History, 2008–2010.
Lost in Space, developed by Matt Sazama and Burk Sharpless, Netflix, 2018–present.
The Lottery, created by Tomothy J. Sexton, Lifetime, 2014.
Maddigan's Quest, created by Margaret Mahy, Gavin Strawhan, and Rachel Lang, TV3 (New Zealand), 2006.
The Magicians, created by Sera Gamble and John McNamara, Syfy, 2015–present.
Marvel's Agents of S.H.I.E.L.D., created by Joss Whedon, Jed Whedon, and Maurissa Tancharoen, ABC, 2013–2020.
Miracle Workers, created by Simon Rich, TBS, 2019–present.
Os Mutantes: Caminhos do Coração, created by Tiago Santiago, Rede Record (Brazil), 2008–2009.

Appendix 1: Apocalypse Television Series

The New Tomorrow, created by Raymond Thompson and Harry Duffin, Seven Network (Australia), 2005.
No Tomorrow, developed by Corinne Brinkerhoff, The CW, 2016–2017.
Not with a Bang, produced by London Weekend Television, ITV (UK), 1990.
Now Apocalypse, created by Gregg Araki, Starz, 2019.
Odyssey 5, created by Manny Coto, Showtime, 2002.
The 100, created by Jason Rothenberg, The CW, 2014–present.
Outcasts, created by Ben Richards, BBC One (UK), 2011.
The Passage, developed by Liz Heldens, Fox, 2019.
Planet of the Apes, developed by Anthony Wilson, CBS, 1974.
Power Rangers R.P.M., created by Haim Saban, Toei Company, and Eddie Guzelian, ABC, 2009.
The Rain, created by Jenny Ann Balverde, Esben Toft Jacobsen, and Christian Potavilo, Netflix (Denmark), 2018–2020.
The Refugees, created by Ramón Campos, Gema R. Neira, Cristóbal Garrido, and Adolfo Valor, laSexta (Spain), 2015.
Revolution, created by Eric Kripke, NBC, 2012–2014.
Salvation, created by Liz Kruger, Craig Shapiro, and Matt Wheeler, CBS, 2017–2018.
The Strain, created by Guillermo del Toro and Chuck Hogan, FX, 2014–2017.
Survivors, created by Adrian Hodges and Terry Nation, BBC (UK), 2008–2010.
Survivors, created by Terry Nation, BBC (UK), 1975–1977.
Terminator: The Sarah Connor Chronicles, created by Josh Friedman, Fox, 2008–2009.
Terra Nova, created by Kelly Marcel and Craig Silverstein, Fox, 2011.
3%, created by Pedro Aguilera, Netflix, 2016–2018.
Thundarr the Barbarian, created by Steve Gerber, Joe Ruby, and Ken Spears, ABC, 1980–1981.
Thunderstone, created by Jonathan M. Shiff, Network Ten (Australia), 1999–2000.
Travelers, created by Brad Wright, Showcase (Canada), 2016–2018.
The Tribe, created by Raymond Thompson and Harry Duffin, Channel 5 (UK), 1999–2003.
The Tripods, adapted by Alick Rowe and Christopher Penfold, BBC (UK), 1984–1985.
12 Monkeys, created by Travis Fickett and Terry Matalas, Syfy, 2015–2018.
2030 CE, created by Dennis Foon, Yan Moore, and Angela Bruce, YTV (Canada), 2002–2003.
The Umbrella Academy, adaptation by Steve Blackman, Netflix, 2019.
Under the Dome, adaptation by Brian K. Vaughan, CBS, 2013–2015.
V, created by Kenneth Johnson, NBC, 1984–1985.
V, developed by Scott Peters, ABC, 2009–2011.
Van Helsing, created by Neil LaBute, Syfy, 2016–present.
The Walking Dead, created by Frank Darabont, AMC, 2010–present.
War of the Worlds, created by Greg Strangis, Syndicated, 1988–1990.
Wayward Pines, created by Chad Hodge, Fox, 2015–2016.
Westworld, created by Jonathan Nolan and Lisa Joy, HBO, 2016–present.
Woops!, created by Gary Jacobs, Fox, 1992.
You, Me and the Apocalypse, created by Iain Hollands, Sky One (UK), 2015.
Z Nation, created by Karl Schaefer and Craig Engler, Syfy, 2014–2018.
Zoo, created by Josh Appelbaum, André Nemec, Jeff Pinkner, and Scott Rosenberg, CBS, 2015–2017.

Appendix 2
"Darkness"

Lord Byron

I had a dream, which was not all a dream.
The bright sun was extinguish'd, and the stars
Did wander darkling in the eternal space,
Rayless, and pathless, and the icy earth
Swung blind and blackening in the moonless air;
Morn came and went—and came, and brought no day,
And men forgot their passions in the dread
Of this their desolation; and all hearts
Were chill'd into a selfish prayer for light:
And they did live by watchfires—and the thrones,
The palaces of crowned kings—the huts,
The habitations of all things which dwell,
Were burnt for beacons; cities were consum'd,
And men were gather'd round their blazing homes
To look once more into each other's face;
Happy were those who dwelt within the eye
Of the volcanos, and their mountain-torch:
A fearful hope was all the world contain'd;
Forests were set on fire—but hour by hour
They fell and faded—and the crackling trunks
Extinguish'd with a crash—and all was black.
The brows of men by the despairing light
Wore an unearthly aspect, as by fits
The flashes fell upon them; some lay down
And hid their eyes and wept; and some did rest
Their chins upon their clenched hands, and smil'd;
And others hurried to and fro, and fed
Their funeral piles with fuel, and look'd up
With mad disquietude on the dull sky,
The pall of a past world; and then again
With curses cast them down upon the dust,
And gnash'd their teeth and howl'd: the wild birds shriek'd
And, terrified, did flutter on the ground,
And flap their useless wings; the wildest brutes
Came tame and tremulous; and vipers crawl'd

Appendix 2: "Darkness" by Lord Byron

And twin'd themselves among the multitude,
Hissing, but stingless—they were slain for food.
And War, which for a moment was no more,
Did glut himself again: a meal was bought
With blood, and each sate sullenly apart
Gorging himself in gloom: no love was left;
All earth was but one thought—and that was death
Immediate and inglorious; and the pang
Of famine fed upon all entrails—men
Died, and their bones were tombless as their flesh;
The meagre by the meagre were devour'd,
Even dogs assail'd their masters, all save one,
And he was faithful to a corse, and kept
The birds and beasts and famish'd men at bay,
Till hunger clung them, or the dropping dead
Lur'd their lank jaws; himself sought out no food,
But with a piteous and perpetual moan,
And a quick desolate cry, licking the hand
Which answer'd not with a caress—he died.
The crowd was famish'd by degrees; but two
Of an enormous city did survive,
And they were enemies: they met beside
The dying embers of an altar-place
Where had been heap'd a mass of holy things
For an unholy usage; they rak'd up,
And shivering scrap'd with their cold skeleton hands
The feeble ashes, and their feeble breath
Blew for a little life, and made a flame
Which was a mockery; then they lifted up
Their eyes as it grew lighter, and beheld
Each other's aspects—saw, and shriek'd, and died—
Even of their mutual hideousness they died,
Unknowing who he was upon whose brow
Famine had written Fiend. The world was void,
The populous and the powerful was a lump,
Seasonless, herbless, treeless, manless, lifeless—
A lump of death—a chaos of hard clay.
The rivers, lakes and ocean all stood still,
And nothing stirr'd within their silent depths;
Ships sailorless lay rotting on the sea,
And their masts fell down piecemeal: as they dropp'd
They slept on the abyss without a surge—
The waves were dead; the tides were in their grave,
The moon, their mistress, had expir'd before;
The winds were wither'd in the stagnant air,
And the clouds perish'd; Darkness had no need
Of aid from them—She was the Universe.

About the Contributors

Emiliano **Aguilar** graduated with an MA from the Universidad de Buenos Aires (UBA)—Facultad de Filosofía y Letras (Argentina). He works as researcher in film history (Ubacyt). He has published in journals such as *Lindes* and *Letraceluloide* and has chapters in *Orphan Black and Philosophy* (ed. Greene); *The Man in the High Castle and Philosophy* (ed. Krajewski); and *Giant Creatures in Our World* (ed. Mustachio and Barr).

William S. **Allen** is a lecturer of philosophy at Morgan State University in Baltimore. His primary philosophical interests are in social and political philosophy and philosophy of race. Specifically, his research involves critiquing liberal political philosophy in application to racial justice. This is his second foray into the world of popular culture and philosophy, having contributed to *The Wire and Philosophy* (2013).

Michael G. **Cornelius**, Ph.D., University of Rhode Island, is the author or editor of 19 books and 70+ essays in anthologies and in journals, including *Fifteenth-Century Studies, Studies in Medieval and Renaissance Teaching, CLUES, White Crane Journal, The Delta Epsilon Sigma Journal, Pennsylvania Literary Journal, Magazine Americana*, and *SCOTIA: A Journal of Scottish Studies*. He is a professor of English at Wilson College in Chambersburg, Pennsylvania.

John **Elia** is an associate professor and Thérèse Murray Goodwin '49 Chair in Philosophy at Wilson College in Chambersburg, Pennsylvania. His scholarship is focused on moral and practical virtues as they're expressed in popular culture, with special attention to environmental virtue, hope, and the Anthropocene. He has published on topics ranging from humiliation in *The Office* and integrity in *Mad Men* to reverence in sword and sandal films like *Spartacus* and *300*.

Adam **Ellerbrock** received an MA in humanities from Wilson College. His master's thesis focused on the role of cultural memory within the dystopias of *Brave New World, 1984*, and *Blade Runner*. He contributes to a variety of blogs, writes freelance articles and essays, and is putting the finishing touches on his debut science fiction/fantasy novel.

C. Anne **Engert** came to academia late in life, completing her MA in English at California State University Stanislaus in 2013 at the age of 59. She has published short stories and poetry, but her academic interests lie in the unexpected intersection of various contemporary pop-culture forms and Early Modern life and literature. As a child of the Cold War era, she is also interested in all things apocalypse.

Sherry **Ginn**, Ph.D., University of South Carolina, focuses on how psychology and neuroscience are illustrated in popular culture. She has written or edited books on women in SF television, sex in SF, time-travel in TV, TV's *Farscape* and *Fringe*, the

TV series of Joss Whedon, Whedon's *Dollhouse*, the companions of *Doctor Who* and Marvel's Black Widow. She is researching female characters in SF television and psychology in Joss Whedon.

Juan Ignacio **Juvé**, MA, social sciences, Universidad de Buenos Aires (UBA)—Facultad de Ciencias Sociales, is a lecturer in sociology, horror cinema and popular culture, and works at Escuela Superior de Comercio Carlos Pellegrini (UBA). He has published in the journals *Lindes*, *Vitae Pensiero*, and in books, including *Science Fiction and the Abolition of Man* (ed. Boone and Neece); *The Rwandan Genocide on Film* (ed. Edwards); and *Requiem for a Nation* (ed. Cavallini).

JZ **Long** is an associate professor of communications at Wilson College in Chambersburg, Pennsylvania, and holds degrees in political and cultural economy, popular culture, and a Ph.D. in cultural studies from George Mason University. His publications include analyses of the Hummer automobile, comic books, and popular cinema. His research focuses on the First Amendment, the Federal Communications Commission, and cyberpower and cyber governance.

E. Leigh **McKagen** is a Ph.D. student in the Alliance for Social, Political, Ethical, and Cultural Thought (ASPECT) program at Virginia Tech, where she also teaches courses in history. Her research uses postcolonial and ecofeminist theories to critically examine science fiction. Her dissertation deconstructs liberal imperial narratives in contemporary science fiction television and then explores alternatives to create the space for a non-imperial vision of the future.

Sebastian **Müller** is a Ph.D. candidate and lecturer at the University of Bayreuth. He participated in the German Research Foundation Project "Contemporary American Risk Fiction" in 2017. His doctoral project focuses on spaces in post-apocalyptic television series, including *Terra Nova* (2011), *Defiance* (2013–2015) and *The 100* (2014–present). Research interests include science fiction television and space studies, and race and gender identity in African American literature.

Fernando-Gabriel **Pagnoni Berns** is a Ph.D. student and a professor at Universidad de Buenos Aires (UBA)—Facultad de Filosofía y Letras (Argentina). The director of the horror cinema research group "Grite," he has published articles on Argentinian and international cinema and drama in numerous journals and book chapters. He is working on a book about the Spanish horror television series, *Historias para no Dormir*.

Tony **Perrello** is an English professor at California State University, Stanislaus, and has been teaching the literature of the Middle Ages and Renaissance for 20 years. He has published several essays on issues related to early British literature and has taken an interest in horror on film and television. He is co-authoring a book-length study, *Horrifying Renaissance Drama*, linking two surprisingly conversant fields of enquiry—horror film and Renaissance theater.

Derek R. **Sweet** is an associate professor of communication studies at Luther College, and writes and teaches about the intersection of rhetoric, popular culture, and politics. Whether addressing the epideictic speeches of Barack Obama or episodes of *Star Wars: The Clone Wars*, his work focuses on how rhetorical texts invite audience members to come together as public arbiters and engage matters of political consequence.

Christina **Wilkins** is a researcher in television and literature. She has written articles about religion, identity, and mental health in popular culture and is the author of *God Is (Un)Dead,* which looks at how the vampire figures in the post–9/11 world. She is working on an article on nostalgia and *Westworld* alongside a research project on mental health and contemporary literature.

Index

acknowledgment 138, 140–141, 144–148
Adams, Douglas 177, 183
Anthropocene 87–88, 100, 102–103, 105–106, 108, 110, 174–176, 178, 183
apocalyptic cycle 164–165
authority 34, 63–65, 132–134

Battlestar Galactica 48–49, 102–111, 125, 130
Beck, Ulrich 72–73, 80, 120
Buffy the Vampire Slayer 8, 12

Cadillacs and Dinosaurs 12, 16, 86–101
Campbell, Joseph 15–16, 102, 107–110
capitalism 62, 64, 87, 88, 118
Capitalocene 88
captivity narrative 90
carrier 74, 76–77, 79–80, 82–83
carrier bag theory of fiction 106–111
Caruth, Cathy 164, 167–168
Centers for Disease Control (CDC) 3, 23, 73, 77–80, 83
certainty 118–119
Chernobyl 2, 87
Chthulucene 88, 100
class struggles 5, 58, 61, 65–68, 164
clown 18, 174, 177–179, 182–184
community 24, 51–55, 61, 119–120, 134, 140
competition 36, 40–42, 48–49, 50–52, 55
consumption 7, 118
containment 73, 77, 79–80, 82–83
contingency 118–119, 174, 176, 177–180
cooperation 15, 24, 25, 29, 30–31, 40–42, 48–52, 54–55, 56
Cousin de Grainville, Jean-Baptiste 8
counter-memory 164, 170–172
counter-trauma *see* trauma
Crying Indian PSA 89–90

Deleuze, Gilles 13–14, 17, 18, 118
democracy 37, 63–64, 66
Doctor Who 8, 12
Doomsday Clock 14
Doomsday Preppers 16, 113–121

ethos 138
everyday heroism/heroes 102, 108–110
evolution 14, 41, 177, 180–181; *see also* evolutionary psychology
evolutionary psychology 40, 43–45
extinction level event (ELE) 3, 158

faith 4, 7, 9, 10, 16, 17, 34, 80, 98, 117, 124–125, 127–129, 132–135, 158
Falling Skies 47–48, 50–52, 54, 56
fascism 64
feminism 56, 60, 67
feudalistic system 63, 64
frontier 87, 88–95, 98, 170
Fukushima Daiichi 2, 19

Grimes, Rick 11, 13, 30–32, 34–35, 37, 48, 52–55, 56
Guattari, Félix 118

The Handmaid's Tale 17, 40–50, 55
Haraway, Donna 88, 100, 102, 104, 105–108, 110–111
Hawthorne, Nathaniel 91
Heise, Ursula 72, 174, 176–177, 179–180
heroic narrative *see* everyday heroism
Hobbes, Thomas 15, 23–34, 36–38, 95–96
Hyde, Michael 138, 140–141, 145–146, 148

identity 11, 17, 34, 44, 67, 90, 133, 153–155, 157, 159, 160–161, 165–167, 169, 171–172
imagination 15, 53, 61, 72, 99, 177, 181
Intermediate-Range Nuclear Forces (INF) Treaty 2
interminable middle *see* Deleuze, Gilles

Johnson, Mark 86, 94, 97
Jung, Carl 99, 100

Kermode, Frank 6–7

Lakoff, George 86, 94, 97
The Last Man on Earth 174–184
Latour, Bruno 96
Left Behind 125, 129, 131
The Leftovers 124–148
Le Guin, Ursula 106, 107, 110
Leviathan 26, 38
Lewis, R.W.B. 91
liberalism 33–34
liminality 7, 124, 134
Locke, John 33

machinatio vitae (machinery of life) 87–88, 90, 94–96, 98
The Magicians (book trilogy) 149, 150, 151, 159

The Magicians (television series) 13, 17, 19, 149–161
meme 164, 165–167
memory 146, 156–157, 165, 171, 172
Messiah 132, 133, 134, 144
mythistory 164, 172

nature-as-machine 87, 88, 94–98; *see also machinatio vitae*
nature/culture divide 96
9/11 *see* terrorism

The 100 24, 31, 37
outbreak narrative 14, 72–74, 77–80, 82–83

paranoia 61
Paris Accords/Agreement 2
personal apocalypse 16, 17, 138, 140–144, 146–148, 151–152, 158–159
perverse cooperation 49–50
Pitetti, Connor 4–6, 18
Plato 25–26, 38
post-humanism 150–154, 156–161
post-nature 174–176, 178, 180–184
psychological egoism 25–27, 29
Purdy, Jedediah 88, 100

quarantine 78–81, 83

Rapture 4, 7, 9, 117, 124–125, 127, 129, 131–132, 137, 139, 142
reconstruction of the country 62, 63, 69
redemption 10, 98, 125–126, 130, 134
regeneration through violence 91–92, 93, 95
The Republic 26
risk 72–83, 120–121
risk management *see* risk
Rosen, Elizabeth 71, 130, 138

Schrag, Calvin O. 138, 140, 147
Schultz, Mark 86, 100; *see also Xenozoic Tales*
secular apocalypse 8, 117, 125, 126, 132, 142

self *see* identity
seriality 59, 72, 82, 83
sexual selection 41–42, 44–45, 48–53
Shelley, Mary 8
skinheads 64
Slotkin, Richard 89–90, 91–92
social contract 28, 29, 32, 38, 180, 182, 183
social death 138, 141–142, 145
social selection 41, 42, 50–51, 53–54
Star Trek (franchise) 5, 6, 8, 20
Star Trek: The Next Generation 5, 6, 12
State of Nature 23–24, 27–32, 36–38
The Strain 12, 16, 23–24, 72–83, 125, 130
structuring metaphors 89, 98
superspreader 74, 76
survival narrative 107–108, 110
Survivors (television series) 58–69

techno-capitalism *see* capitalism
terrorism 11, 175
threefold crisis 88
time (nature of) *see* time loops
time loops 149–150, 155–157, 161
trauma 11, 129, 134, 140, 145, 164–172
Two Treatises of Government see Locke, John

utopia 4, 5, 6, 7, 12, 20, 90

Wald, Priscilla *see* outbreak narrative
The Walking Dead 10, 11–13, 19, 24, 30–31, 34–37, 40, 41, 48, 50, 52–55, 56, 72, 82, 125, 130
Wells, H.G. 8
Westworld 12, 163–172
winter of discontent 58–60, 66, 68–69
wonder 151–152, 159, 161
world as frontier *see* frontier

Xenozoic Tales 86, 96, 100

Z Nation 36, 72, 82
Žižek, Slavoj 99

www.ingramcontent.com/pod-product-compliance
Lightning Source LLC
Chambersburg PA
CBHW032044300426
44117CB00009B/1188